# THE HOLY SPIRT WITHIN

## JESUS SON OF GOD

Copyright © 2017 Lynda Hackford

All rights reserved worldwide.

No part of the book may be copied or changed in any format, sold, or used in a way other than what is outlined in this book, under any circumstances, without the prior written permission of the publisher.

**Publisher:**
Inspiring Publishers
P.O. Box 159, Calwell, ACT Australia 2905
Email: publishaspg@gmail.com
http://www.inspiringpublishers.com

National Library of Australia Cataloguing-in-Publication entry

Author: Hackford, Lynda

Title: **Jesus Son of God**/*Lynda Hackford*.

ISBN: 9781925477962 (pbk)

Subjects: Jesus Christ—Biblical teaching.
         Bible—Commentaries.
         Bible—Inspiration.
         God—Biblical teaching.

# Contents

Introduction ............................................................................. 5

Jesus Son of God Changed My Life ................................... 10

Receiving the Holy Spirit ..................................................... 30

The Spirit of Truth ................................................................ 34

No Favourtism with God the Father .................................. 40

"Christ Jesus" ........................................................................ 53

Hardened Heart .................................................................... 59

Miracles of Christ ................................................................. 72

The Cross and Jesus ............................................................ 89

The Holy Spirit .................................................................... 102

Faith Believing .................................................................... 110

Relationship in Christ "Not Religion" .............................. 116

The Fruits of the Spirit ...................................................... 125

Page of Prayers and Promises ......................................... 144

Promises of God ............................................................................ 147

The 10 Commandments ................................................................ 152

The Power of God Almighty ......................................................... 156

Spiritual Darkness (the Watchers) ............................................... 179

A God to Worship .......................................................................... 193

Inner Spiritual Warfare ................................................................. 196

Draw your Strength from Jesus Christ ....................................... 217

Jesus Message of Love ................................................................ 237

# Introduction

**WELCOME TO JESUS SON OF GOD,** I hope to bring you as much learning about the Holy Bible, especially Jesus Christ, helping you the reader to fully understand the meaning and principles of the words of our Lord, and how it can mean so much to our daily life.

To learn about our Father in Heaven is going to bring you an experience that you will never forget, living for our Lord; trusting in him and loving him with all your heart and soul, learning to have faith and understanding; for the importance in Christ is keeping faith and trust, for God so loves his children.

The lord our God is always with you, the word of God however is fading in our world with so many people today not trusting and believing in the Holy Bible and the word of God our father, our children think that God is not cool and never mind the sheer thought of religion; and not understanding what they believe religion to be, it's just that now; there are so many different religious beliefs that exist.

I have tried to explain to many that God isn't a religion, God the father is love, faith, trust, peace, joy and happiness for this is only what he wants for us to have in our lives, religion is what people have turned it out to be; it's also people that have turned religion and faith into a mockery of the different religious practices and peoples different beliefs in their God.

Sadly though this has been going on since before Jesus was even born, so what has really changed? Religious beliefs, reader it's that simple. The Holy Bible today is still one of the most searched after books, and is also today one of the most popular books brought.

Many thousands of people who have brought the Bible have done so because they believe that they need God, or because they whole heartedly believe in a higher power, but not necessarily believing in God; so they purchase the Bible for answers.

There are many answers in the Bible which can help all of our day to day problems physically, mentally and emotionally.

Many people stop reading the Bible, not because they don't believe in God or a higher power, but because they find the Bible way too hard to understand; so it gets pushed aside; I can understand this for I found it very difficult to comprehend myself and also didn't take it back up until I hit rock bottom.

But this is why I am now lead to write this book, to help you to understand the scriptures better, to bring you new light in the Holy Bible I want something different for people in understanding in the word of God so that people can turn to the Father and not turn away from him because they feel that God doesn't love them, because they have sinned for example.

But before I start I will be writing many other stories about the life and meanings of how important Jesus is too us, and also some stories about my life struggles and how the Lord has changed my life and the life of others, little prayers which I have called them speaking the words of grace for you to pray to God; when you need him most or daily, whichever is best for you. AMEN

I really want you the reader to embrace the lord and feel his love for you, to learn that you as I have can actually turn to God to help you with the many troubles we experience in our everyday life, and to trust God to help us get through it.

The other subjects to follow will also help you to understand the New Testament completely, and how it effects you on the emotional levels of your life. You will truly have your eyes reopened, your love and faith will become stronger and you will become a new child in our Lord God, Jesus Christ.

# INTRODUCTION ✝ 7

I will have some scriptures that will be from the New Testament in the stories and also scripture from the Old Testament which is still important because it's the Holy Bible, the word of God. The New Testament is focused on Jesus Christ where as the Old Testament focuses on the laws of the 10 commandments and the Law of Moses, where as the New Testament was Jesus Christ law of love, peace, joy and happiness, and forgiveness of sin.

Jesus Christ was God incarnate, and he was born to die on the cross to save us all from our sins, in other words Jesus Christ came to give all God's children a second chance to save us all from sin, so that is where born again as Christians' came from, so we can repent from all of our sins, to change our ways, to be saved and to live life eternal in the kingdom of God.

This is why I find now that our world as we know it is actually in such a big turmoil, after learning so much from the scriptures (and I haven't even scratched the surface, in my eyes) that I realize the word of God has even been taken out of our schools, our Children haven't even got the choice to even get to know our father and Jesus, and the reason is because our world is so multi cultural and there are so many different religious beliefs, turning our children of today non believers of God or any kind of religious belief.

This I believe is what is turning our world into one big religious battlefield all really fighting over one God or who they believe to be their God or their religious leader. Don't get me wrong I believe whole heartedly that absolutely nobody should judge anyone in their belief of their God, because God does not want you to judge anyone, for he is the judge.

But people on the other hand do judge peoples beliefs, "not God" and this is the sole reason for our world's problems; today right now some country or someone is getting murdered or bombed over their religious beliefs, when they should not judge, and keep their belief where it belongs close to their heart and there religious background, for its their right.

My belief is whatever happened to all our rights as individual's free will to believe in the God or higher being we choose to worship and love, and to stop judging. The religious Christians are targeted just for being Christians, but Christianity is believing in the word of God and in Jesus Christ, but what many believers of their God or Faith whether being a 7th Day Adventist, Jehovah Witness, Roman Catholic, Church of England, Protestants, Mormons and of course the list is much longer; but the point people need to have is to respect all peoples rights to the belief and faith of one another.

In my eyes and many of the religions I just wrote about believe there is only one God, and it's the one God in heaven that I love and believe in, AMEN for it's my free will and your right. Nobody should be made to be frightened and live in fear, what is our world coming to, people should stay focused on God and the word of God and their religion and not worry about someone else's.

The word of God is powerful and its truth and it will have such an impact on your life, the word of God will bring truth, love and honour, respect, and loyalty to God, others and yourself, wisdom will follow then joy, happiness and Gods unmerited favour, with all of this how can you not want God in your life, how could one not want to be reborn again into Gods kingdom.

If you need God in your life, then you have made the right decision in purchasing this book, and my prayer book, First prayer book; My peace I give unto you; then you are on the right path and a change is already beginning in your life, God is working in you now; to enhance the transformation in you as a new child in Christ Jesus. The Bibles words and teachings as followers of God and Christ Jesus will bring you closer to God's word bringing you hope when you need it, rescuing you and anointing you, when you reach out to him, finding hope and the ultimate love of God and our Lord and Saviour "Jesus Christ.

So we should all pray not tomorrow but today, find yourself and walk in the light with Christ, he is love and kindness and he will hear your voice he will feel your tears of happiness and sadness.

You will feel his joy rushing over you like rushing water; God wants you; but you must believe and trust by keeping in the word, keeping faith because God and Jesus are the givers of life, by transforming your life giving you a second chance, through the death of our Lord Jesus Christ on the cross.

## SPEAK THE WORD OF GRACE PRAYER

Thank you Jesus, that because I have received your love and that you have given me the authority to become a beloved child of God. I believe in you, Adhere to and to rely on your word, your grace, and to trust in your name.

Father in Heaven, thank you for your gracious hand of favour on my life; I choose to believe that with you all things are possible. I know that you are making a way where there seems to be no way. So my Lord I will worship you on your goodness all the days of my life, in the name of my Lord Jesus Christ I pray, AMEN

# Jesus Son of God Changed My Life

**I BELIEVE THAT BECOMING** a born again Christian can and will change you and your life; I became a Minister of God and it was one of the best decisions' that I have done in my life, becoming closer to my Lord and Saviour and being transformed to a new person.

I had so many struggles in my life I was truly on my knees in a dark and unforgiving world that we live in; many of my problems were family, work, health; however many of us do go through simular problems some even much worse and I am aware of this, (not looking for sympathy) but reaching to you my Lord God for understanding in my times of trouble.

Stress ended up for me being such a major problem which ended up effecting my health on a big scale and then my families well being.

Stress I could never have imagined what it can do to someone and how it can affect so many people and the levels of emotion and depression it can cause; I had skin cancer which was treated then returned, I had it on my face and extremely close to my eyes one was near my tear duct on my right eye.

When it was done the results came back that it was all clear, the surgeon had done a very good job, the one that was near my right tear duct (a stitch) was still there for over a year and a half it was very difficult to remove for awhile because it was so close to me eye which was very annoying but I got use to it, about 2 years later I discovered that it had returned I was shattered in a very emotional way, I didn't want to go under the knife again and go through all that and continue to work in my business facing customers.

Then on top of that I lost my beloved mother, and then there were problems one after the other within my business, machinery breakdowns , power failures which cost me a fortune in lost stock, family problems occurred on a huge level, and much more..... Everything in my life was falling all around me, this is when I believed I had no one to turn to but my Father in Heaven, I thought no one else will listen, maybe God will.

I started praying and praying no answer, and I just kept on praying with many many heartfelt tears and still no answer, well that's what I thought anyway; But that wasn't the truth, my Father and Jesus were listening to my prayers.

I realized that our Lord listens to your prayers but answers them in his own appointed time, and also when he feels that you are ready to accept his help. Ready to follow him with all your heart and soul, and I was truly ready to accept my Lord God and My Lord Jesus Christ.

My life started to turn around, and without me realising to start with, until one day I realized I wasn't crying all the time and I felt different in my heart; I decided to go and see the doctor and ask him if I could use the cancer cream he looked and tried to take out the stitch and it was finally removed, but the cancer was still too close to my right tear duct and he refused and said it was too dangerous with the cream and that I needed to book in to see the specialist again the same specialist that removed it the first time, I had cancer removed on my left side as well also near my eye and near my cheek which also had returned.

But no one would let me try the cream I asked the specialist before surgery and he said no and second time around still the answer was no; I was devastated I had all these horrible thoughts going through my mind and how scared I was going to be again, not to mention all the other problems going on in my life, I truly was a mess, I was still on my knees begging my father in heaven to please help me, please Father I want to try the cream please I want it to work.

Then one night Father told me to get a second opinion, which I never really considered for fear of what the answer would be because I had already spoken to my doctors and also because I lived 200km away from any other doctors and I was suffering deep inside. I listened to what God was telling me deep within my spirit and I made an appointment closing my business for the day and of I went to see another doctor.

All the way their I kept thinking what is this doctor going to tell me about the cancer that doctors and specialists haven't already told me (the knife) I was scared but God was telling me differently, so have faith in God. I arrived at the doctors; and in I went, nervously yes you bet. The doctor examined me and I explained to the doctor that I wanted to try the new cancer cream, on the internet the doctor went and researched the trials already done on the cream and other patients, and he showed me the results.

It wasn't great, but I was still willing to give it a try, the doctor went through all the pros and about how close the cancer was to my eyes and the importance of trying to keep the cream away from my eyes and then came from the doctor all the negative results about the affects of using the cream and not being out in the sunlight with the cream on, but the good news was still he was going to let me try it and see how it goes. Hallelujah, Amen.

I couldn't believe what I was hearing; God was right, from that day on my life turned around and to this day I still thank God for the renewal of my life and the change that he has made to my life. The cream has worked and it has been 4years now and I am still free from it, I have small red scaring when I have no makeup on, I actually found more cancer when I was applying the cream that I never noticed, neither did any doctor discover it, so in the end the treatment was very rough but **THANK YOU MY FATHER.**

My thoughts changed, my heart wasn't aching, my grieving for my mother subsided which was going on for more than 5 years it was as

# JESUS SON OF GOD CHANGED MY LIFE ✝ 13

though I had lost a huge part of my life; which I did my beloved mum, not to also mention the daily crying (grieving) and the effect that it had on my family, they didn't know what to do for me (I didn't know what to do for me).

I will however never forget the day my wonderful young son said to me, mum you are always crying; wow what do you say to something like that, but yes he was correct I was living a very unhappy life and it was because of all the negative influences and stress around my life and the health issues as well, I remember my doctor saying to me that if I didn't get the stress in my life under control it would kill me.

Do I believe that God heard my cries absolutely without any doubt, has God changed my life around, yes. Has God entered into my Holy Spirit, Yes without any doubt, Do I love God and Jesus with all my heart and soul YES without and doubt. My Lord has taken away the darkness that was plaguing my life and now I see things so much differently, but understand that darkness still has its way of sneaking into your life but you will get understanding regarding this throughout my book, and my Prayer book.

I talk to God and Jesus everyday whether in pray daily or through ministering to people or through scripture, my Lord is with me all the time, and you do need him daily it's just many do not understand how much and on what levels, however you can be guaranteed Jesus will guide you.

I was being lead by God to give more of myself to him to all the children in the world to God's chosen people to help them, to become a devout loyal follower of God's word, so I become a minister/pastor to spread the gospel to teach the Gospel in Gods church the God within us all which is the house of God, and ministering in the words and prayers in my Books, (God wrote).

Many may wonder, do I make mistakes of the flesh YES of course I do, I am no different than most people out in the world, But I know my God loves me and will forgive me and each day God and Jesus teaches me to be more and more in the word and not the flesh of the world and there is a difference, God the Father wants us to become more Godly and to forgive others not just yourself. If God has forgiven me how can I not forgive others, so I have learnt to not judge others and to forgive others for their mistakes, It comes down to who am I to not forgive when I have made so many mistakes myself.

Everyone makes mistakes not only from today but from past mistakes, many people turn away from our Father because of the flesh sins that they have done and they fear God and his wrath, but this is where I want you to clearly think about what I have to tell you.

Our God our Father is a loving caring Father and will forgive us of our sins, if you repent from all of your sins and that you truly believe in God and Jesus and that Jesus died on the cross for all of our sins and rose up again to our Father in heaven, then you can be saved and forgiven for your sins, so please do not turn away from Jesus, and instead turn to our Lord and Saviour for forgiveness, the words from your mouth can save you, and change you; turning your life around.

Prayers are so important to me and my new life in God the Father and Jesus, and how I have prayed in my times of trouble, the feelings that I have are so hard to explain; guess it's something that you have to go through with yourself and God, but if you are already their then you know what I mean. And if you are not there yet, when you find God you will understand, hoping and praying that this book and my Prayer book will help you on your way, because Jesus will be guiding you to the word.

I was giving away to some of my customers a cross which there were 4 different styles to choose from, I am also glad to say that I never had to many people refuse one; One customer had said to me that she will always carry her cross in her purse to keep her safe; another had told me that 3yrs ago her 28yr old son had committed suicide by hanging, because he had all his life a crippling disease.

This man had asked his mum that if he did commit suicide would Jesus accept him and love him if he took his own life, his mum told me that she said to her son that she didn't know and couldn't answer that truthfully to him.

# JESUS SON OF GOD CHANGED MY LIFE ✝ 15

She said to me that the cross meant a lot to her, I told her that her son would not have the crippling disease in Gods kingdom and that he would be safe, his faith and love in Jesus Christ was strong and he would be lead to Jesus, and Jesus would accept her son, her son loved Jesus and believed in Jesus, and this is why he was thinking of Jesus in his time of sorrow and stress of leaving our world and returning to the Father.

His mother didn't in her heart believe that her son would ever really go through taking his own life, the lady she found her son and tried desperately to bring him back with mouth to mouth resuscitation. The ladies faith and spirit gave me so much comfort, why you may be thinking, it's because so many people that I have spoken to over the years lose their faith in God because he took their loved one, regardless of whether by accident or been born the way they were or by illness, suffering ECT.

Our Father in heaven is a loving God and he doesn't want us to suffer, God is in charge of heaven and Jesus, our world its left to us to make our own decisions for its our free will; He also takes care of us when we arrive in heaven, to tell us what we have done wrong here on Earth (the world). The amount of people that stop believing in God in their grieving is many thousands, they don't blame Satan for they simply do not even want to go there thinking on that level, that's to full on. Then God; that's different, he's almighty and powerful he could have stopped this from happening, we can blame God then. WHY

Why? Because people expect God to be there for them, because he is loving and caring, but the real problem is that people only turn to God and Jesus when its good and ready for them only and (if I have the time) on their terms, and when it doesn't go according to what they believe is right, then someone is to blame (may as well be the Lord).

Unfair...God deserves better than that, he wants 100% of his children, and to believe in him 100%, and not to blame him for every little thing that does go wrong in our world. We are to blame for a lot as well and then what about prayers and faith in God the Father and his word (the Bible), I've come to realise and understand that a lot of people's views about our Father is when it's good for them and when they choose to need him, and in essence this is still ok with our father, because you need him. AMEN

God will listen to people, who call on him, but you must continue to have faith all the time and believe in the word of God, and the Holy Bible is a good place to start and continue to acknowledge over and over again and reading it as many time as the word of God will teach you also time and time again in the Greatest book in the world the Holy Bible.

Many ministers/Pastors who have been preaching for 30yrs+ say that no matter how many times they have read the Bible they find and learn something different each time, I myself find that fascinating, it's never ending learning and interpreting, it's never ending just like life really in the kingdom of heaven if you truly believe and love Jesus. You live your life here on Earth for such a short space of time, but with love, faith and belief in our Father in heaven you can have eternal peace in Gods kingdom in Heaven, for he promises us that, those who love him. AMEN

This takes you to a whole new level of spiritualism, the love the faith and the believing, the healing in your heart when you truly truly believe in God and what he can bring to your life.

I have just realised while writing this that I have always had and felt that something wasn't right and was missing in my life and I have just typed it for you; my faith and truly finding and believing in God and Jesus, for where my Father has brought me to today that even with many struggles that we all struggle with daily my heart for my father is fulfilled I just want to continue to grow in the word for I know that I will never completely know it all until I am with my Father to find what is truth, writing for my God (no Gods readers, his children) to bring you what is missing in your life, true love in God and faith, is a blessing from God to us all.

I could not imagine my life now without praying to my Father everyday to help guide me: I believe prayer is the most important and the most helpful to the one doing the praying. But it is also possible to

# JESUS SON OF GOD CHANGED MY LIFE

raise "positive energies" and to even evoke spirit beings (Angles) that we are all given when born. But understand that we cannot depend on miracles to happen without true faith believing.

Our Lord Jesus Christ our Saviour says, faith as a grain of mustard seed can move mountains". But let us not be disheartened when God hands us a shovel. In other words it is all of our personal responsibility to work towards that change we need to see, for faith without works is dead (St James), therefore prayers without action are indeed worthless, and how true.

Prayer is best when used in its most powerful form, Prayer mostly will benefit the person praying and sometimes in their own private place and sometimes with only a very few deep meaningful words, among the highest form of prayer is asking God to reveal himself to you, call out to God silently in prayerful meditation; and God he loves your most intimate private space.

Intense prayer done over long periods of time can develop into the power of concentration, which then can lead to even more intense forms of prayer in a deep spiritual realm. All forms of prayer are good but the purest form of prayer is to stay focused on developing the relationship between yourself and God for this kind of prayer deep within your Holy Spirit will awaken love that's divine for God and Jesus; a devoted love and bond, and in turn this will affect all whom you are around, bringing peace, joy and happiness.

Every Christian must believe and remember that God created this world; we can only see a small fraction of the magnitude of its brilliance and size, whereas God the creator sees its big picture.' This world that we live in is based on pairs of opposites: positive and negative, day and night, male and female, then there is good and bad (evil) light and darkness, Light being God; darkness being evil, ECT then we have the opposite of duality which is unity.

We can all unite together with God only when we have transcended into the realm of duality through intense prayer. Although some will find this very hard to understand this, but it's a fact that in order for the creation to continue, evil must be present, so God cast Satan to Earth.

If however all of the negativity that exists in our world were to be removed, it would only collapse back into its pre creation state. Many now ask us then why does evil have to exist in our world, to only bring the question around to why the creation must exist; god needs to fix what Satan destroyed.

Evil exists all over the world, so one can suggest that God would have eradicated all evil a long time ago, if he hadn't have wanted it in our world today. Our world as we know it is however a proving ground to make us very spiritual beings to be able to become strong so we can resist and overcome evil; We can however avoid evil by preventing others from doing evil to us from overcoming evil doings to others which is one of Gods commandments, our love, believing and trust in God; to help us to overcome evil, by faith.

Looking at a different angle, we can wear strong shoes, but we cannot remove the thorns on the pathway to life, I believe that prayers does change us and for those that we pray for, I also strongly believe that after we have prayed we need to go out and do great things, for God and others.

The bible teaches us to pray without ceasing but also calls us to love one another including our enemies and to work for social justice. Jesus also tells us to do well to those who do evil to us and to pray for them as well, amen.

Wow you must be thinking of many people, whom you don't want to forgive for many reasons, But I was watching a religious show and a woman had a son that was murdered and she was having a very difficult time in forgiving her son's killer, she even went to see the young man who had killed her son just to see him to look at his face and to see if he had any remorse and then left.

Months had past and she turned to God to help her to overcome her grief, and she was beginning to understand the importance of forgiveness within our Christian faith, she gave it much deep thought and decided to take a video taken of her son's funeral which showed everyone's emotional grief of the loss of this young man and the young man in his coffin, and put it on when enclosed all the photos of her beloved son, then took them to his killer.

# JESUS SON OF GOD CHANGED MY LIFE ✝ 19

As you can imagine this was very deep in emotion and eventually the young man broke down as was the grieving mother, and she looked at the young man who was about the same age as her son and said I FORGIVE YOU as now I can see that you to now are showing remorse for my son, the young man then said; my young sister was killed by a hit and run driver who didn't care that he had hit my sister and then drove of and left her to die.

He said to the mother I have learnt a lesson and I was thinking that I have done the same thing to another family and now I too am grieving and I am inside as to the killer of my sister I too am asking you to forgive me and thank you, and has kept a photo of the young man he murdered as a reminder of the life he took for no reason at all.

I found that story so unbelievable in love, forgiveness and the working of God to comfort 2 very sad people, and the faith in letting them both move on through the grace of transforming two people's lives, and the tragedies of all lives involved; in learning about forgiveness and what it means to them and God.

The strength of both of them in the end was so amazing and what faith it would have given the people who were watching to see what God can do to heal and transform peoples love, faith and the real meaning of what forgiveness can do too many people's lives.

As children of God we need to be light and to have hope in the midst of an evil and a very hurting world; and we have to stay focused and be the hands, feet and voice of our loving caring gracious Father and his beloved son Jesus Christ our Lord and saviour, we become what we believe, we are in a fight for life, we must stay focused on the beauty of our Lord Jesus and not the world of anger, crime, and unbelievers.

I pray to God daily for healing for those who have lost loved ones and the people less fortunate than us and the elderly and Gods little suffering children who have been born into our world off suffering and deserve so much better, and the ones who have lost their lives for simply being in the wrong place at the wrong time, and it happens all too often.

I also pray hard that I will maintain my touch of grace and composure so as to have the ability to provide solace and strength for our precious brothers and sisters which have faced the loss of loved ones, I have suffered as many people have; and some the loss has been great; for some have lost all their family member in one go, that grief would just be unimaginable.

## PRAYER IS THE ANSWER FOR PEACE, WE ARE TOLD IN THE BIBLE TO PRAY WITHOUT CEASING.

God can and will he mend your broken heart, yes absolutely, he will send in the comforter like he did for me; however our world is in sin right now; and Gods word doesn't put up with sin. God is still and always will be love and mercifulness, But God at the same time is still by far our judge and He will never put up with sin, without you judging yourself not others for what you have done and by repentance, and doing so with a meaningful heart and of deep sorrow for all your sins, showing God your love for him is deep.

The lord is near to all who call on him he will hear everyone who needs him, to all who call on him in truth in their hearts, God says if my children which are called by name shall humble themselves and pray and seek my face, then I will hear them from heaven, I will forgive them their sins and I will heal the land.

"The test of all prayers always lies in the answer to many questions: Do we love our neighbour better because of what they may or may not have? Do we continue to keep on our same old path of selfishness or do we stay fulfilled in having prayed for something better, although we give no evidence of the sincerity in our hearts for our requests just by living consistently with our prayer? If our selfishness has given place to kindness, we shall never meet this great duty simply by asking that it may be done. However we need to take up the cross before we can even enjoy the fruits of our hope and faith, in our saviour Jesus Christ, AMEN

I think this is a good guide for us all; if we as Christians are sincerely living for what we have asked and prayed to our Father for, and for our prayers to bear any good fruits; then really what are we storing up in our own thoughts? Are we contributing to the hatred of our world by

# JESUS SON OF GOD CHANGED MY LIFE ✝ 21

hating those who commit acts of hatred or because we actually are feeding another person who talks about someone whom they hate by adding into the comments and making the other person happy because they think you agree, you may even not like that person that they hate and then you also may feel good because you have got it of your chest, is this not something to think about really?

Should we not see everyone as deserving of love regardless of what you think; it's hard, we have all been in this situation, sometimes we are drawn into it by someone else's conversation and you don't know the person but you still make a negative comment to a person you don't even know, (not good, right) but it does happen, this is what we need to watch out for because this is a sin and this is one we need to repent for by asking for forgiveness from our Father.

It can take a great deal of humility to love someone who does evil things and we have all at one stage or another heard about and maybe know someone like that, but with God it has been asked for us to do so. It's easy to love someone who loves us but the true test of love and faith and trust in God is to love someone who you feel isn't that loving, hard you may be thinking?

My prayer for you is to say; "teach me Father God to love in the way that you love; I have had my struggles with someone who is upsetting me and I don't want to feel this way anymore, I ask you my lord to show me how to forgive this person in my heart so I can forgive them and then I can heal and send healing and blessings to the one hurting me, so I can live in your commandments to love one another and to forgive and pray for the ones who hurt me, I love you Lord and thank you for hearing my prayers. AMEN

You can try and draw on your own sense of love but I can guarantee, you will fail because we all don't know the true meaning of love, and this is why the world we live in is failing at a horrendous rate, But if we all draw on the love of our true Father in heaven I believe with all my heart and soul that we can help eliminate hate and evil and indeed keep it out of our lives and this can be done also by prayers and believing and asking Jesus to unite us, all as Gods beloved children unite in mind, body and soul.

Prayers can be very powerful when words are carefully chosen. Prayers; with all the right action can and will promote a better world for us to live in, now you may be asking yourself what then is the right action to take? Our world now is filled with so much hatred, war, murder, rape ECT... are these not hate differences, or as Believers in God are we not longing for promoting a better society with our hands up facing God to those in need, and are we not trying to make peace with everyone so that the world can radiate with others, feeling the radiance of the world and bringing smiling faces to the ones that you may meet in the streets and within our family environments, would this not be a world also without fear.

Here comes now the biggest question that is all too often said about God; "why" God isn't fixing our world if he is a loving caring God? My question back to the many who ask this question is how do we know that God isn't trying too; where is your love coming from, or your trust, and hope in our Father, I suspect and have trust, hope and faith that he is fixing it for the ones who love him with all their heart and soul; and one may ask what is your contribution.

Many need to understand that all the manipulation on the part of man has created the mess we are in and our world as we know it today isn't getting any better we see it on the daily news on television, our computers ECT or we will read it in the daily papers, and we are not learning anything from it; except to turn the other cheek and hope it will just fix itself, just like us trying to fix a failing relationship; however our relationship should be the word of God; the right one to be asking and pray for his mercy and help, the bible says that we are what we sow, and what we will end up reaping, which means if you want better lives then you must sow right (good things) and then we will be able to reap the rewards of good "sounds like a fair deal"

While we our living in a harsh world we are more and more turning away from our beloved Father, and as long as the world continues to do this it can only result in more pain and suffering, leading to

# JESUS SON OF GOD CHANGED MY LIFE ✝ 23

no hope for the ones that cause this pain and suffering unless they turn their lives around and be rescued by God by finding the way; the truth and the light, by reaching out and finding hope in our Lord Jesus Christ.

Jesus Christ is the light and way "not tomorrow but today", he can reach deep inside your Holy Spirit, his life and death has deep meaning in my heart and soul, I reach deep inside to have him by my side, his spirit in me brings comfort not tomorrow but today, I want him to hear my voice and prayers. Jesus' teachings reveal truth with regards to spiritual enlightenment to his followers; and you need to understand that no other being has introduced such loving perfection to the world, you must seek and know this truth and it will set you free. Jesus is indeed "the way, the truth and the life".

Jesus also says I love those who love me, and those who seek me early and diligently shall find me, For God so loved the world that he gave his only begotten son, that whosoever believeth in me should not perish but have everlasting life, this everlasting life you can have through him, he died to set you free from all your sins, life is in the spilt blood of Jesus Christ, the only begotten son of God, the Father.

## SPEAK THE WORD OF GRACE PRAYER

Thankyou God, for loving me so much that you gave up your only son, so that if I believe in Jesus "and I truly do" that I will not perish, but have everlasting life. I know that you didn't send your son to condemn me, but that I find salvation and learn the truth so that it will set me free, to bring and to make me safe and sound through my Lord and saviour, your son whom you are well pleased "Jesus Christ" Thankyou my Father for hearing my Prayers, I will focus on you and your words to bring and keep me close to you. AMEN

The love of God the Father is an attribute of God and a description of his being, God alone is of divine love and the source of all truth and love. His Love is unconditional and is consistently seeking the highest good of the one who is loved and God's love for his beloved son was clearly demonstrated at Calvary when Jesus died for all of our sins; and because God first loved us, so then we should also learn to love others as well, for it is written.

> **LORD, I GIVE YOU MY HEART**
> **I GIVE YOU MY SOUL,**
> **I LIVE FOR YOU ALONE AND**
> **EVERY BREATH THAT**
> **I TAKE, AND EVERY MOMENT**
> **I AM AWAKE**
> **I PUT MY TRUST AND FAITH IN YOU,**
> **I ASK YOU MY LORD TO TEACH ME;**
> **GIVE ME WISDOM,**
> **HAVE YOUR WAY IN ME,**
> **OH MY GRACIOUS LORD AND SAVIOUR.**

God wants us to depend entirely on him, he wants us to lean on, trust in and rely on him. Actually, that is a part of the definition of faith, are we not now partners with God, which that now means that we have our own responsibilities, however we must lean on Jesus in order to do the things that are our part.

God called me to become a Minister, to help mission feed all his little children, to write this book to help you to understand the word of God a lot more and to help and teach you through your understanding to stay close to God and his word, he anointed me and gifted me to do what I need to do, but that still doesn't mean that I don't need my father in heaven, because I still have to trust in God and remember how much that I truly need him.

Sometimes we may think that we do not need God and his help with something or things that we have done over and over again successfully we truly do think why would we need help with something we already know that we can do but It is dangerous to become self reliant, isn't this something to think about "right" in our faith believing in our walk with God.

The Bible speaks frequently of the self confident fools, people who think they are self sufficient and can take care of themselves are being foolish, and eventually that will be proven to everyone including themselves.

An independent attitude is part of the baby stage of Christianity, for a mature Christian knows that they can truly do nothing of any real value apart from our Lord Jesus Christ. Of course, we can do things but that doesn't mean they will be done right or that we will enjoy them or that they will produce any real lasting fruit, we need Jesus to get our lives on the right pathway.

When our Lord says we can do nothing apart from him, he means things will not work properly in our lives unless we invite him into everything, and it is Jesus presence that can eliminate much of the struggle we experience in our lives; it makes impossible things possible, my hard things easier and all my frustrating things peaceful; but do not ever be afraid to say, "oh help me Lord, I can't do this without you, I will struggle too much in my everyday life, I need your love, peace and joy that you promise that you can give me to grow in faith, believing; for without it I am nothing.

I truly with all my heart and soul believe that God can change your lives around with love and faith, but the problem within our society is that many people believe that the good things that happens to them is because of them alone; but when things go wrong, well you probably have guessed it " Gods fault.

I know that the things that has happened in my life is purely because I lost faith in people and in myself, so bad things continued to happen because of this, until I called on God to change my life. I want to give you an example from the bible; so have you ever wondered if God can really do what he has promised? Abraham had good reason to Doubt God, for God had promised him and his wife Sarah a child even though he and his wife were far beyond child bearing years.

Yet Gods word tells us that Abraham's faith grew as he waited for the fulfilment of Gods promise. No unbelief or distrust made him waver concerning the promise of God, but he grew strong and was empowered by faith as he gave praise and glory to God.

God promised Abraham that he would have an heir from his own body, but many years came and went and still there was no child as a result of Abraham and Sarah's relationship. Abraham still stood in faith, believing that what God had said would come to pass. As he stood, he was attacked with thoughts of doubt, and the spirit of unbelief pressed him to disobey God.

Disobedience in a situation like this can simply be given up when God prompts us to continue on. Disobedience is disregarding the voice of the Lord, or whenever God is speaking to us personally, for many think that the small voice is their thoughts and not God's leading, which only leads us to ignoring the voice of God.

Abraham continued though to remain steadfast; he kept praising and giving glory to God, and as he did so he continued to grow stronger in faith. He felt confident that God would keep his word, and God did. Praise the Lord, AMEN

God says that we should walk by faith and not by sight; however we have faith in what we see, it is reality to us you hear many people say if I can't see it, it doesn't exist, I need proof; they see it so therefore they believe it; but there is more invisible that is around us; this is where are faith should be; we should not make decisions by what we can see and feel. We have to search our hearts, this is where our faith abides, and lives, from there. The kingdom of God is and always will be within us, and we should follow those inner feelings to reach our father in heaven, which will also lead us to righteousness, peace, and joy in the Holy Spirit.

Feelings can be misleading to us and also steal our faith, more than any other single influence; the problem with feelings is that they change within us constantly. We can feel one way a thousand times and about the same thing in as much as a week or a month.

One minute we can feel like doing something and in our next breath we can totally change our minds and we don't do it. This is the sole reason why people and our feelings provoke us into saying things that we always regret because it was unwise and it can also get many of us into a lot of trouble, but we can't change it then, and it is therefore too late; some problems we can however talk about expressing how we are actually feeling to either ourselves or someone else.

I can associate with this a lot and I want you to truly understand that your feelings are not like anyone else's; I run a business 7 days a week 365 days a year and this is very challenging and with it many moods and feelings that I get from people (public) that I have to deal with, and it's hard to focus and keep faith when someone can just walk through your door and change your feelings in a split second and yes it's that easy.

God has changed my life around so much that his faith helps me to get back on track a lot quicker than ever before, and if I do happen to take a while and keep my focus on who has upset me, God is right there helping me, by faith , trust and prayer.

Do you believe the God of your feelings or the God of the Holy Bible? This is a question we must all think about; ask yourself, more than anything. I have many people who have come in and talked to me in my life and in business about how they feel, and needing help. I try to really think about what they are going through and then try to remind myself that we should all tell each other what the word of God says, not just about how we are feeling, all answers to our worldly problems are in the word of God.

Our feelings do not relay truth to us, but satin on the other hand uses our feelings to deceive and lead us astray. Emotions are unreliable; they can put us on a roller coaster ride and when you fall of; well this is just a matter of time? So we should not rely or believe nor trust them when we are feeling this way.

You must respond to our Holy Spirit only, not with our heads as many people do, for this is where the spirit of God abides, and always be assured that you will have peace. So please start listening and feeling with your heart and not your emotions, before making any major decisions, by learning to walk in and by faith, not by things that you can see and touch, and feel.

When we walk by faith, we start to regulate our lives and conduct ourselves by our convictions or belief respecting our relationship with God and divine things, with trust and Holy fervour; then we walk not by sight or appearance.

The more that we love Jesus, the more we will be able to operate in self-control, it is so easy for us to say no to our selfish desires, and yes to God because of the love that Christians have for our Lord Jesus Christ, and isn't that what our Holy Spirit urges us to do.

For as our love for God grows, we will not want to offend him in any way or form, and in doing something wrong you will find that your Holy Spirit will become grieved and we will want it fixed because we want to do what God wants us to do, obedient's in Christ will give us great Joy, peace and happiness in our everyday lives.

Our walk with Jesus will become progressive and we will do better and better in every aspect as we continue in his word, please do not get discouraged with yourself however if you feel that you are not their yet or where you want to be; but instead try thanking God for not being where you use to be, for believe me I have no one else to thank but God and Jesus for where I am today and I certainly would not want the old suffering and unhappy me back, when I have My Father and My Lord and Saviour Jesus Christ on my side.

You must understand that if you have a lot of negativity in your life (like I did) and like many other believers who are also tormented by negative thinking about themselves, they think about how God must be so displeased with them because of all their weaknesses and failures.

So how much time do you really waste, living under condemnation? Noticed how I have asked you how much time wasted, because that is exactly what that kind of thinking is and does to you, it only wastes your life.

I often think about all the years that I have wasted that I cannot bring back, and also I think of all the wasted years without my Lord, because I could have had so much more happiness in my life instead of spending so much time crying about things that I could not change; without my Father and Jesus.

Now this doesn't mean that I want you to start thinking about how bad you may have been before you found Christ Jesus as I too did that, but instead I want you to do something different and I ask you to instead, think about the fact that you have been made the righteousness of God in him.

Remembering that thoughts turn into action, so if you change and want to behave better, you do have to change you're thinking first; because if you don't then all I can say is that if you keep thinking how terrible you are, as you will find out ,that you will only start to act worse.

Every time a negative condemning thought comes to your mind, remind yourself that God the Father loves you and meditate on him, and that you have been made in the righteousness of God in Christ. Let God work in you through his word and feel the change in you and how much for the better that you are becoming. For every day you are growing spiritually and God has a huge plan for your life, these are the truths and reality that you must stay focused on, positive thoughts through Christ.

# RECEIVING THE HOLY SPIRIT

**THE HOLY SPIRIT GUIDES** believers into the whole truth, and Jesus is the leader guiding you to a process of sanctification in your life. This is partially accomplished by his convicted works in you so every time we get off track or go in a wrong direction, the Holy Spirit convicts us that our behaviour or our decision is wrong and we need leading back on the right path of righteousness.

You now may be thinking how is this accomplished? It's by a "knowing" in our Holy Spirit that what we are doing is not right. When you and I feel convicted, we should repent, all through the Bible it teaches us to repent, asking for forgiveness, for no more or less that is required or even acceptable.

If we are able to and willing to cooperate with the Holy Spirit, we can move on to what I call spiritual awareness, maturity in a different level; this is where we can release all our thoughts and blessings and prayers to God our Father into our lives. If however, we ignore the Holy Spirits conviction and tend to go on in our own way which many of us tend to do then we will start to find things very difficult and our lives will not be blessed as a result of this, you cannot bear the good fruits that God has to bless us with, which will give us all the love, peace, joy and happiness that do desires for us.

# RECEIVING THE HOLY SPIRIT ✝ 31

Do you think that Satan wants these blessings for us? Satan he does not want us to be convicted of the Holy Spirit, neither does he even want us to understand that we are under conviction, He wants us to think it's us; our own fault, he always has a counterfeit for all the good things that God has to offer us, understanding this is highly important to move forward in God.

Satan has us thinking that something's appear to be similar to what God offers, he is a counterfeit he is only out to destroy you, but only if we accept it without thinking from our heart that It doesn't feel right, we cannot think with our head, if received; it will only bring us destruction instead of blessings, which is what Satan is planning to keep you away from God.

I believe that Satan's counterfeit for true godly convictions is only condemnation; for condemnation always produces the feelings of guilt which will only bring you grief into your life making you feel down in every way possible, when we feel this way we are moving away from God making it harder for us to be with God, and Satan can easily access us, causing us this grief and heartache, and confusion.

It's heaviness in your heart and your mind which will also lead you to have bad thoughts and lead your mind to wonder, leading to negativity and sadness which will filter around you and your home and your family environment, and this is exactly what Satan wants to steal and rob you; from your life, the more lives he can destroy the better he feels, not you.

Now our Father in heaven on the other hand, sent our Lord Jesus Christ to set us free and to give us righteousness, peace and joy, our Holy Spirits should be filled with the love and light of God that he gives to us it should not feel heavy and full of burdens; that we are unable to bear we cannot carry our sins; however Jesus came to bear them he died for us so Jesus alone is able to do so, and we must receive his love through God and ministry through the scriptures of God's word.

Did you know that the Holy Spirit given to us by God that it actually speaks to our conscience to convict us of our sin and to convince us to repent, which means to turn and to head in the right direction which God is trying to lead us to rather than the wrong one in which most are heading because of our sin nature.

Learning about condemnation has taken a long time for me; because I condemned myself every time the Holy Spirit convicted me of something in my life that was not of God's will; because Godly conviction is meant to lift us out of a situation and to help us to move up higher in Gods will and plan for our lives and condemnation on the other hand it only pulls us deeper down and puts us under such a heavy burden of guilt, negativity and sadness, which easily leads to depression.

It is a normal part of life to have the feelings of guilt when we feel we are being convicted of our sins, especially when you find God and want to walk in righteousness; however to keep these guilty feelings after you have repented of sin is not healthy for you nor is it Gods will for us to continually feel that way, and God understands that it is also destructive to you mentally and emotionally leading you away from your Holy Spirit.

**In John 16:8:14** He says, When he comes, he will convict and convince the world and bring demonstration to it about sin and about righteousness, uprightness' of the heart and right standing with God and about judgement about sin, because they do not believe me ,trust and rely on me about righteousness, uprightness in the heart and right standing in God, because I go to my Father, and you will see me no longer; about Judgement, because the ruler of this world Satan is judged and condemned and sentence already is passed upon him.

I Jesus have still many things to say to you, but you are not able to bear them or to take them upon you or to grasp them now; but when he the Spirit of truth, the truth given Spirit comes, he will guide you into truth, the whole truth, for he will not speak his own message but he will tell whatever he hears from the Father; he will give the message that has been given to him, and he will announce and declare to you the things that are to come. That will happen in the future.

He will honour and glorify me, because he will take of what is mine and will reveal, declare and transmit it to you. For everything the Father has is mine, that is what I meant when I said that he the Spirit will take the things that are mine and will reveal it to you, and a little while you will no longer see me, and again after a short while you will see me.

# THE SPIRIT OF TRUTH

**JESUS TOLD HIS DISCIPLES** that he had many things to say to them that they were unable to bear. But he promised that the Holy Spirit would come and lead them into all truth and continue to teach them.

When Jesus spoke these words, he was talking to men with whom he had spent a few years with. They were with him day and night, yet he indicated that he had so much more to teach them.

We might think that if Jesus were with us for a few years and personally getting to know our Lord and Saviour Jesus Christ we would have learnt so much, and then to be able to teach people what Jesus taught you **wow** what an honour. Jesus said to expect more because he will always have things to teach us and something to say to us about new situations that we are facing and in the near future we will face.

Jesus he always knew the right thing to say and do because he only did what he saw his Father in heaven do, and as our Lord, we can trust him to personally lead us on the right path every single day. Jesus said, it is written in the book of the profits, that we should all be taught of God in person for our teachings, and that everyone that has listened to their Holy Spirit and learns from the Father, will come to me first.

Our Father in Heaven knew we needed help in understanding his plan for us and this is the reasoning behind why he sent the Holy Spirit to live inside of us, inside every Christian that believes and trusts in God and his beloved son Jesus Christ. He is our guide our teacher;

he is of the full truth and our comforter, for God will send you in the comforter; as he did for me.

Our Father in Heaven and Jesus; I will turn to with all my heart and soul; I need them often so I pray and ask for help and guidance. I owe them so much on a personal level; they have given me comfort when I have needed it the most and they have saved me from total destruction and given me a reason to live.

My Holy Spirit is so in tune to me every day that I do know when I am letting my Father down, my Holy Spirit tells me, I do know what is right and what is wrong as most of us do; but I am still of flesh and I do make mistakes and we have so much as people to learn on a spiritual level.

But I love learning and writing this book to you; all from my Father and Jesus, when I first started writing this book I was so stuck on where to start, so I just went for it, not putting too much thought in it at all. But my Father told me to walk away from it and NOW.

I knew that God the Father was not happy with what I was writing and I walked away from what I was doing, and thinking what was I doing wrong and as you can imagine I was very upset and crying that God was not happy with me. (So I thought anyway)

I asked and prayed for him to please help me and that I was sorry, but God he wasn't upset as I was with myself, you see although my (our) Father wasn't happy He wanted me to put my own input into this book of what he has done for my life, so that others can understand what he can also do for others and to take them into a journey of love, peace, joy and happiness and to trust and rely on him. Because to teach people on life and God, it needs to come from God and your Holy Spirit (God within), not just writing from the Holy Bible, so my Father showed me the way to teach you and helping you to understand. AMEN

## DAILY PRINCIPLES OF YOUR LIFE

Everyone desperately needs the God power of the Holy Spirit in our lives not just today but everyday just to keep your everyday struggles under control and to keep focus on God, and we need to thank God because it is available to each and every one of us; it's up to everyone of Gods faithful ones (believers) to ask for it! Christianity is not a religious activity as many people think and I have spoken to many that think that way, a born again Christian to some, think it is almost voodoo. But it's a way of life and living a life in Our Lord and our Saviour Jesus Christ, and the Holy Spirit that wants us to be involved in every area of our lives, and YES every area.

We all need this amazing power and Jesus has promised that, you shall receive this power when the Holy Spirit has come upon you; I do not, or let's say cannot imagine any person who could hope and pray for inability and weakness; who could possibly want to suffer "right" Gods desire for us is to be powerful and to live and enjoy a fulfilled life, lives that will include total victory over Satan and all of his wicked plots and schemes to kill and destroy you, God tells us to be strong, because Satan is a defeated foe.

The Holy Spirit is the power of God, and when he comes into our lives we can feel and have this amazing power, it can and does transform your life, your mind, and through Jesus Christ, faith and believing it has the power to heal. We can even say that our power level is completely dependent on this power; and our wanting to surrender ourselves to God with all of our heart and soul.

Have you truly given yourself totally in your heart to God (the Holy Spirit) Have you asked and received him into your everyday area of your life; or have you held yourself back because you do not want any interference from anything or anyone into your already full life, not even to God because you are way too busy.

I mentioned spiritual maturity previously in the book; this spiritual maturity is a process. It is where you release areas of your life to our Lord, "giving" a little of yourself to him each and every day; and the more that we release to God the better off our lives will become. We often become so use to how we live our lives that we cling onto the very things that will make us miserable; becoming almost stagnant and refusing to let go because we become afraid of changes in all areas of your life, and many do not like change.

The answer is to all whom want God in your life is to trust God and know for certain that everything that he asks you to do; can only be for your own good, and that it will indeed make your life better, changing you and your family; they will feel the difference in you making the family home environment lighter because you have let the good of God's light in.

The power of the Holy Spirit enables us to be what God wants us to be, we haven't done the best Job, now it is God's turn to work and change us; do you noticed now by watching and observing that people received power to "be" witnesses for Jesus Christ in our everyday lives, the Bible talks frequently about witnesses, not power to do witnessing; God wants us to become what he has in mind for us, for when we become what he wants us to be like then we will begin to do better because we are reborn in Christ and we will be what God wants us to be like and do what God wants us to do.

**Not power to do witnessing**; let me explain; while doing witnessing is a good thing the key to the kingdom is to be a witness for Christ in our everyday living, while people can show up in church and think that will be good enough, however Gods greatest desire is for each believer to become Christ like in all of our thoughts, attitudes, words and deeds, this is what brings around change in you.

Many people make the mistake of being concerned about what is happening in our own and "everyone else's" circumstances, but clearly our priority should be what's going on in our hearts, and our minds for God is more interested in us changing our circumstances, and this can only be done by inviting him in, letting him have his way in your life, and watch the miracles and experience the increase of the Holy Spirits power of the God within.

I have always used the word infinity for the love I have for my Family, myself and my Husband and our son Tristan; when we say to each other how much do we love each other; we always say Infinity, I even had a necklace designed into an infinity sign with our initials inside, to symbolize our love for each other. I also believe that the key word for God is infinity, if you think about it God created our world and the universe and its infinite, it's never ending and always growing is that not clearly power beyond our comprehension.

That's also the love that we all as Christians should feel for God and Jesus Lets go deeper? God wants us to do without his almighty power until he feels we are ready and can handle it correctly, like an approval from the almighty one. Have you seen people in church with their hands held high waiting for the outpouring of the Holy Spirit to enter them, AMEN when we should actually be waiting and approach God with a right attitude and then say to our Father, I will wait for you my Lord indefinitely, until you feel I am ready to accept and receive the Holy Spirit from you, the almighty power from on high.

Many need God desperately I know I did, but God still made me wait until I really hit rock bottom, so I clearly understand why God wants us to wait until he thinks we can handle and comprehend a fraction of the true meaning of God, his wants in our lives, and his work.

Now the reason for me saying a fraction is because we could never handle the truth completely, for that's how God works, he says it's not for us to know for many reasons, we are flesh and live completely in the flesh so for God there is no way we could except the truth no matter how much we say we love him, never mind the ones that do not believe. Even Jesus doesn't know when he is coming back to our world? Now that is truth for it is written.

Thinking about waiting for God in the flesh for indefinitely is a lot for people in the flesh to even comprehend, and the reason for that is the energy levels we have, even if we think that we can wait for God, people can only have so much patience and then right back into the flesh we go, it always takes over, God hasn't done what we want quick enough or how can God let that happen ECT, constantly falling back to our old ways covering the same grounds and over and over again, no wonder many say we are predictable.

Some make progress and then become impatient and lose sight of the big picture, what needs to happen is to gain trust and maintain trust in God; we must stand fast in the liberties that are given and not to submit again to bondage we have once put off.

# THE SPIRIT OF TRUTH ✝ 39

People do not understand that God is always working for us, is it not only because we cannot see or feel God working in our behalf; we have inherited through Jesus the promise of love, faith, trust and patience, is that not righteousness, unmerited favour.

The mindset we need to have is this: Oh God please hear my prayers I have come to the end of myself, I have tried so many things and much more, everything I can possibly think of and for many years, Now I have fallen so far and I truly need your help and support to put me back in favour with you. I now understand that I cannot do this without you, I know I am nothing without you; so I am waiting, I will have patience, for I know that I am being tested, I am willing to wait indefinitely for you God, for as long as it takes, I have lost sight of myself and the truth. I need to understand and find wisdom through you My Lord, I need to be saved. AMEN

# NO FAVOURTISM WITH GOD THE FATHER

**WE MUST LOVE AS GOD LOVES,** so we must not show partiality, for God is impartial; this does not mean that we cannot be more involved with certain people than others. It does however mean that we cannot treat some people one way and other people differently. We cannot be kind to those who we class as friends and then turn your back on people who are of no interest or importance to you, thinking like that is wrong, we are all brothers and sisters.

I know many people with whom I am not interested in at all never mind trying to have a deep personal relationship with them for instance I wouldn't share a coffee ECT; for I know for one reason or another that it would not benefit either of us"understand" however this does not mean that these people are bad or not good enough for me, it's just a casual relationship Hi and By, trying not to be rude to them and it would be a vice versa situation I am sure.

However though I have struggled with this for many years; simply because of my business and having to deal with many people on a day to day basis; and then there is family issues, now for that simple reason I have needed God and Jesus on my side just to help me get through the daily struggles of dealing with difficult people and not trying to get involved in their problems.

I needed to stay on a fruitful path a path of righteousness, I believe now that God puts you in a position to see how you react with difficult times and people, as he did with me to see how I am reacting, and how I am treated and how I am treating people now to how I use to act with people before becoming reborn as a Christian and at times I am sure I failed.

God is also teaching me to treat people also with respect, to make them feel of value regardless of their behaviour, and trust me this is difficult, as sometimes I still have my thoughts but that is as far as it can go, learning to keep your mouth to yourself, to listen to people when they are talking to me, regardless of what they are also talking about, and not to judge them.

God has given me several people like that in my life and no doubt you as well, and as learning with God's help, I can only appreciate it very much, I have said to God gee thanks Lord and got the response back before I even finished the words, "well how else are you going to learn" But now God has taught me to have all respect for people, and even when I have my moments I understand perfectly that Its wrong and keep with God in heart at all times. For judge and you will be judged, for we will all bow before God as it is written.

Our walk with love in God is readily seen by how we treat people who cannot do us any good; if we truly want to love as God loves, we will treat everyone equally with honour and respect, it's going to be sometimes really hard for you and the people that you come across in your lifetime and its certainly going to be a struggle as it was for me, but I can tell you that it has to be right standing with God.

## EPHESIANS 3:16:19

May he grant you out of the rich treasury, his glory to be strengthened and reinforced with mighty power in the inner man by the Holy Spirit (The God dwelling within you personally). May Christ dwell in your hearts by faith; and may you be rooted deeply in love and founded securely on love.

That you may have the power and to be strong, so you too can comprehend and grasp with all the saints (Gods devoted people) what is the breadth and length and height and depth of it.

So that you may really come to know the love Of Christ Jesus, which far surpasses mere knowledge without experience; that you may be filled through all your being, unto all the fullness of God may have the richest measure of the divine presence, and to become a body Holy filled and flooded with God himself.

Just imagine having your personality filled with the Holy Spirit of the living God and your every being a body filled with God himself. I just love that thought and when I am down and ask God for help and then start to feel better in myself because of God within, it's the ultimate love. You can't get better than that can you; believing in God and everything that he can do for you because of your love, trust and joy in loving and believing in him, how can one not want what God can give; to give up your old ways for Christ Jesus; and to become a follower of Christ. (Take up your cross).

Christians should not hold back any area of their lives from God for in doing so it will be an area that cannot be filled with his spirit, your heart needs to be surrendered to God, and your time is his, so is your money, your talents which are a gift from God, your family which is chosen from birth; for your life is mapped out for you, your careers, your thoughts, attitudes and desires. God watches everything you do in your life, and he also wants to be involved in your life so that he is an ear away for when you need him, so call on God and Jesus when you need them.

**JESUS IS OUR KING AND OUR SAVIOUR HE SITS AT THE RIGHT HAND OF GOD AND MANY CHRISTIANS NEED TO REMEMBER THAT HE DIED TO GIVE US A SECOND CHANCE TO HAVE LIFE IN THE KINGDOM OF HEAVEN.**

I lived what I can only described was a defeated life for many years; let me explain what I mean by this. I was not fully surrendered; I still had areas of my life that I claimed as my own, I accepted Jesus as my lord and saviour, I even owned the bible but had not yet acknowledged it correctly (in the word); I even had Jesus enough in my heart to stay out of Hell, but I hadn't accepted Jesus as my Lord in every area of my life; not enough for me anyway that I could possibly think that I had victory to walk in the grace of God and be totally free and saved with the Holy Spirit of my lord and Saviour; and there is a difference.

Their isn't many people out in the world If not all; who doesn't need the blessedness of being filled with the Holy Spirit, for everyone of us needs saving to some extent, we have all sinned even the best of us and there are plenty of people out in the world that think that they are good enough and perfect enough and don't need saving, because this is what our world is all about, don't people understand that God knew us all and all about our lives before we were even put in our mother's womb, you cannot hide from God he knows our sins, thoughts, and our hearts.

Complete surrender to God brings good changes into our lives and in doing so will open doors to things that we long for in hope, love, peace, joy and happiness; and yet even though this is what people want and need; we waste all our energy trying to obtain access to them our own way without inviting our Lord in. But I encourage you today to surrender yourself and every area of it to God so that you can receive the Holy Spirit in every area of your life. AMEN

## AND LET THE LORD BLESS YOU AND KEEP YOU; AND LET THE LORD MAKE HIS FACE SHINE UPON YOU.....

In the supernatural realm with God, nothing is impossible for there is more in the invisible than the visible; in the natural world many things are impossible, because without God you are nothing. But God wants us to be happy and to believe in him, and for us to believe in striving for the greater things, and to be making bigger plans, and not to be afraid to ask God for blessings, for God so loves his children and does want the best for them as we do for our children that we bring into this world, all we want from our children is loyalty, but so does God want that from us.

In the bible the Lord says that we have not yet asked for it, and we can be straight to the point about it, and ask for great things, so children of God are you up to that challenge, to ask your Father for anything; Sometimes when our desires seem overwhelmingly huge we cannot always see the way to accomplishing them, we should remember that even though we do not know the way, see any future of our goals, we must understand and keep our faith in our Lord and saviour to show us the way.

Our God is a loving and caring God, and he has a way for us to do everything he places in our hearts, we have our dreams and our visions, some people truly rely on their dreams and visions, to get them through life.

However God does not give them to us to tease us and frustrate us; we must though keep our faith in him all the way through to the end, not just for a short time until you get bored with the idea and give up, and everything looks too much for us to handle (like climbing mount Everest)! It is untold what people can actually do, even for the people that appear to not be able to do anything. God does not usually call people who are capable, for if he did, and then God would not get the Glory. AMEN

God does choose people frequently in the world that are over their heads completely and are truly ready in their hearts to accept him as the God of love peace, joy, truth and happiness and if they do not realize this straight away, like me; they will soon enough. You need to stand up on the inside, for God knows when you are ready in your heart, you cannot hide anything.

Taking those steps of faith as you receive them directly from God, we usually want to wait until we feel ready before we step out, but if we feel ready, then we tend to lean on ourselves instead of god. We should always know and find our weaknesses' and know God; know his strengths and faithfulness that he has; his beloved children. Remember that he is able to do many great works within you, far and above everything that you could possibly imagine or think! God is able to do exceedingly and abundantly above and beyond all we could dare

# NO FAVOURTISM WITH GOD THE FATHER ✝ 45

to hope for, ask and think, according to his almighty power that is at work in us, it is Gods power, but it is done through us.

But we also need to co operate with God, This means that we need to be daring in our faith and especially in our prayers, so I encourage you to go beyond yourself and stretch your faith into new realms, go beyond your "highest prayers" Desires, thoughts, hopes or dreams.

Do not be discouraged with yourself, however just because you have not yet arrived at a place of perfection in your thoughts and behaviour. God would not be angry with you if God came back today and found you just as you are, as long as he sees that you have the right attitude and are co operating with the works he is doing in you.

God he knows that you are at work and in progress in trying to change and become more in touch with God and yourself, and I want to tell you that you will be for as long as you are here on our earthly realm, but enjoy where you are, on the way to where you are going.

## SPEAK THE WORD OF GRACE PRAYER

God, I pray that my love may abound more and more and extend to its fullest development in knowledge and all keen insight, so that I may display itself in greater depths of acquaintance and more comprehensive discernment. AMEN

Strength comes from the joy of the Lord, Rejoicing in all things; and cultivates real joy in your life, for joy is more than emotional happiness; it can be anything from extreme hilarity to a calm delight.

The Joy that God and Jesus has brought into my life truly amazes me every single day and there is not a day that goes by that I cannot give anyone thanks for that joy, peace and happiness accept my lord, and you too can have this as well if you give yourself to God like I did, the tears that I cry now are because of the love that God has brought to my life and I find myself not getting upset over such minor little things that I would blow right out of potion, now I think how could I have ever acted like that, how could I have possibly had those thoughts, how could I have possibly said those angry words to that person, whether they were wrong or not, how could I have used such bad language.

These are the changes that God has brought into my life and yes God has made me a new person and yes God can change you as well, give him a chance, for God and Jesus are worth it and God wants you to understand that he wants you because you are worth the saving, repent for your sins and God will be well pleased.

God will always finish his works that he has started in you, to keep working in his beloved believers, God has called us unto himself and started a good works in us, and he will finish it, that is a promise, from our Lord.

But of course we must have a devoted part to play, which is to believe in our Lord Jesus' words, for they will transform you, pray always, and always be thankful to our Father, never be overcome by Evil, overcome evil by Good. Conform and be established in God, which is to keep believing in God to be delivered, co operating with the sanctifying works of the Holy Spirit in our lives.

I know it is frustrating sometimes to feel that we are in the middle of something and do not know how to go forward, but to also know that we cannot go back to our old way, we must walk by faith, not by sight, let Gods love control us, live for Jesus for he died and rose for us.

Christ must be in you, to have power over the enemy, have sufficiency in everything, let your harvest increase, you are a blessing to the Lord, be devoted to Jesus, Do not be let astray from God, you have fellowship with the lord Jesus and the Holy Spirit.

We love Jesus "right" and we do want to go all the way through to the finish with Jesus by our side, but we are in the flesh still and at times it is difficult, comprehending what is right and what is not, it's the fear, to want to get it right; But Jesus himself does understand this, he was born of flesh, to understand our way, however we sometimes forget that Jesus lived in the fleshly body that we have, while he was here on the Earth, so he does understand what it's like to be tempted, Jesus was tempted by the devil, in the desert, and he had passed; so must we.

You may experience temptation to sin, or even just to want to quit and give up because you find it to difficult, but turn back to God for

# NO FAVOURTISM WITH GOD THE FATHER ✝ 47

he will indeed strengthen you to go all the way to the finish with him, reach out to Jesus, rely on him to help you, trust, faith and reliance, its important; it may be uncomfortable sometimes but you will be pleased in the end, if you allow the Lord to go with you, and let him work in you.

Many people today start things and never finish which isn't pleasing to God, I myself have done this and you can pretty much say that this is most of us; In fact it's not a good representation of many people who have the desire to be in righteousness with God to work with integrity, although many of us just want to make the right decision and get it right, having the fear of making a wrong decision to start with and sometimes it works. It's easy to start something because all of our emotions are being driven by the excitement of stating something new, not putting enough thought behind it.

When people's feelings are no longer supporting them it is seen in their character and this is sometimes a good time to be spending it alone with God, he can bring you back to a place where he wants you, he brought you to him, let's not forget that, so he wants you to turn back to him, it's also in Gods character to finish what he had started; not to give in, like we do. We need to respect Jesus and keep the commitment we started in Christ, it's a much better place to be than where we were before we turned to God.

You may want to even ask yourself at times if where you are in your life today is a challenging time. Know that God can work through you in any circumstances to further you along in the word of the Gospel to build your Holy Spirit, strengthening you, just as he did for Paul in Philippians 1:12:14 working in yourself for Christ, for when your are struggling God knows that your are serving him, ask God to continue to show you how you can better serve him, and the word of God, you will see in your Bible how Paul was in prison, and how Paul drew his strength from the Lord and the Gospel, God revealing himself in such a way that strengthening his belief, and his love from the knowledge of the word of God.

This needs to always be our way of thinking, one thing that many fellow Christians face when walking with the Lord is keeping up with good behaviour, perfect behaviour is even better, walking the right path to righteousness is all we want to achieve, but with God's help we can keep going and get better at acknowledging our poor behaviour bringing it completely back to God to fix, helping us to keep pressing forward to achieve our goals.

    I want to share with you what happened to me today as an example of how Jesus works in us, I had a phone call from a man who was obviously trying to sell me a product, which we have all had at one time or another, but I was busy writing this book and didn't want to be disturbed by anyone, this was my time with the Lord and his message to you, I have very little time I think you have the message "right", so I answered the phone in the usual manner, hello and who I was and who is speaking and what do you need and want, blah, blah, blah, I was polite don't get me wrong.

    The man said he wanted to speak to the owner, but I said to him sorry the owner wasn't here, available, you all get the message right, I was pushing him of, he replied, when will she be back, (not wanting him to disturb me tomorrow) I replied, she has gone on holidays and that she would not be back for weeks, (just to stop him from not calling back, and I can continue to not be disturbed by telephone calls), but also knowing that he did have the opportunity to call back at a later time "right".

    But he called me a liar and hung up, well that through me, dumb founded me, and then it hit me, I was lying, then I felt guilty, (how could I just lie to him and especially while I am writing the word of God and teaching others about him, when I have sinned), how could I do this to God, I felt like you couldn't imagine, a hypocrite was one, I was so upset and I cried hard, I lied and God doesn't like liars.

    I am teaching people to be of God, I lied to someone, mind you not intentionally in my heart, no excuses though, but not thinking properly, I just had no intentions what so ever to harm anyone, even though the man was only just doing his job. I told my husband and he tried his hardest to comfort me as much as he could, and to some extent he did, but I explained to him that I should know better.

# NO FAVOURTISM WITH GOD THE FATHER ✝ 49

I don't want to use God as an excuse that I know he would forgive me, and yes I did tell God straight away just to let him know that I didn't realize that at the time I was sinning, which is also silly for God already knew what happened, he is the mighty God, that knows all.

However about 15min or so later I was serving a customer and had to go into the kitchen when God said to me to pray for the man, well that stopped me in my tracks, and made me think, why would God ask me to pray for this poor man when I was the one lying to him,

Then God gave me the answer, this man called me a liar and he also upset me, which is a bigger sin, he judged me, he accused me, and he intentionally wanted to upset me and he did; for also in the bible; God doesn't except people who argue and call people to their faces names or on the phone as it's the same principle, name calling only comes under a proud heart, or a puffed up ego; which is the leaven.

All this is what the man had done over the phone, my intensions in Gods eyes even though I was also wrong, I wasn't out to harm this man at all, but his intensions on the other hand was different, and to upset and cause me grief.

Lessons for me to learn by God, as it turned out, I also teach you what God wants you to know about how he works for me to you, next comes something to think about, that I have learned by this whole phone experience, do you know why God never lets us achieve perfect behaviour? If we ever did, we would derive our sense of worth from our perfection and performance rather than from Gods love and grace.

If we think more deeply about this, if you and I behaved perfectly all the time, we would start to think God owed us an answer to our prayers, because of our obedience to all the rules and regulations. So do you know what God does? He will leave us weaknesses so that we can turn to him, (like I did when I lied on the phone) he knows we could never be perfect all the time, that's our wish, when we love God, with all our heart and soul; however we do need to turn constantly to him to ask for and confess what we have done wrong, and asking god for his help.

Our weaknesses helps keep us dependent on God, whether we like it or not. God is not going to let us work our way into a sense of peace and fulfilment. But he will allow us to work ourselves into a fit and frenzy. Why you ask?

It's so that we can realize that the works of the flesh produce nothing but upset and misery and frustration, which is exactly how I feel today.

Now you may be thinking is that so, and what are we suppose to do? My answer to you is simple, TRUST in God, relax, and enjoy your life. For we really need to learn to enjoy God more. That will not only help us, it will also take the pressure off the people around us. We need to also quit demanding perfection from ourselves and everyone around us. We need to start to enjoy people around us that we come in contact with in our everyday lives accepting them just as they are, for that is also what we expect, believing in the righteousness in yourself, believing in god and our Lord Jesus Christ, making that your focus and goal.

The Holy Bible is a teaching tool, a guide to put you in right standing with God and Jesus, it presents detailed instructions and advice; to tell us what kind of way we should be living and thinking, things that will keep us on the good things that keep us happy, not on things that tear us down, for its our thoughts that affect our moods and our attitudes and affecting the people we come in contact with, which can rub off on them changing their moods, so in fact everything God is trying to teach us in the bible is for our own good, he already knows what we want and think and what makes us happy and unhappy.

But when people are thinking wrong thoughts, they become miserable and then often this can turn into depression, affecting again everyone that you are in contact with, usually affecting family in a strong way, and this is not Gods work or how he wants his children to feel.

Thinking about what you are thinking about is very important to every believer of God, for this is when Satan will work on you and deceive people into thinking that the source of their misery or problems is something other than what usually is, they think that it's a

# NO FAVOURTISM WITH GOD THE FATHER ✝ 51

normal behavioural pattern, thinking I always feel this way and it will pass, how wrong they are; Satan will play with your thoughts to make you feel that they are your thoughts, he can and does have a lot to do with how you can feel.

He is a manipulator playing with your head and he is good at it, making you think that you are unhappy due to what is going on in your circumstances, but your unhappiness is because of your thoughts and his influences that he is taking advantage of, which is you.

For many years I truly believed I was unhappy because of things that was going on in my life, the way people were treating me, what they were doing and were not doing to me, I blamed my unhappiness, misery; on my husband, my children, my family members, anyone I could, I thought I would be happy if they were different, if they would be more attentive to my feelings and needs, but it really just doesn't work that way, as many people would hopefully understand.

But my beloved Lord helped me to finally understand and face the truth, it's your thoughts that need to change, you cannot expect people to change their ways especially if they cannot see and do not want to see your views regardless, of what they are, for people are individuals and don't see eye to eye of your ways, for they as well as you and I are still walking in the flesh.

I also strongly urge you to think about what you are thinking about, when you change the things you allow your mind to dwell on; you will be on your way to a greater sense of freedom, wholeness and victory.

We all have daily needs and wants but did you even consider that sometimes what you want might not actually be what you need? We however can thank God that he knows what we need, even before we realize it, and God will always be faithful to us and provide. I thank God/Jesus everyday for what he has provided and brought to my life for myself and my family.

My life has become dramatically changed through my faith and my deep devoted love for my Lord and Saviour Jesus Christ, become a Pastor/disciple and follower of the Lord, sending prayers, blessings and teaching to all who read this book, praying the prayers from the prayer section, is transforming your life as the reader, which is bringing you closer to the Lord, transforming your own life through your own faith and love of the Lord, is fulfilling.

The Lord God is working in me to transfer all my knowledge and wisdom given to be passed on to you, which is all the word of God, for the word of God provides people with everyday life changing experiences and answers, in the bible there are 3.000 promises from God that he will give you, find them and have faith and trust in the Lord and he will provide;

There is nothing in the Holy Bible where you cannot find an answer to any problem that arises in your life, you have to read the whole Bible to understand what I am trying to explain to you; you have to work with God, to call also upon Jesus, when you find the answer, so that these changes can be powered with strength by the Lord so it will start working in the areas of your life, by Grace, love, peace and joy.

# "Christ Jesus"

**MANY SPEAK OF JESUS CHRIST,** not fully understanding the title of Christ, Christ is in essence a confession of faith, and it literally means "The Anointed one." The Messiah would be anointed by Gods Spirit to be the preeminent Prophet, Priest, and our King. And with his confession, thou art the Christ, the son of the living God."

Our Lord and Saviour was with God from the beginning of time, yes from Adam until his resurrection, it was Jesus that walked with Adam in the Garden of Eden, Jesus States I am the beginning I am the end, The Holy Bible is Jesus from the beginning of Genesis to the New Testament/ revelations.

## JOHN 4:29

Come and see a man, "which told me all things that I ever did: is this not the Christ and we believe and are sure that thou art the Christ, the son of the living God.

The most important relationship you could ever have or want is the Holy Scriptures in your life, to have a close personal relationship with Jesus Christ, to receive him as your Lord and saviour, walking with him on a day to day basis, he will transform your Holy Spirit filling it with the greatest of Love, you entering into the deepest of love, that you can never have with anyone that you have ever known except Jesus.

## SPEAKING THE WORDS OF GRACE

Thankyou Jesus, for walking with me, training me every day, walking in love, faith and righteousness, thank you for loving me, and freeing me from all the pain and suffering that I have been through, you have also freed me from all of my sins, you took them for me when you suffered and died on the cross, you have shown me real love that you have for Fathers children, a sacrifice, out of love, through your shed blood. Amen

The book of revelations was written by John dated around 70-95 AD, there are many different perspectives and interpretations of the book of revelations however it can be difficult to understand, but it is also to remind us all that we do have an enemy, who is Satan.

Many people do not even realize that there is a spiritual war being waged between the forces of God and the forces of Satan, but the best news is that when Jesus Christ returns with his army of Angel by his side, he will ultimately win.

As the struggle unfolds, there will be days of deception and the anti Christ will arise, deceiving many who will listen to his lies as he pretends that he is our Lord, but through the scriptures we are pre warned, and through our Holy Spirit, we can live will discernment during these times and look forward to the second coming of our beloved Jesus Christ, who will bring a thousand years of peace.

As a devout Christian, and follower of Jesus Christ, you the reader and everyone throughout history of the Holy Bible, are the true winners, living forever with Jesus in our Fathers blessed realm, keep in mind that the book of revelations is also a revelation it's unveiling; and gives us a picture into our Lord Jesus Christ.

It's a teaching tool for us to know who Jesus is and how he lived his life until his death and his resurrection, the power that Jesus had over his enemies and the love that he had for church and the teachings of his father's word, Jesus is an inspiration to all who believe in him and in our Father and his word.

The Holy Bible is the book of undeniable truth about our Lord, many do not realize and understand that our Lord Jesus is in the beginning and the end of revelations; he is the Holy Bible; Jesus is the son of God and the son of man, he is worthy of all the grace, love, glory and the soul reason why his beloved people have followed him and the word of his and our father for over 2000yrs, all over the world, he states he is the way the truth and the life.

That is unbelievable power and love beyond most people's comprehension of true faith and following, Jesus Christs followers, his disciples, Christians believe in our mind, body and Holy Spirit, that we are going to see our Lord Jesus again, and that the truth is he is coming back, to save us from condemnation; to give his believers life forever in the kingdom of Heaven and that Earth will have a 1000 yrs of peace.

Our Lord he wants us to be saved for he loves us; this is why we must stand strong in our faith and not to turn away from him when we are having a tough ride in our lives, standing firm in our belief with no doubt give us the strength that we need to push forward in believing that Jesus will get us through all our problems, including our sicknesses, and diseases; no matter what obstacles' we have to face in our lives.

I truly do believe that the Holy Scriptures is an individual test of our love of Jesus Christ and every individuals beliefs and faith, in what is written and how we interpret the word of God, many wonder if how they interpret it is wrong and many will argue about how it is interpreted, but listen, who is right and who is wrong, in how you see the word of God.

The truth is in your strong belief in God and the kingdom of heaven and that Jesus died for us to save us from all of our sins, past, present and future and that he did indeed, died on the cross to save us, I believe that this is the most important test, your love and faith in your heart, that is what God is looking for, how deep is your belief, because one day all who do not believe are certainly going to believe, AMEN.

Another example to give you is that doors that open for true believers, the ones that have at times struggled, but still have not denied his existence, the door will not be closed on them; they will remain open. And the doors that remain closed for the non believers in God, and his son Jesus Christ; they have hardened hearts and have closed the door on him, some of them, not all, believe in another God, and not the word of God, and believe he did not make Heaven and Earth, and all things great and small.

Our God he already knows what is in your heart and the record of your life, fear God, is where this also comes in for we cannot hide anything from our mighty God, all is written in the Lambs book of life, and he already knew us before we were even born, denying what we have done and pushing it under a mat so to speak is a waste of time, it is better to remember all that you have done and repent for all sins for our forgiveness from our Lord God almighty to have everlasting life in the kingdom of God, also remembering that Jesus leaves the door open for many hearts, for he will not force his way into your life, you must welcome our Lord into your life.

God he wants us to serve him unconditionally and wholeheartedly, he does not like us not putting in an effort 100%, God is worthy of the effort and much more; would you like your loved ones, your children to like you only a little bit, our Father is the same, we are his children and he wants us to love him, not too much to ask for is it.

In **revelations 3:15:16** Jesus says I know your works, when you are cold or hot, so then because you are lukewarm, and neither hot nor cold, will I spew you out of my mouth.

The church is likened to lukewarm water, or as being virtually worthless, Christ Jesus says, he will "spew them out" or reject them from his company. Christ says spiritually the people of the church are poor, blind and naked; true wealth however is only found in the grace of God, is this not God telling his children that he wants us to serve him with enthusiasm and with all their heart and soul, for is this not what following him is all about, is this not what the word of God is teaching us, for God does not appreciate any half-hearted efforts, this is also well clear in revelations 3:15:16 It warns his children about being lukewarm and teaches us that being neither lukewarm nor cold, that it isn't acceptable to God.

Actually, he would prefer that we be cold towards him rather than being lukewarm, strange you may be thinking; for doesn't cold mean that you do not care? I'll explain; God's desire is that we feel that our hearts are on fire with excitement over him, and rightly so, he can work miracles in your life and he deserves this kind of devotion and love, for God's word and his principles, are only for our benefits' and our lives.

Now this is the reason why God would prefer us to be cold than to be lukewarm, now you may also be thinking isn't lukewarm better than nothing? I also believe that it is because lukewarm people are easily deceived into thinking that they are doing what they should be doing when in fact they are not, seeing and believing only what is in their eyes.

They are offering sacrifices and not wholeheartedly in obedient with Christ, for example, they may go to church even confess their sins, and do so only as an obligation but in reality they do not even want to be there at all, maybe they are there only out of pressure from a wife or a husband/ mother or father who wants them to be there, however when a person is totally cold towards God, at least God knows that it can be dealt with more easily, there is hope in the near future , than for someone who is totally deceived by darkness.

Another good example is if God was moving towards you, what would you do? Or if you found yourself face to face with Jesus Christ, I mean now, not when we pass on to the other side, for that will no doubt happen, but face to face with then now; would you work with God and be so pleased to be standing next to them feeling that you are in the presence of divine royalty, and feeling the love that comes with them, to know that they loved you enough to talk towards you, I know how I would feel, and that is totally blessed, beyond imagination, or would you be rebellious and still not believe, letting them just walk right by you, leaving you behind.

If you do not want this at all start now by evaluating your life and the truth in the Holy Bibles word, to have God on your side, and to be in Gods kingdom when your spirit leaves your fleshly body behind, then as far as I am concerned life isn't worth much at all if our Lord Jesus isn't the centre of attention in my life, and if he isn't there for me in the end to hold out his hand and take me to see my Father in Heaven, but sadly though many people waste most of their lives before they realise that this is a fact; and some never will.

God he never does anything halfway, and we should not either, whatever your task may be, work at it wholeheartedly as something for the lord and not for others, this means we are to be good, faithful, loyal, profitable and hardworking, for example employees obey your human employers in everything, not only serving, when they are watching you to win their appreciation; but also wholeheartedly fearing the Lord.

So whatever work that you do you must put your full self into it, as those who are serving not merely other people, but truly serving the Lord, remember that as your reward, you will receive the inheritance of the Lord, for you are in essence working for the Lord, the messiah, but don't worry whoever is doing wrong will be paid in kind for his wrong, and God will not show favouritism, employers treat your workers justly and fairly, for remember that you too have a master in Heaven. Amen.

Remember as well that God wants us to do our jobs well and with good attitudes, and not to be twofaced towards each other, for we need to be as real, sincere, honest, and trustworthy to each other at all times; God wants us to commit our works to him, and this includes your thoughts so that they can be establishes, for the Lord your God who knows your thoughts of his children/man, and God knows what is also vanity.

# Hardened Heart

**I FIND THAT A LOT** that is going on in people's lives stems from either work, or their home environment, and even when you are out socialising with your friends; everything has a lot to do with your thoughts and how you are behaving, and to be able to recognise that your behaviour is not at its best, and this is either your good or bad behaviour.

Unfortunately one of people's biggest problems is to learn to control their thoughts and feelings which will lead to anger and bad words to each other; and all this results in only ungodliness and a hardened Heart (spirit). I have experienced this all too well in my business and having to deal with customers, my staffs problems and behaviour and then there is your family members.

I have learned that it is Hard to stand firm with God when you are dealing with so much of what life is already throwing at you, at one time before I gave myself to God I was so determined that nobody was ever going to hurt me again so I tried ever so hard to harden my heart, and do you know all that it did was to influence the things that I said, because although I tried hard to say things that was right; and trying to please almost every impossible situations in trying to please others, including loved ones, by the time my thoughts had passed through my soul and picked up on the negativity and harshness and bitterness hidden inside of me, my words only came out harsh and hard, and I knew in my soul this was hurting me more,

For I knew that deep down inside of my heart that I just didn't want a hardened heart, I knew it wasn't me at all, I knew I wasn't the person I was portraying, I would cry and say to people I can't do this it isn't me, all I was doing was literally hurting myself even more because I was feeling bad, for being not nice, I was not harming anyone else but me and grieving my Holy Spirit, and I wasn't being very Godly.

I was spiralling into a very dark place a place which I really disliked and I could really feel it as well, and the dark side enjoyed trying to keep me away from turning to God, you know no matter how right you may think your heart is before our father, if you have pride and anger, and resentment in your Holy Spirit, you cannot speak words from your mouth without releasing negativity and emotions, that are pleasing to yourself, anyone that is on the receiving end, nor the one that is most important in your life, and that is God the Father.

Now the answer to how to get rid of it out of your life and why it is important to eliminate it, and why I begged God for his mercy and to help me in my life, because Jesus has told us in Matthew 12:34 it is out of the abundance of the heart or the Spirit that the mouth speaks.

**IN MY HEART AND MY SOUL, LORD I GIVE YOU CONTROL, CONSUME ME FROM THE INSIDE OUT, LORD, LET JUSTICE AND PRAISE BECOME MY EMBRACE, TO LOVE YOU FROM THE INSIDE OUT, AMEN.**

I knew that God had to do some serious work in me, from the inside out, and My prayers were indeed answered, my Lord did do a miracle within me, he reformed me into a new gentleness and turned me back into the caring for others person I once was, He helped me restore my relationship with my children, he restored my heart from grieving for my beloved mother which was what destroyed everything in my life, grieving is a terrible thing to go through, I needed my lords help to overcome my spiralling life that was out of control, including my mouth.

My Lord he sent in the comforter to help my grieving and because I indeed to and wanted to turn to God/Jesus for the healing of my

# HARDENED HEART ✝ 61

heart and my illnesses and my skin cancer, there is not one person on this planet that could stand in front of me today and tell me that this is all a coincidence, when I know in my Holy Spirit that this has happened to me because I grieved and turned to my Lord and My Father in Heaven for help, and that I have seen and heard enough in my life to know what is real and what is not.

What God has revealed to me was which speaks of a capable person, a daughter of God, that out of my mouth must be Godly, to speak and to be taught in wisdom, and that on my tongue must be the law of kindness, giving to others of which God has given to me, caring, feeding and praying to Gods beloved children, and the elderly, sending healing, peace and happiness to all who are suffering.

Not a person with a hammer for a tongue, many of you who hear this will understand where I am coming from, for if you cannot relate to this, then you are bound to be associated with someone who is like that, you could also relate to being mistreated, and abused, have some deep down hatred towards someone that you could be holding onto for many years, have distrust in someone, and have anger that is stored up and you are ready to fire at the next poor unfortunate person that says the wrong thing to you.

But what do you think God wants us to learn really, to keep hanging on to all of this anger, and don't get me wrong I am still not perfect in Gods eyes or even in mine enough for me to be happy, because of my love for God, my fear of God; I got very annoyed at some holiday travellers today; the worst time to own a shop as far as I am concerned, but on the other hand I still am very happy that God has sent these customers to me,

I do understand that this is also teaching to me from God to recognise my annoyances and to learn from them, to put them into respective, and understand what God would do and think, for instance free coffee for the driver that the government put in many, many years ago, we did do it but removed it because we put in a very expensive coffee machine, now I have still got customers wanting it and abusing the new machine by taking more than they should, now I am struggling with do

I continue to keep giving or do I stop and let the new machine pay for what I am giving as a service, as it is my free will to refuse, and the customer's choice to travel without expecting me to give them something for free, when I do not longer do this service, then a lady came in expecting me to feed her children and to pay me later when I have lost a lot of money to unpaid giving, so I feed her little girl by giving her a new baby bottle full of milk and refused to feed the family because I knew that they drank alcohol, Now I put it down to the fact that God would want me to have given to the child, than to worry about getting upset with the travellers wanting something for free when I do not provide the service which is my choice and that I am providing them with a new service that I have paid for to please them.

Now was I wrong in Gods eyes by not giving a free service to everyone that walks in my door, because of a sign done by the government years ago, put onto my shoulders and not being reimbursed for their service that they expected me to do, that I have done for ten years without reimbursement, or was the real test and the most important one was to have a good heart and to give the child a full belly of milk that was crying for a bottle and was hungry.

I thank God as I know the answer in my heart and I do now feel better, these people are adults and they are not suffering neither are they poor except, just wanting something for free, because they think they are entitled to it, when in fact they are not, I am providing them with a service by being opened, and I am entitled to say no, there is the kindness side which bothered me, to give by being kind, but I did so by giving to one of Gods defenceless children, not an adult that should not expect something for nothing when they are travelling.

Over the many years of being in business I have given and opened my heart to many who have been in need, I should not feel guilty and God doesn't want me to feel guilty when I have given so much and will continue to give, we need to accept what God gives us to finally understand and to be happy with our lives, for fearing God and trying to keep his commandments is the only solution to our everyday problems that we face with in life.

Our God is the ultimate Judge, so we need to do things his way, so as to be rewarded accordingly by God, now I think that being rewarded by God is the ultimate gift that we can ever have, it's worth trying very hard to live up to what God our Father wants.

This is the reason why I turn to God as often as I can, I need answers from him to help me to heal, and yes sometimes on a daily basis, to be healed from pain and suffering of past, present and future afflictions, to help us to develop the kindness and the gentleness that he does want us to possess, to let Gods healing powers work fulfil our Holy Spirits, to hear finally words of love, peace and calmness flowing out into others.

Some people will still ask "so what is the secret to happiness and fulfilment in life? I believe it is making sure that we are obeying Gods will and giving ourselves to what God has called us to do; will that always be that easy you ask? "No' not at all, doing God's will is not without its challenges, for we will struggle; for example I still struggle at times and my husband struggles as well, we were taking yesterday about someone close to us who isn't doing what is right with God and what is written in scripture which bothers me, and his behaviour.

I am concerned about his lifestyle because when it falls apart on him he turns to me all the time, then when it doesn't work out his way, goes down the line to the next person, and mind you he is nearly fifty years old, but what we struggle with is actually talking about his ups and downs of his lifestyle and his ungodliness lifestyle, I have baptized him, prayed with him, talked to him about God, anointed him with oil, and still he went straight back to his ungodly behaviour, yet he says I believe and love God.

We came to an understanding that as much as we care for him I must put my love for God first, I have done back flips to help him and that includes giving him a job and paying many of his bills, but enough is enough, he has to live his life the way he chooses, we have been all given our free will, I have made many of my own bad mistakes, but I found our Lord, and have repented and asked for forgiveness, now it's up to everyone else to do the same when its right for them, he can be still saved by the grace of God the same as others who have turned their lives to our Lord and saviour Jesus Christ, there is only one Judge and that is the Lord.

As Christians we understand that God wants us to forgive and love, and to pray for him and the lifestyle he chooses, not to discuss or curse his lifestyle, we get tired and frustrated for we are dragged into it, trying to save someone who is just not ready to be saved, however now it becomes a "good kind of tired" that comes from doing what we were supposed to do that is right standing with God, you see acknowledging by our words that we know we are doing wrong is also right with God for we are confessing our sins for putting someone down and talking about them, whether it's a family member or someone you know; for with God it does not matter who it is because it is against his word.

I hope that gives you a little insight understanding and realization that you cannot do everything, then deciding with God's help what you can and cannot do; it will make you more effective at the things that you are suppose to do and it will greatly increase the levels of peace that God can bring into your life. Peace brought into your life brings power and grace for without this you will only stay frustrated and weak, understand that sometimes you will still feel that way; as I do, but it is so much easier to bring God back into your thoughts and recognize the way you are feeling, as God brings you back to grace and peace, for this understanding; feeling under Gods grace keeps Gods presence with you.

As you the reader; evaluate how you are spending your time and what you are doing with this time in your life, apply this to yourself, if you are totally at peace right now in your life continue to keep it and think about your state of mind and what is keeping you in peace, and if you do not have this peace, think about what is taking your peace away, stop and listen to all the complaining within yourself, what has upset you, who has upset you is someone feeding you the problems?

Listening and learning to understand how you think will open up many doors to your state of mind; you will learn to listen to your mind chatter, and the voices of information that you can receive from the divine as they talk to you, how open are you to this information? Even

# HARDENED HEART ✝ 65

in your regular everyday living, hearing yourself on a regular basis and everyone else around you is going to be a real eye opener, you will therefore need to re-assess what is going on to make important changes as you become closer to how you should be living your new life in Jesus Christ, making positive changes and guidance.

Many people do not understand the mind chatter that is going on inside of them, the positive thoughts and the negative ones, people believe that it is their thoughts because it is their body, and they were born that way, "WRONG" many people even in the medical side of it, people who have had medical conditions have been miss diagnosed, don't get me wrong there are genuine cases, but evil thoughts do not come from God only good thoughts and a good heart, evil thoughts are put into someone by dark forces, which is explained throughout the bible.

For example when Judas he betrayed and was exposed at the Last Supper and peter tried to interfere will Jesus' destiny, Jesus said to him get behind me Satan, Dark or negative thoughts are not given to anyone by God they are from Satan, scary to many yes, but he cannot hurt you unless you let him or another way to put it, INVITE him in to your thoughts, understanding and programming your thoughts is a lesson,

This is very deep; and a lot to take in, but when you start listening to your thoughts you can ask the negative thoughts to leave and ask God to give you back your happy positive peaceful thoughts, negative dark thoughts cannot stay with you for the goodness of God, for God is stronger and more powerful, praying for guidance and teaching is also a positive programming you should continue to teach yourself.

God he does not either want us to all hate our lives and others, growing bitter (like I was). His greatest desire is for us to enjoy being in control and being in his will, to depend on him and to call upon him when we need him; to be satisfied at all times and to have peace, joy and happiness, in doing so we can rely on God and receive his blessings for when you are negative, you do not need him and he cannot help you until you invite him in.

## SPEAK THE WORDS OF GRACE

God, I want to please you always and I ask for your wisdom to come into my life, and your knowledge, I ask for joy, peace and happiness to be brought upon me, I do thankyou my Father for everything that I already have in my life, right now, I want grace flowing into my Holy Spirit, lifting me up as many times as I call upon you when I need lifting up, Oh I thank you for hearing my prayers, may grace abound in me, and my tears flow like a river with my love for you my gracious Lord.
## AMEN

Many people do live their lives to the fullest and yet there are so many people who have ended their lives, and there are many thinking about doing so now; and there are the ones who try to make people's lives as miserable as they possibly can because they are not happy, why? Because it is all they have ended up knowing, and living like this for a long period of time they do not know any other way to function, not knowing how to behave better. But unfortunately they make life extremely sad and difficult for the people and families they live with and associate with, and this can even be with people they have to work with,

One of Jesus sayings is; and I know your thoughts, and I say to you that a kingdom, (Household); that is divided against itself is being brought to desolation and laid to waste, and no city or household divided against itself will last or continue to stand.

So how many people have you met in your life so far that are like this, for Jesus has it so right, because I have met a few, "and listen to me" have we at times not been to same, I had no idea that so many people had problems with mercy, I have known people in my life people who were very young, distant family members and people I just knew from customers who have taken their own lives and before they were even thirty, very sad; some people however show no mercy and just want to drag you down no matter how much they understand that it is hurting you, for its not about you, it's all about them and how they feel.

I believe people who are like that should carry a sign with them titled "I desire More mercy" They need to understand that this kind of

# HARDENED HEART ✟ 67

mercy required from them is Love, kindness, and understanding, and this is what Jesus is also requiring from us which is in everyone, their Holy Spirit; I have been badly hurt from family, and have been in a dark place and have indeed turned to God for his help, **Jesus mercy is great**; he says that those who mourn are blessed and that they will have the comforter sent to them and have this comfort. **AMEN**

The comforting of God which is ministered by his Holy Spirit is so awesome that it is worth having a problem just to be able to receive it and experience what Jesus can give you, as with most things of God, for it goes far beyond any kind of ordinary comfort that you could receive on our earthly existence, it's a total release of all anxiety and stress, at first you do not even realise that a change has come upon you, I didn't until what I felt was a few days later when I stopped and realized that I had not cried for my mum, I wasn't feeling down, I wasn't angry with the world, I felt completely different in myself, I even felt happy; that Is when I realized that it was because of my prayers to God, that he had answered me, I just could not deny what had happened to me, you do not just wake up one day and everything has gone just in the blink of an eye, and I felt the presence of God upon me, it is the inner knowing which God gives you, a knowing and understanding of what has happened, a miracle only given by divine intervention, sending in the comforter.

What really made it clear to me is that it is written in scripture that if you pray and you are sincere about what you are praying for, and you believe in what God can do for you, and that you are in grief, God will sent in the comforter, to help you get through your troubled times, yes it gave me what I was looking for, the complete trust, faith and reliance in the truth of the word of God, and nobody can ever tell me anything different, I know what I was going through and I know what I prayed for, and to this day, my relationship with my children is solid, my family we are all talking again, I do not grieve for my mum now as much, which was totally effecting my life,

I have this complete reassurance that she is safe and doing just fine, it was me suffering not my mum, and the other side of it is that everything that I have wanted and thought about even in my business has come through for me, This by the way has nothing to do with possessions nor money, I just would not ask God for money, I believe that I have all the riches in the world, by finding what has given me; a new start and that is my Lord and my Father in Heaven.

Let God be your source of comfort, when you are hurting; just ask the Lord like I did to comfort you, and then wait in his glorious presence while he works miracles on you in your heart and emotions, for he will not fail you.

It has taken me awhile to understand the significance of what Jesus had delivered to me, and to share with you the reader, but slowly I discovered two things about myself, and that was I wasn't being as merciful as I thought, I was becoming detached; from the real me.

I even began to realize that I was being raised by the people I was around and listening too, their negativeness was becoming mine, an atmosphere in which I had not really been experiencing in my life, not at the level that it had climbed to anyway, we all experience some in our lives for that is relatively normal, but every day, day in and day out is another level of complete misery.

When I realized that I had reached a place where I needed that mercifulness back within my true heart, a place where I wasn't able to be, I become angry because I saw that the people I was around and had been listening too and agreeing with just to keep the peace, I knew in my heart I was trapped kind of for me in two different worlds with no escape, I had no one to turn too, because everyone only saw their own point of view, no one was willing to see where I was coming from even when I tried to explain that I was trapped, with every ones point of views, this was even the people I employed.

I knew I needed Gods help in me to have his love and his grace in my life and that I needed to show God my gratitude. The bible teaches you that you have to love one another including your neighbour and yourself because sometimes you are trying to give to people something that you yourself are not getting back in return or that you just do not have.

When reality sets in within yourself, and you realize that if you do not receive Gods love flow through you and give to someone else? If you do not receive God's mercy when you make mistakes (for there will still be more mistakes to come) you will not then have a stored up supply of mercy from which to draw others.

So with God's grace once again I have learned to be a merciful person and to give to others in need, and I do enjoy the mercy of God every day of my own life, I do try very hard to not let people get me down as much, and it isn't easy and yes it does still happen, so I won't be a hypocrite, but I try to bring myself back as quick as I can to the grace of God, by keeping my focus on my Lord and saviour to help me to get through,

The good thing is that when I have sinned and sometimes we do not know what God classes as sin for we do not know all of them, but have comfort in knowing that you will receive God's mercy immediately, for I know in my Spirit that I am wrong for your Spirit will tell you; and God he knows yours and my thoughts (fearing the Lord) to say sorry for all your mistakes made, and refuse to live under condemnation. (Guilt)

We must admit to our sins and to repent, ask for God's forgiveness and allow our gracious Lord if you can receive his mercy, and allow yourself to press forward, for in reality mercy is for people who do not deserve it, remember that for yourself and for others.

Isn't it exciting to know that with God all things are possible for us, for in our human thinking when we hit a brick wall, so to speak, and come up against something that is impossible for us? We feel frustrated and hopeless; but with the grace of God that never has to happen; for when we put our trust in Jesus another world emerges up inside of us with an overflow of love, grace, peace, and emotions in our Holy Spirit, a world of possibilities that we would never have thought possible in our worldly existence.

How many times have you just exhausted yourself trying to accomplish something and when you finally gave up and turned it over to God because you have put trust and faith in him to fix it, you see that he has done it for you will ease; what you have struggled with for a long time, this has happened to me over and over again and it never ceases to amaze me what God can do and if I forget then he will certainly remind me.

I am glad that we can serve our God who is ready and willing to help his beloved and devoted children; for if you didn't have this within yourself and for God, then you without doubt will feel helpless and frustrated, I always like to believe that there is hope, no matter how bad things get and look.

The miracles of God are phenomenal to be able to create our amazing world and all creatures great and small, and to be able to turn a hard and sinful, hateful, and bitter heart and turn it into butter, and turn that person into a loving and caring, and forgiving person, then as far as I am concerned our Lord Jesus can help anyone and do anything, sometimes we just do not realise what a miracle our salvation is until we have received it.

When you turn to God like yourself and I did, you don't know what to expect, then what do you really expect; you feel a difference in yourself but not immediately it's a gradual healing of God; we have decided with God who in essence drew us to him, you have become a new born person in Christ, and starting over a brand new life, just by accepting our Lord and saviour Jesus Christ, have you noticed the key word, (accepting) the reason for me pointing that out to you is this? God can only draw us to him; it is completely up to us to accept his invitation, when we accept; then it is again up to us to put in 110% in accomplishing the works of God. How great a feeling is that, you can't ask for much more in life, than to have God on your side, no wonder the Holy Bible is the greatest book ever sort after.

Jesus he can indeed change your life around and indeed he has healed the sick and performed many miraculous miracles, he has fixed marriages through trust and faith and healing; helped people with finances through the same reasons faith....ect, and let's not forget that he fed over 5 thousand people with only a few fish and a couple of loaves of bread; and the best of all reader is that Jesus has walked on water, now that alone gets my vote of greatness, AMEN so nothing is impossible for God(right) impossible for us, but with God, "again" all things are possible.

All believers in Christ Jesus need to continue to pray and keep faith and believing, so God can continue to keep working with us, but if we just give up and I am not talking about giving up one day because you don't feel well or you feel that someone has annoyed you today I am talking about just giving up without any real effort at all into God, prayers ect... in doing this what do you think will happen?

Let me tell you that you will only have the doors closed for you that God has in store; planned for you, now putting it to you this way do you think God is going to miss out on this great opportunity or yourself; let's face it you turn to God for a reason, why would you pick and choose your time to open and close this doorway to a wonderful God with a wonderful heart, he only wants the best for his beloved children, so you need to ask God to take away the mess that is piling up in your life, in your marriage, your family, work, children....ect, turning them into the miracles of Jesus Christ whom is our Lord and our saviour.

## SPEAK THE WORDS OF GRACE

My Heavenly Father I pray that you send me miracles in my life in the areas that you know need fixing, for I have many struggles and I need your help, fill me with your word and your grace, for I lose sight, and I want to live in your heart forever and in the grace of God **AMEN**

# Miracles of Christ

**JESUS WAS A MIRACLE** worker through the love of our Father God, for Jesus so loved the people and the word of God, that so many people were afraid to go to Jesus for any of his miracles, so their lack of faith in Jesus had a lot to do with it, doubts of his miracles for some feared our Lord and many questioned his abilities. Now when you think about it how many people do you know in your life right now that are just like that question themselves, lacking faith.

Have you yourself made a commitment to do whatever it takes to help a person to find and seek Jesus out, have you asked your Holy Spirit to help you to break through the walls of unbelief, for unbelief can harbour also a lot of grief and anger, trust ect....

**1st** Jesus did many wondrous things in his time; his first miracle was the **Healing of a leper** And a leper came to Jesus begging him on his knees and saying to him, if you are willing, are you able to make me clean. Jesus he was moved by this man's plea, and he had sympathy and pity on him, so Jesus reached out his hand and he touched the leper and he said to him, I am willing; be made clean, and at once the leper was completely cleaned, healed by the miracle of Jesus.

**2nd** So as Jesus went into Capernaum, a centurion came up to Jesus and was begging him, and saying to our Lord, my servant boy is lying in my house Paralysed and he is distressed with intense pain; Jesus said

# MIRACLES OF CHRIST ✟ 73

to the man, I will come with you and I will restore and cure the boy to make him healed.

But the centurion said to Jesus I feel I am not worthy or fit to have you come into my house; but only speak the words, and that my servant boy will be cured, Jesus said go, for it has been done for you for you have believed.

**3rd The Healing of Peters mother-in-law**; Jesus went in to peter's house, where he saw his mother- in- law lying ill with fever. Jesus touched her hand and the fever left her body, and the woman got up and started to wait on Jesus, when morning came many had heard about all the miracles that Jesus had done and many had come and they were under the power of Demons, and Jesus drove them out, the spirit of darkness with words; and restored them all to health, all the people who came to him sick.

**4th Stilling the storm;** Jesus and his disciples went into a boat and Jesus said to them; let us go over to the other side of the lake (sea), and after a while and when Jesus was asleep suddenly behold arose a violent storm on the sea, the boat was being covered by the waves; but Jesus he was still sleeping,

His disciples they went and awoken him saying, Lord; please come rescue us and save us for we shall all but perish, and Jesus spoke and said to them, why are you all timid and afraid, O you of little faith? Then Jesus he got up and he rebuked the winds and the sea, and then there was a great and wondrous calm. All Jesus disciples were stunned with bewildered with wonder and marvelled, saying, what kind of man is this; that even the winds and the sea obeys him!

Wouldn't you like Jesus standing next to you and your family all the time to protect you? Many of you have all answered yes I am sure, but did you know that you already have, Just its put in a different way, Jesus he done a miracle while still in a human form, but he is much stronger in the spirit form, he has unlimited power and that power needs to be brought out into you, with calling on him and having the trust and belief that his disciples were struggling with, but there is no need for you to be struggling as long as you keep believing and have faith, especially when you realise that you do actually have the faith, you are reading this book, you already love Jesus the Holy one, I know I will always need him In my life, more than anyone can imagine, I love that closeness and the need to call on him when I need him the most, to talk to someone who understands, **me.**

There are not many if any who have not encountered many storms in their lifetime, and sometimes trying to control them consumes you, physically, mentally and emotionally. It's sometimes something you cannot foresee coming until it's upon you out of nowhere, many know it's going to erupt because it's something they cannot stop and don't want to because they feel they are right, and they know it's going to cause many problems, these are raging storms, and they are many.

The disciples of Jesus found themselves in a storm that would have been terrifying, could you even imagine yourself being in a small boat out in the middle of the sea and all your friends were on board and this raging storm came out of nowhere and the waves were filling it with crashing waves filling the boat with water and throwing you from side to side and lightning and the thunder loud and ferociousness, scary ah, the disciples at this stage probably were not as excited now as they were when they started on this voyage. God can call us to destinations to be tested to see how we can handle the tests put before us, and he doesn't always tell us what is going to happen along the way? Sometimes it can start out as blessings and finish with the blessings from the other side and other times a storm can rage right in the middle of the journey; this is the place of testing from God, to see if we can stand the storm and break through it or crumble in a heap with no way of escape.

As you can see sometimes storms can range from something very minor and sometimes they can turn into a raging full blown storm, now the disciples found themselves in a raging storm and listen this was no April show it was what we call today as a cyclone, the disciple would probably never had encountered this kind of weather in the middle of

# MIRACLES OF CHRIST ✝ 75

the sea before, but they were following the instructions of the messiah who knew what was going to happen, for this was a test of their faith; and yes he was asleep peacefully in this raging storm.

**5th Devils entering a herd of swine;** When Jesus and his disciples arrived on the other side of the sea to the region of Gerasenes, Jesus got out of the boat there to meet him out of the tombs was a man who was under the power of an unclean spirit; this man continually lived among the tombs; and no one could subdue him anymore; not even with chains; for he had been bound with shackles on his feet and handcuffs for his hands, but the man he just wrenched them apart, the shackles he just rubbed and grounded them together until they broke and fell apart into pieces; and no one had the strength enough to restrain or to tame him any longer.

Night and day among the tombs; and on the mountains he was always screaming, shrieking, and beating, bruising and cutting himself with stones, then from a distance he clapped his eyes on Jesus, he ran and fell onto his knees before him in homage, crying out in a loud voice; he said, what have you to do with me Jesus, son of the highest God? What is there even in common with us; I solemnly implore you by God, to not torment me.

However Jesus was commanding saying; come out of this man, you unclean spirit! Then Jesus he asked him, what is your name? And he replied to Jesus, my name is Legion, for we are many. And he kept on begging Jesus urgently to not send them away out on the region.

Now there was a great herd of hogs that were grazing in the hillside, and the Demons they begged Jesus saying, send us to these hogs so that we may go into them! So Jesus he did give them permission. Then the unclean spirits left the man and entered the herd of hogs, which numbered about 2,000, then on entering the herd rushed down the steep slope headlong into the sea where they all drowned.

All the hog feeders ran away and told all the town folks what they had seen all that had taken place; then they had all come to see Jesus with an intense look on their faces, searching Jesus up and down and looking upon the man that had been a demoniac who was sitting their completely clothed and in his right state of mind, who had the legions of demons; now the crowd who were now seized with alarm and struck with fear, began to beg Jesus and his followers to leave their neighbourhood at once.

**6th Healing of a Paralytic;** Jesus having returned to Capernaum, after some days, it was rumoured that he was in the house; so many people came and gathered together; however there was no longer any more room for them, not even around the door; but Jesus he was discussing the word of God.

Then more people arrived and they brought with them a man who was paralytic, whom was being carried by 4 men; however when the men could not get anywhere to see Jesus because of the huge crowds that had come to see Jesus themselves, the men dug through the roof just above where Jesus was standing in the house, when the 4 men had scooped out an opening in the roof, they let down a thick padded quilt or mat upon which the paralysed man lay upon.

When Jesus saw the strong faith and confidence that these men had in God through him he said to the paralysed man, son you are forgiven of your sins, all guilt is now removed.

This readers is very moving; you have to look deep within one's self to realise that there are so many people out there in our society that really need Jesus Christ to release and help them to overcome many problems, they actually do need his healing; the paralysed man had doubt in himself; to ever be healed, without the faith and love of his friends in bringing him to Jesus, I would most definitely say without question that the paralysed man would never have turned to Jesus otherwise; how many people are out there today who are just as paralysed as this man, they have doubt, fear and question faith; How great it would be to be able to reach out to someone like that today to make a difference and commitment in turning their lives around to Jesus and get them to trust and have faith in Jesus Christ; to breakthrough there walls of unbelief, praise our Lord Jesus Christ. **AMEN**

**7th Raising the ruler's daughter;** A ruler of the synagogue came up, whose name was Jairus; seeking to speak with Jesus, when he had approached Jesus he bowed at his feet; and he begged him deeply, saying, my little girl she is at the point of death, please come and lay your hands on her, so that she may be healed and live.

So Jesus he went with him and a huge crowd they followed; and pressed him on every side, when Jesus had arrived at the house of the ruler of the synagogue he looked inside and he observed many people weeping and crying loudly; when Jesus went inside he said to the many crying, why are you making such an uproar and crying? This little girl she is not dead but merely sleeping?

Then the large crowd began to laugh and mock Jesus so he asked for them to leave and he closed the door so they could not witness what he was doing and discussing with the Childs father and mother, and the few that was with them; then Jesus he went in to where the little girl was lying.

Gripping the girls hand firmly, Jesus he said to her; Talitha Cumi- which means translated, little girl; I say to you, arise from the sleep of death! Then straight away the girl stood to her feet and started to walk around, the child was of the age of 12; the people that were there where utterly astonished and overcome with such joy and amazement.

Jesus he strictly commanded the crowd and the Childs family members to not let anyone know about the miracle that has just taken place, he warned them to keep their silence; then after saying these things he said to her parents, give the child something to eat, then he left.

**8th The healing of the Haemorrhaging woman;** There was a woman who had been living with a blood flow for almost 12 years, and she had endured so much suffering especially under the hands of physicians and she had spent all that she had, but was still no better off but instead she was getting worse.

Now the woman had heard the reports concerning Jesus, when she had heard that Jesus was coming down the streets, so she came up behind him and she kept saying to herself, If only I could just touch his garment I know I will be healed.

After the woman got close enough she reach forward and touched the hem of his garment and immediately her blood flow had stopped, and she felt it in her body that she had just been healed. However Jesus also felt and recognised in himself that the power proceeding from him had gone forth, he turned around and immediately looked into the crown and spoke saying, who is the one that has just touched my clothing?

But the disciples said to Jesus, My Lord can you not see the amount of people that are here with us on all sides, and you ask who has just touched you, but still Jesus kept looking around to see, but the woman knowing what she had just done, although frightened, she fell at his feet and proceeded to tell Jesus the truth and why she needed to touch his garment.

Then Jesus he said to her, daughter your faith, trust and confidence in me and Father God, has now restored you to health, go now in peace and be continually healed and freed from your distressed bodily disease.

Can you ever imagine readers to have a condition that causes you that much stress, and prolonged for 12 years, can you imagine the hopelessness that you would feel, how many of us would have the faith that this woman had, she had put all her confidence in the physicians to heal her using every cent that she had, with nothing left for her to continue in faith, that one day she would be completely healed.

Many of us today also put faith into doctor's hands and find that we are not healed and then put faith into the hands of another doctor to heal us, just like I had done with my skin cancer, not many doctors of today would heal you without being paid, we have medical insurances and Medicare, which didn't exist in Jesus' day.

Never the less this woman pressed on, determined to reach Jesus as she pushed her way through the crowd, her faith healed her with the touch of his clothing, my prayers and faith in the Lord, is what has healed me as well, and your faith in the power of our Lord and Saviour Jesus Christ can also heal you, **AMEN.**

Whatever you are facing in your life today and no matter the length of time you have been suffering, let me encourage you to keep pressing on no matter how hard and difficult the situation becomes, reach out also to Jesus to touch and heal your life, your family will feel the difference in you and you will also feel the difference in yourself, and your environment will be filled with more light.

**9th Healing two blind men;** With all the news spreading throughout the districts, Jesus was walking when two blind men were following him with the crowd, when they started shouting at Jesus loudly: have pity and mercy on us Jesus son of David!

Jesus he arrived at the house which was his destination, he went in and in also came the two blind men; Jesus he said to them, do you believe that I am able to heal you? Then they replied to him, yes my Lord, then Jesus he touched their eyes, saying; according to your faith and trust and reliance, on the power invested in me, be healed to you.

And then they had opened their eyes and could see, Jesus strictly said to the men see that you tell no one of the healing works that I have performed on you this day, but as soon as the men had left, they spread the news around throughout all the districts of the miraculous healing that Jesus had done to restore their eyesight.

**9th The healing of a Devil possessed- dumb man;** Jesus had not gone too far after healing the two blind men when behold a dumb man under the power of a demon was brought to Jesus, when Jesus had driven out the demon, the dumb man began to speak, and the crowd of people were stunned with wonder, saying; never before has anything like this been seen in Israel, but the Pharisees said, he drives out Demons through and with the help of the prince of Demons.

But our Lord Jesus just went about doing his marvellous works of healing to villages and cities, teaching in their synagogues proclaiming the good news of the Gospel of the Holy kingdom, curing all kinds of diseases and weaknesses among the people.

**10th Healing of a man's withered hand;** When Jesus had left the synagogues behold a man was there with one withered hand, and they said to Jesus, it is lawful and allowable to cure people on the Sabbath days? -That they might accuse him.

But Jesus said to them, what man is there among you, that if one of his sheep it was to fall into a ditch on the Sabbath, would you not take hold of it and lift it out? So how much better and of more value is a man than a sheep! So it is lawful and allowable to do good on the Sabbath days.

Then Jesus he said to the man, reach out your hand, and the man reached out his hand and it was restored, as sound as the first one, but the Pharisees went out and held a consultation against Jesus, how they may get rid of him.

But as Jesus was already aware of this, Jesus went away from there; now many people followed Jesus, and he healed and he cured all of them, however Jesus he asked of them to not make it publicly known of the miracles that he had done on them.

**11th Curing a Devil Possessed, dumb man;** In and on his name the Gentiles (the people outside of Israel) set all their hopes on Jesus. And a blind and dumb man was brought to Jesus that was under the power of a Demon, Jesus he did cure him so that the blind and dumb man both spoke and his eyes restored.

And all the crowds of people they were stunned and bewildered with wonder and said, this cannot be the son of David, can it? But the Pharisees, hearing this, said, this man drives out Demons only and by the help of Beelzebub, the price of demons.

Jesus knowing their thoughts, he said to them, any kingdom that is divided against itself being brought to desolation and laid to waste, and no city or house divided against itself will last or continue to stand? And if I drive out the Demons from Beelzebub, by whose help do your sons drive them out? For this reason they shall be your judges, but it is by the spirit of God that I drive out the demons, and then the kingdom of God has come upon you, before you expected it to or how can a person go into a strong mans house and carry of his goods without first binding the strong man, for only then may he plunder the house?

He who is not with me is against me and he who does not gather with me and for my side scatters, therefore I tell you, even sin and blasphemy can be forgiven of men, but blasphemy against the Holy Spirit shall not and cannot be forgiven.

And whoever speaks a word against the son of man will be forgiven, but whoever speaks against the spirit, the Holy one, will not be forgiven, either in this world and the age to come.

**12th Feeding the five thousand;** Jesus went to the far side of the Sea of Galilee, which is the sea of Tiberias, a great crowd has been following Jesus and where he was going, for they had seen the signs and the miracles which he was continually performing upon those who were sick.

Jesus he walked up the mountain and he sat down there with his disciples, now the Passover, the feast of the Jews was approaching, as Jesus looked up he saw a large amount of people coming towards him, and he said to Phillip, where are we to buy bread, so that all of these people can eat?

But this was only said to test Phillip, for he knew already what he had to do, and Phillip answered Jesus; two hundred Pennies or $40.00 in our currency, worth of bread is not enough for everyone will only receive very little.

Another one of Jesus' disciples Andrew, Simon Peter's brother, said to him, there is a little boy here who has with him 5 Barley loaves, and 2 small fish; but what are they among so many people? Jesus said; make all the people sit down, now the ground was covered with thick grass at the spot, so the people sitted themselves down, about 5000 men, not including women and children.

Jesus he took the loaves and when he had given thanks, he distributed to the disciples, and the disciples distributed to the sitted people; as also he did with the fish as much as they wanted, when they all had enough, he said to the disciples, gather up now the fragments the broken pieces left over so that nothing can be lost and wasted.

So accordingly they gathered them up, and they filled 12 small wicker hand baskets with fragments left over by those who had eaten from the 5 barley loaves, when the people saw the miracle that Jesus had performed, they began to say, surely and beyond any doubt this is the Prophet who is to come into this world!

Everybody knows that your body lets you know when you are hungry (right) because your stomach it will get upset, it will growl; you may get a headache, and feel even light headed, and then there are some people that may even really had felt very sick, can you imagine how the people that Jesus fed with the bread and the fish, felt; Jesus, he had a lot of compassion for these people and he never wanted them to go hungry especially the little children.

Many Christian believers understand the importance of your Holy Spirit which is where God and Jesus reside, the God and the life within you, well our Holy Spirit needs to be fed as well, by keeping peace, love, forgiveness and happiness within yourself otherwise you can grieve your Holy Spirit very much, which in turn doesn't make God very happy either, for he is a loving caring God and by your Holy Spirit grieving you will feel and know the difference and you can turn your feelings and your love back to God and heal.

So in essence just as you need to feed your body daily it is necessary also to feed daily on the bread of life, the word of the living God and spending as much time with him as we can, this will also keep you focused on life by staying on the right path of righteousness, walking the straight pathway, and "yes" we will lead of this path, occasionally, however God does expect that, he knows that we are not perfect, and if we were all perfect then we wouldn't need God, and we do, right.

The biggest problem that we all face is the intrusion of darkness, this is the other reason the children of God need to stay in the light so that he can protect what he loves very much, parents are suppose to protect their children, we know that even our children stray, as some of us have, but we all wake up eventually, well most of us anyway, but the fact is that God understands that some of his children will not return to him, some are lead to darkness and will not escape, some are lead because they are curious and think this is just a big game of defiance, some because they get mixed up in cults, some drugs, porn and the list can just go on.

The word of God is not just a test of your faith and your belief and trust in God but it is protection and the hope and faith that you as a believer get through your struggles, and ask God for forgiveness by repentance, and you will live forever in the kingdom of God, for God keeps his promises. AMEN.

**13th Walking on the Sea;** after Jesus had fed all the 5000 people Jesus ordered his disciples into the boat, and asked them to go before him to the other side, while he sent away the crowds of people, after dismissing the large crowds of people Jesus he went up to the hills by himself and he prayed, and when evening approached Jesus he was still on the hillside alone.

However the boat by this time was already way out to Sea, many furlongs (a furlong is one-eighth of a mile) distance from land, the boat was now being tossed and beaten by the high winds and waves, the winds were very much against them, and the water was beginning to fill the boat.

On the fourth watch of the night, Jesus he came to them; walking on water, but when his disciples saw a figure that was walking on the water they were terrified and said it is a ghost! And they began to scream out with fright. But Jesus spoke to them saying, take courage it is I, do not be afraid; and Peter answered him, Lord; if it is you, command me to come on the water.

Jesus he commanded him to come, so Peter he got out of the boat and he began to walk out onto the water towards Jesus, When Peter began to understand and realise what he was actually doing and set his mind and focus on the fierce wind in his face, and the rough Seas, he began to panic.

Peter he became very frightened, when he lost all his faith and concentration he began to sink into the Sea, he cried out to Jesus, Lord please save me, for I will surely die, Jesus he came to him lifting him out of the water and he held him, and said to Peter, Oh you of little faith, why did you doubt?

When they returned into the boat, all the winds and the Sea began to cease, all was very calm and peaceful, the disciples in the boat all knelt before Jesus and worshipped him saying, truly my Lord you are the Son of God.

All our lives we need faith, hope and trust, and many give up and loose the peacefulness, if we begin to understand what we give up when we lose sight of this, we would all have very different life styles, and pathways.

## SPEAK THE WORD OF GRACE

My Lord Jesus I pray in your name that I will keep my faith and trust and reliance on you, enough faith to not doubt when I pray, putting all my faith in you so that I can turn and trust in you in my troubled times, to know and understand that you will always be by my side, I will be faithful as you are faithful, so that you will never have to say to me Oh you of little faith. AMEN.

**14th The Withering Fig;** Jesus and his disciples went into Bethany and they lodged there, in the early dawn of the next day, as Jesus was coming back from the city, and he was hungry; however he only saw one single leafy fig tree above the roadside, When Jesus he approached it he found nothing but leaves on it, seeing in the fig tree that fruit will almost always appear at the same times as the leaves; so Jesus spoke to the tree saying to it, you will never again grow fruit on you! And the tree it withered away before him.

When the disciple had seen this happen before their eyes they said to Jesus as they marvelled greatly; Lord, how is it that the fig tree has withered away all at once, and Jesus he replied, truly I say to you, that if you have no faith and you do not have any doubt, you will not only do what has to be done to the fig tree, but even if you also say to this mountain, be taken up and cast into the Sea, it will be done, so whatever you ask for in prayer, having faith and believing, you will then receive.

How many people have been in a situation when they have considered just for a moment that if they had believed and trusted in themselves and the Lord that the situation that they are in; the outcome could have been very different, I know I have no doubt that you the reader have been in the same situation,

This is what Jesus is trying to teach us and what he was trying to tell his disciples in the boat with Peter and the fig tree, You can achieve much more in your life if you pray and you just believe in what you are praying for, keeping faith, the power of the truth and the word of the Holy Scriptures is what comes out of one's mouth, the power that resides within your Spirit.

Just as no branch can bear fruit of itself without abiding in the vine, as Jesus says dwell in me and I will dwell in you, live in me and I will live in you; for neither can you bear fruit unless you abide in me. Amen

This is so very much the truth, I have found that saying of Jesus very inspiring even at my most difficult situations, we need to have this in our lives knowing that the Lord God resides in you if you keep love and trust and faith in him that he will support your every need, living and walking with the Lord every single day, how glorious is that to every Christian believer.

**15th Turning water into wine;** Jesus and his disciples where invited to a wedding in Cana of Galilee, and Mary the mother of Jesus was also there; now while at the wedding Jesus' mother approached him and said, Jesus my son what are we to do for the wine it has run dry, Jesus said to his mother, dear woman; what has that to really do with you or with me that they have run dry? Leave it to me.

Jesus' mother said to the servants, whatever he says to you, you do it; now there were six water pots made of stone there, as the Jewish custom of purification ceremonial washing; which held around 20-30 gallons a piece, now Jesus he said to them, go and fill each of the pots with water, so they took the pots and they filled them to the brim, then Jesus had asked them to draw some of it out and to take it to the manager of the feast, so they proceeded to do so and took him some.

When the manager had tasted the water, which was now turning to wine and not knowing of where it had come from, for only the servants who had drawn the water knew, he called to the bridegroom, and he said to him; everyone else serves his best wine first; and when the people drunk freely, then he will serve that which is not the good wine until now!

This was one of Jesus' **1st** miracles which was performed in Cana of Galilee, all of his miracles manifested his power and his glory displaying his greatness openly; his disciples they believed him, trusted him, and they relied on him very much so, following Jesus' to the end, and after his death, and there's.

Have you ever wondered how great it would have been to have lived over 2000yrs ago and walked with Jesus as one of his disciple's, one of his devoted followers; or to just follow him as the multitude crowds have done, to watch with your eyes the manifesting of the miracles of our beloved Lord and Saviour Jesus Christ; when I feel the way I do about my Lord I wish I could have been there and I think I would have not been that scared at seeing his miracles, it would have been amazing to watch, But realistically those days were really tough and not very merciful, especially the Romans and the other King leaders and followers that Gave Jesus a hard time with his faith and Belief in God, so in general I guess it's easier to say because I'm here now and not living in those times.

As a Minister (Pastor) and follower of Jesus Christ, I guess I would do anything to be standing by his side to witness his works, but obviously I can't? But you know I think we are lucky now also to have the knowledge that we have been given from the Holy Bible and Jesus' teaching, many of what we are reading has had to be decoded from another language but it is the truth and it was written by the followers Of Jesus and the word of God and his chosen people to relay this information back to his children of the light, for it is them who will spread the word in any form possible to plant the seed of God back into our society and the Children of the next generation.

There is a lot of information that's been missing over 2000 yrs and more, the disciples of Jesus only knew a fraction of what was given up freely by Jesus to them, what he believed that they could understand, for he already knew that one of them was going to betray him, so how much faith would many of the people had; the followers that believed and the unbelievers you even had highly religious priest, that believed in God but still had Jesus crucified, for the fear that they had in him and what he could do, they could see the power that he had, and in people.

Jesus' disciples however still obeyed him even when he asked them to go and fill the pots with water, when they needed wine because it had run dry, they didn't argue with him, not believing in him, saying Lord it is only water, they did not disobey his orders at all; rightly so, you do not disobey God, right.

Let's think about life over 2000yrs ago to what is going on in our world as we know it today and focus on what has really changed; are people back then really that much more different? Do people read and think they are barbaric I would hate to live in those days; and our technology is so much more intelligent?

I suggest that we all need to put more thought into that, for we are no different, neither is our behaviour it is not even less barbaric than in those days than today, rape, murder, drugs, violence, adultery, ect even our technology much of it was thought of many thousands of years ago all we have done is perfected it to our technology, makeup, jewellery, houses, cups, plates, knives, forks, spoons, curtains, chairs, beds, pillows, blankets, fruit and vegetables, confectionery, money, taxes, jails, law enforcement, properties, market places, shops, eateries, shearing, butcher shops, cake bakeries, real estate agents, and really I can just add so much more to that list, now these places were all back in the day of Jesus Christ, how do you think that we become to know about them, these existed in the beginning of the days of Moses and probably even before Noah. Eye opener isn't it; this is what really made me think, how perfect do we think that we really are?

So how much has it really changed, or is it simply how we think and perceive it, or the fact that many people are too wrapped up in the world today that they give a comment if asked or just don't give it a thought either way, and too many do not even give thought about the subject of the church or our Lord and saviour Jesus Christ; for many only want to get on with their lives without too many obstacles' and what they would class as problems until they need the Lord when something goes wrong, and at some point we all need to believe in something?

You see many want to put thoughts into their lives; but with very little thought into anything that has to do with faith, love, trust and believing in anything beyond themselves as sad as it is it is a fact and we need not kid ourselves for we have all done it and know someone like this; But our Lord he has died for us so that we can have a second chance to change and repent, for he died for our sins.

So in fact today we are very lucky in our faith as Christians and believers in our Lord Jesus Christ and the sacrifice that he has done for us to be born again in Christ, for me that is the greatest gift that anyone could give you, to have faith, trust, and believing and having hope in our lives; magnified by believing that Jesus died for us, our Holy Spirit transformed in such a way, that it changes you permanently; believing in our one true God and the word and truth of the Holy Bible.

# The Cross and Jesus

**THE FEAST OF THE PASSOVER** was on the **12th** day of the month (April) it was the first feast on the Jewish yearly Calender, this is done by Jewish faith and believing, done in commemoration of the national deliverance from Egypt in the exodus of Moses.

The custom of the Passover become a religion of its own down to the fact that nothing was to go wrong in the leading up to the Passover custom, Jesus he made his final prediction of his death two days before Passover; when Jesus said to his disciples, that in two days it will be Passover and the son of man will be delivered up treacherously to be crucified.

While Jesus was talking to his disciples, the chief priests and the elders of the people gathered in the open courts of the palace of the high priests, whose name was Caiaphas; and they consulted together in order to arrest Jesus; and by planning secretly to put Jesus to death. But there plan was also not to do this during the feast of Passover because they knew that this would cause the people protest and cause problems.

However while this was being put to plan, Jesus had arrived back in Bethany and he came to the house of Simon the Leper, and a woman approached him with a alabaster flask of very expensive perfume, and she had poured this onto the head of Jesus as he was seated at the table.

The disciple seeing this became very indignant, saying; for what is the purpose of the waste of this precious perfume; for the perfume can be sold for a large sum of money and the money can then be distributed to the poor.

But Jesus understanding this very well said to his disciples, why are you bothering this woman with your concerns for has she not done a gracious and noble thing for me; have you also not poor among you, but you will not always have me.

The poor will always be in the land so therefore I command you that you should open wide your hands to your brothers and to the needy, and to the poor in your land.

And for pouring this perfume on my body, this woman has made my body ready for burial; so truly, truly I say to you, wherever the good news of the Gospel is preached in the whole world, what this woman has done will be told also, in memory of her.

There were 12 disciples of Jesus, and one of them was named Judas Iscariot, now he had left them and he was on his way to see the high priest, and he had said to the high priest on arrival, what are you willing to pay me if I hand him over to you? On agreement, the high priests weighed up 30 pieces of silver (about $21.60) and they paid Judas and from that moment Judas sought out to complete his mission to betray Jesus.

On the first day of unleavened bread Passover week, the disciples came to Jesus and said to him, where would you like us to prepare, your Passover supper my Lord; and Jesus answered, go into the city to a certain man and say to him, The master said; my time is near; I will keep the Passover at your house with my disciples.

Accordingly the disciples did as Jesus had directed them to do, and they made ready the Passover supper, when it was the evening, he was sitting at the table with the twelve disciples and as they were eating, Jesus said solemnly I say unto you, that one of you will betray me.

Then disciples were extremely upset with pain and stress, deeply hurt at what Jesus was saying to them; then the disciples began to say to him one after the other, surely my Lord it cannot be me; can it?

# THE CROSS AND JESUS ✝ 91

Jesus he replied, he who has just dipped his hand in the same dish with me is the one who will betray me.

The son of man is going just as it is written of him; but woe to the man by whom the son of man is betrayed! For it would have been better for that man to have not been born at all, Judas the betrayer, said; surely it is not I, is it; Master? Jesus said to him, you have stated the fact.

Now as they were eating, Jesus took bread and he praised God, gave thanks and asked him to bless it; and when Jesus he had broken the unleavened bread, he gave to his disciples and said take and eat for this is my body which is for you, then Jesus he took in his hand the Holy cup and when he had given thanks he handed the cup to the disciples and he said to them, drink of this cup all of you; for this is my blood of the new covenant (testament) it is poured out for many for the forgiveness of sins.

I say to you, I shall not drink again of this fruit of the vine until the day when I drink it with you new, in my father's kingdom, when they had sung a song of hymns; they went out to the mountain of olives.

Then Jesus he said to them, you will all be offended and stumble and fall, denying me, and because of me this night; for it is written, I will strike the shepherd, and the sheep will scatter, but after I am raised up to life again I will go ahead of you and see you n Galilee.

Then Peter he said to him, my Lord although they all are offended and stumble and fall away because of you, I will never deny you, then Jesus he said to Peter, solemnly I declare to you Peter, that before this night ends, this very night, before a single rooster crows, you will deny me and disown me three times.

Peter was saddened and sure of his thoughts and feelings said to Jesus, my Lord, even if I must die with you, I will not deny you, and all his disciples agreed and said the same thing, then Jesus went with them to a place called Gethsemane, and Jesus told his disciples, sit down here while I go over yonder and pray to the Father.

Then Jesus he took with him Peter and the two sons of Zebedee, and he became grief stricken and was deeply distress for he knew what was ahead of him, then he said to the disciples that was with him, my soul is deeply stressed and deeply grieved, I feel that I am dying of sorrow, so I ask of you to stay here and keep awake and keep watch over me, and then he walked a little further away from where he prayed last, then again he threw himself to the ground on his face and prayed again to the Father saying, my Father if it is possible, let this cup pass away from me, nevertheless not what I desire but as you will desire.

When Jesus he came back to where the disciples were waiting and keeping watch he found that they had all fallen asleep; and Jesus he said to Peter, what; are you not suppose to be keeping a watch for me for just 1 hour? All of you must keep watch over me and pray that you may not come into temptation; for the spirit indeed is willing, but the flesh it is weak.

Then again he went away for a second time and prayed, my Father, if this cannot pass unless I drink it; your will; it will be done, and again when Jesus he had returned to his disciples he had found that they had again fallen asleep; so he left them and went and prayed for the third time, using the same words to the Father.

When he returned to his disciples he said to them are you all still sleeping and taking your rest? I say to you, behold the hour is now at hand, for the son of man is being betrayed into the hands of especially wicked sinners. Get up now for we need to be going; see now my betrayer is now at hand; but as Jesus was still speaking, Judas; one of the 12 disciples came up, and with him stood a great many with swords, lanterns, and torches, and also were the chief priests and the elders of the people.

Then because Jesus knew what was to befall him, he walked out towards them and he said who are you seeking? And they replied to Jesus saying, we are here for Jesus of Nazarene; and Jesus he replied back, have I not told you that I am he, so if it is me that you are seeking, let these men go on their way.

Judas had given them a sign, saying; the one that I kiss he is the man that you are seeking; then Judas he approached Jesus and he said to him hail, Master! And then he kissed and embraced him, then Jesus he said to him friend for why are you here? Then the soldiers came up to Jesus and struck him and arrested him.

Then with anger for them laying their hands on Jesus, one of the disciples that was with Jesus had a sword and he drew it and he struck the high priest servant and cut of his right ear; the servants name was Malchus, then Jesus said to the disciple; put the sword back away in its sheath! For the cup which my Father has given to me, shall I not drink it? So the troops and their captain and the guards of the Jews seized Jesus and bound him.

And they brought him first to Annas, for he was the Father in- Law of Caiaphas, who was the High Priest that year. It was Caiaphas who had counselled the Jews that was expedient and for their welfare that one man should die for the people.

Now Simon Peter and another of Jesus' disciples were following Jesus; and that disciple was known to the high priest, and so he entered along with Jesus into the court of the palace of the high priest; but peter was standing outside at the door, so the other disciple who were known to the high priest went out and spoke to the maid who kept watch at the door and she brought Peter inside.

Then the maid who was in charge at the door said to Peter, are you not also one of the disciples of this man? And Peter he said, no I am not! Now the servants and the guard attendants had made a fire of coals, for it was cold, and they were standing and warming themselves; and Peter was with them standing and also warming himself,

The High Priest he started to question Jesus about who his disciples were and about his teachings, but Jesus he answered him saying; I have spoken openly to the world and I have always taught in the synagogue and in the temple, where the Jews congregate and I have spoken nothing secretly; for all that have come; have come to listen to my teachings freely and by their choice not mine.

I ask you; why are you High Priest asking me these things, why are you not asking those who have attended which have heart my words and what I have said to them? But when Jesus had said these words; one of the guard attendants struck Jesus saying, is this how you answer a High Priest.

Then Jesus replied; If I had said anything wrong, spoken abusively, or if there was any evil in what I have said; then you tell me what was wrong with what I had said for you to have struck me in the manner in which you did; so that if you think that what I had spoken was right and properly do you not know that you still did strike me? Then Annas sent Jesus to Caiaphas the High Priest.

Reader Jesus was correct in his approach to the high Priest and the way that our Lord has spoken to the High Priest, for Jesus was still so calm and polite in the presence of the company of where he was taken, the priest did not care at all in what Jesus was saying, because they were frightened of Jesus' beliefs and his power over the people and his teachings of God the Father, and people were calling Jesus the Messiah, the son of God; they heard also about the miracles in which he had been doing, and they wanted Jesus out of the way because they feared that his power and his stronger growing followers would eventually over power them.

But Simon Peter who at this time was still standing and was warming himself, they said to him; are you not also one of his disciples, are you not? But Simon Peter denied Jesus for the second time and he replied, No I am not.

One of the Priests servants a relative of the man who's ear was cut off by Peter, said did I not see you in the garden with Jesus, and again Peter denied ever even associating with Jesus the son of God, and immediately a rooster crowed.

Jesus he was then taken from the presence of Caiaphas and brought to the hall of judgement the Governors' palace and it was very early in the morning; they did not enter into the Judgement hall for they become frightened that they may become unclean but might be fit to eat at the Passover supper; so Pilate he went out to them and asked, what accusations do you have against this man? They replied, if he was not an evil doer we would not be here handing him over to you.

However Pilate replied back, then you take him yourself and judge and sentence him according to your own laws; then the Jews answered, it is not lawful for us to have anyone put to death.

Pilate he went back again into the Judgement hall and called Jesus to him, and asked him; are you the King of the Jews? For your own people and nation and their Chief Priests have delivered you hear to me, so I am asking you, in your own words of what have you done so wrong, for me to judge and sentence you.

Jesus he replied; my kingdom belongs not of this world, if my kingdom were of this world, my followers would have been fighting to keep me from being handed over to the Jews, but as it is my kingdom is not from here, this world.

Pilate then said to Jesus, so then you are a King? Jesus he replied, you say that I am a King, for I say to you yes I am a King; for this is why I am born, and for this that I have come into the world, to bear witness to the truth, everyone who is of the truth hears and listens to my voice.

Pilate replies, so what is the truth? On saying this he went out to the Jews again and said to them, I see no fault in this man, The High Priests replied; but it is your custom that I release one prisoner for you at the Passover, Pilate said then shall I release to you the King of the Jews? Then all the people shouted back again, not him, not this man, but Barabbas!

Pilate replies very well, so then Pilate had taken Jesus and he ordered Jesus to be scourged (flogged and whipped) and the soldiers had made a crown of thorns which they had placed on Jesus' head, and then gave him a purple robe.

The soldiers were cruel and they tormented Jesus and said to him hail King of the Jews; peace to you, long life to you, and they abused and struck Jesus with their hands.

Then Pilate went out again and said to the crowd of people, see here, I bring this man to you so that you may know that I do not find any fault or crime that he has done for the accusations made against him, then the soldiers brought Jesus out with the crown of thorns that they had placed on his head and the purple robe which they had placed on him also; and his beaten body that was covering him through the punishment.

Pilate had then said to the crowd, here is the man Jesus! When the chief priests has seen Jesus and the guards had seen him they all yelled crucify him; crucify him, crucify him, then all the crowds also followed and cried out also, crucify him, (which is what the high priests was counting on) then Pilate replied to them and the crowd take him yourself and you crucify this innocent man, for I say to you again, I do not see any fault in the accusations that you are bringing against this man Jesus?

(This saying of Jesus which is being fulfilled which he had spoken? Signifying what death Jesus was predicting on how he was to die; the Crucifixion)

The Jews answered him saying, we have a law and according to this law the man Jesus should die; for he has claimed and made himself out to be the son of God, so, when Pilate heard this he was alarmed at how callous they were for he knew in his heart the reasons behind the High Priest decisions and determination to have Jesus put to death by crucifixion.

Then Pilate took Jesus and went in the Judgement hall again and he said to Jesus, tell me where are you from? But Jesus he did not answer him, so Pilate he said to Jesus, will you not even speak to me? Do you not know that I have the power (authority) to either release you and that I also have the power to have you crucified.

Jesus he replied to Pilate saying, you do not have the power or authority whatsoever over me, because it has not been given to you from my Father above. For it is this reason the sin and the guilt is of the one who has delivered me over to you that of which is greater.

Upon hearing this in the heart of Pilate he wanted to release Jesus, but it was the Jews pressure on Pilate to have Jesus crucified; saying if you release this man then you will be no friend of Caesar! For if anyone who makes himself out to be a King sets himself up against Caesar.

It's these words that Pilate brought Jesus out to sit down on the judgement seat at a place called the pavement the mosaic pavement, the stone platform in Hebrew, Gabbatha.

Now it was the day of preparation for the Passover, it was the 6th hour, around 12oclock noon; when Pilate had said to the Jews, behold here is your King, but the Jews they still cried out, get rid of him, away with him, crucify him; Pilate being displeased at the crowd, replied

# THE CROSS AND JESUS ✝ 97

to them for compassion, what crucify your King? The Chief Priest answered; we have no King but Caesar. Then Pilate handed Jesus over to them to be crucified, replying I was my hands of this man's innocent blood.

They then took Jesus and led him away, so he went out bearing his own cross, to a spot called the place of the skull in Hebrew it is called Golgotha; it is there that they crucified Jesus, and with him were two others one on either side of Jesus, Jesus being in the middle.

Pilate he wrote a titled inscription on a placard, and he put on it Jesus' cross and written on the placard was the words; Jesus the Nazarene, King of the Jews.

Many of the Jews were reading the placard title for Jesus, for the place where Jesus was to be crucified was near the city, and Pilate had it done so that it was to be understood in Hebrew, Latin and Greek.

When the Chief Priest of the Jews heard about this he said to Pilate, do not have written King of the Jews, for he said I am the King of the Jews; Pilate replied to him what I have written, I have written and It will stand.

When the soldiers had crucified Jesus they had taken his clothing garments and had made four parts of it, one share for each soldier; and they also had his tunic, the long shirt like undergarment, but because the tunic was seamless and woven into one piece from top to bottom the soldiers said to one another let us not tear it; but instead let us cast lots to decide whose it shall be (this was also to fulfil the scriptures: they parted my garment among themselves and for my clothes they cast lots) so the soldiers did those things. (Jesus' own prophesy filled)

By the cross of Jesus stood his mother Mary; his mothers sister Mary the wife of Cleophas, and Mary Magdalene; so Jesus seeing his mother there and the disciples whom he loved standing close to his mother, said to his mother, woman, behold your son! Then Jesus said to his beloved disciples see, here is your mother, and from that hour on the disciples took and cared for Jesus' mother as their own and took her to their home.

Jesus who by this time now knowing that all things where being fulfilled (accomplished; Finished) said in fulfilment of the scriptures said, I thirst; and there was a vessel jar filled with sour vinegar in it, so the soldiers put a sponge in the jar soaked it in the vinegar and placed it upon a reed of hyssop, and held it to Jesus mouth.

When Jesus had received the sour wine he said IT IS FINISHED; then Jesus he bowed down his head and gave up his Holy Spirit, since it was the day of preparation, in order to prevent the bodies from hanging on the cross on the Sabbath for it was very important one, the Jews requested Pilate to have the legs broken and the bodies to be taken away.

So the soldiers came and they broke the legs of the first one, and also of the other one who had been crucified with Jesus, however when it came to Jesus and that they saw that he was indeed dead, they did not break his legs, instead one of the soldiers picked a spear and pieced the side of Jesus and out came water and blood.

The fulfilling of scripture that was to take place was that not one of the legs of Jesus was to be broken, and another was in scripture was that they shall look at who they have pieced, which is in Zech 12:10 and Exod 12:46.

After the soldiers had done this, a man called Joseph of Arimathaea who was a disciple of Jesus came to see Pilate, he had hidden the fact that he was a disciple of Jesus for fear of arrest and being put to death himself; he asked Pilate if he would release the body of Jesus to him, and Pilate he granted him permission, so he took the body of Jesus away, to prepare it for burial.

As Joseph arrived with the body of Jesus his mother Mary and Mary Magdalene were there to sponge and wash his body down, and Nicodemus, he arrived carrying with him mixtures of myrrh and aloes each which weighed around one hundred pounds, after his body was cleaned and prepared, as this preparation for burial is also the traditional custom for the Jewish people, it was wrapped in fine linen cloth with the aromatic spices fit for the King that he was and to this day still is.

He was placed in a new tomb close to where he was crucified in a garden, where no one had yet been laid, because it was close to the day of preparation and that the tomb was close by, it was there that that they lay Jesus to rest.

Now on the first day of the week of Jesus' death, Mary Magdalene came to the tomb, it was very early, it still being dark; and Mary had seen that the stone had been moved from the tomb. So Mary ran and went to see Simon Peter and the other disciples, whom Jesus so tenderly loved, and Mary she said to then, they have taken away our Lord from his tomb, and we do not know where they have laid him.

Upon this that Mary has told him, Peter and the other disciples came out following Mary and they went towards the tomb where Jesus had laid; they came running together, but the other disciples outran Peter and arrived at the tomb first; but as Peter looked down all he saw was the linen clothes worn by Jesus laying there, but he did not see any sight of Jesus, body, so he did not enter the tomb.

Then Simon Peter came up following him, and went into the tomb and he also saw the linen clothes laying there; but the burial napkin which was wrapped around Jesus' head was also laying with the other linen cloths, but was rolled up wrapped and around in a place by itself.

Then the other disciples who had reached the tomb first went in as well, and he had seen the same and was convinced and believed what he had seen, for as yet they did not understand the statement of the scriptures that he must raise again from the dead.

After seeing what had happened they all left and returned back to their homes, however Mary she remained standing outside the tomb of her beloved Jesus, her teacher, Mary her heart was broken and she was sobbing; as Mary Magdalene wept she stooped down and looked into the tomb and Mary she saw two Angels in white sitting there, one at the head and one at the feet of where Jesus' body had laid.

And the two Angels said to Mary, woman why are you sobbing? And Mary she replied, because they have taken my Lord, and I do not know where they have taken him. Then on saying this Mary had turned around and Jesus he was standing there, but she did not recognise him immediately.

Jesus he said woman, why are you crying so, and who is it that you are looking for? And Mary thinking that it could have been the gardener around the tomb, she replied, sir, if you have taken my Lord away from here, tell me where you have put his body so that I may take him.

Jesus he said to her, Mary! Then turning around she said to him in Hebrew (Rabboni) which means teacher; Jesus he said Mary do not touch me or cling to my garments for I have not yet ascended to the Father, but I tell you to go to my brethren and tell them, I am ascending to my Father and your Father and to my God and your God.

Mary she left upon hearing what Jesus' had spoken to her to do and went to see the disciples. Their places of residence, and she told them the news that she had seen Jesus and what he had spoken to her about, and that they were the words spoken by Jesus.

Then it was the first day of the week when it was evening, the disciples who were behind closed doors for the fears of the Jews, Jesus came and stood among the disciples and said, peace to you all; he showed the disciples his marks in his hands and his side, the marks from the crucifixion; so that they can believe it was truly Jesus standing before them.

When the disciples had believed and seen Jesus they were filled with so much joy and peace that they could see that he was still with them, delighted in his presence then Jesus said to them again, peace be with you all, just as the Father has sent me forth, so I am sending you.

And having said that to his beloved disciples, he breathed on them and said to them, receive the Holy Spirit, now having received the Holy Spirit and being led and directed by me, if you forgive the sins of anyone, they are then forgiven, but if you forgive not someone for their sins, then they are not forgiven.

But there was one called Thomas, he was one of the twelve disciple called the twin, he was not with the disciples when Jesus first came, and it did not matter what the disciples had said to him regarding Jesus that they had witnessed in seeing Jesus, he still did not believe the other disciples, he said that he had to witness this with his own eyes, he told the disciples that he had to see Jesus' hands and put his fingers in the marks of Jesus' hands and side before he would believe.

Eight days later his disciples were again at the house, and Thomas was with them, and Jesus he came, thought they were behind closed doors, Jesus he stood among them and again he said peace be with you all; then he said to Thomas reach out your finger here, and see my hands, come and put your hand and place it in my side, do not be faithless and incredulous, but stop your unbelief and now believe, Thomas was given the name (doubting Thomas) and Thomas he answered Jesus, Oh my Lord, My God.

Jesus he again answered Thomas and said, because you have now seen me, Thomas do you now believe and have trust and faith? For blessed and happy and to be envied are those who have seen me and yet have believed and adhered to and trusted and relied on me.

There are so many more miracles that Jesus has performed in front of his disciples that have never been recorded in the Holy Bible, but these are written and recorded in order so that you may believe that Jesus is the Christ, the anointed one, and the son of God, and through believing, and trusting and relying upon Jesus as our Lord and our Saviour, then you too can have eternal life through his name. Amen

# The Holy Spirit

**READERS BEING A DEVOUT CHRISTIAN** you have been sent into the world to do the work that Jesus began to be filled with the Holy Spirit so that you can be empowered to do all the things that he has called us to do, how truly blessed was his disciples to have our Lord Jesus, the Messiah blew his breath of the Holy Spirit onto them; this readers is to be born again in Christ for the forgiveness of all of their sins, so that Jesus can save you from all of your sins and to give the same blessings to save others with the breath of the Holy Spirit.

You can call upon Jesus everyday when you are feeling down and tied, to ask from him saying; please my Lord can you fill me with the Holy Spirit, so that I can get back on track to do your will, I will obey you, for it is not my will, I have turned to you for I want to be a devout follower of you my Lord and my Saviour, Jesus Christ. **Amen**

The forgiveness of sins is the first thing given in being reborn again in Christ, so as a born again Christian myself then I believe that the first duty as a Christian is the forgiveness of sins as believers of Christ.

So although we have the power to forgive sins it always isn't that easy to forgive sins, for I have had problems will, and so may many of you; I have needed to pray as you have to do, for people that have caused you as well, much grief.

However because of my faith and my love for Christ, I must and I do have the need to forgive, and this need and love is supplied by my Holy Spirit given to me, so even if you truly do not want to or whatever your deep reasoning, your pain that has been afflicted upon you; your Holy Spirit also will ask you to forgive them, you must be open to forgive and not ignore what God has given you.

The amazing Holy Spirit will want you to let it all go and to pray for the person, who has caused you grief, and you also must put your trust and faith in God for he will do the healing, he will be the judge not you, he will heal you when you have done your works in yourself, you must remember again to trust, and have ultimate faith in God.

There are many followers who are Christian that have doubt in God? Yes you are reading this correctly, and there are many who even go to church on a weekly and a casual basis, but believe it or not if you do then do not panic or worry too much because you are not alone there, guilt of having these doubts can hinder your feelings, again do not worry too much, actually this can work in your favour?

Ok listen to me, it's actually your Holy Spirit working in you trying hard to keep you in Christ; to not stray of the path of righteousness making you become aware of your feelings, and that's what I love about the Lord for he is always there to work on you and in your favour to bring your doubts to him, remember that God will always know your thoughts and heart better than you actually do; that's a great feeling knowing how much God loves you.

When Jesus he blew the Holy Spirit upon them he told his disciples to wait for the Father to deliver them the power and to not try any great works without receiving this Holy power, and that if the disciples did not wait as Jesus had instructed the disciples understood that they would not receive the power.

Always remember that if you are faithful to our Lord then he also will be faithful to you, he wants you to love and to lean on him, for in doing so our loving Father in heaven in return will lean on you with his loving kindness, now how many Christians today would not want this kind of love and power from the Father, right" because we are all going to need him always to keep us on the right path, for we are of flesh and we will have our ups and downs all the time and we will need Jesus to help us when we turn to our faith and pray for forgiveness and for help.

Now Jesus has promised us that we will have the power when the Holy Spirit has come upon us, now how many would not want this power of Christ upon them, we need to receive it, and I don't know too many people that would ask for weakness and pray for that instead of the Holy Spirit?

I pray and give praise for the empowerment of my Holy Spirit for without it I would find it very difficult to have my old self back, for I also need my Holy Spirit because of my love and devotion to Christ, darkness verses Christ, darkness does not want you turning to God, he will fight to keep you where you were, but God and my faith wins for God will protect and always sent me in the comforters to ease my pain, I have no fear in darkness at all not like I use to, fear of God is what I need in my life to keep me on the right path, I will stay with my faith and I love the Lord with all of my heart and soul, my beliefs are strong and I put trust in what God can do for me than what the world has to throw at me,

My/our Lords only desire is for us to be and stay strong, happy and at peace in our lives and to enjoy it, and that includes victory over darkness and his wicked ways over us, for he is on a rampage looking for Gods children to devour, plot and scheme his way into our lives.

How Jesus works for us to help others can be for a devout Christian can be overcoming with our faith, I had been giving away some crosses of our Lord, and a young lady of about 22yrs old came in my shop, however I was serving another customer and wasn't aware of her being there; I heard movement and realised that someone else was in the shop so I went back around the counter and that's when I saw her; when I received the message from the Lord to give her a cross; so I picked one out of four different styles and asked her what was her name and she replied my name is Sarah.

I went around to the counter to approach her and asked If she would accept the cross of our Lord and Saviour Jesus Christ, and she said yes, with a lot of surprise on her face, we ended up talking, and I talked to her about what the cross meant in Christ; and she asked me about my faith and the Lord and then she told me about all her struggles, then she said to me I believe I was meant to be here today to see me, Sarah told me that the night before she had actually prayed to God for the first time and said to me that she didn't even understand why she had prayed.

I explained to Sarah about how I prayed to Jesus for help and that I was a minister of God's and that even though I was a minister that I was still of the flesh and that even I still get attacked from darkness, Sarah began to cry and she put her arms around me, and I talked more to her about Jesus' love and what he can bring to her life through prayers, faith and love for Jesus Christ our Lord and Saviour.

Sarah never did tell me what she was struggling with and I never asked for that was between her and the Lord, Sarah did tell me that she loves Jesus more now and I held her hands and I prayed for her, for Jesus to hear Sarah's prayers and to let her into his life, for Jesus was already there to receive Sarah and her love for him, you can truly see that this Lady needed and loved Jesus very much, and I truly believe that Jesus sent Sarah to me for this very purpose to strengthen Faith and believing.

When Sarah left she said to me I love you, and I looked at Sarah and said I love you too Sarah, she said to me thank you so much, I explained to her that I don't need the praise Sarah the praise comes from the Lord in Heaven, the healing for us both in Unity; That he has touched us both in our Holy Spirits, that connection will forever never be broken: it's a bond between Jesus, myself and Sarah; the power of the Holy Spirit that was breathed on us by our Lord Jesus.

The Lord has ways to bring people together to help heal people that are in need; he knows the loves of the children whom love him, for he does know are hearts, and the ones that are reaching out for him; Glory to God, for we need to acknowledge this help, and say thank you to the one who sends us this healing comfort, for we cannot do this without the help of our Lord readers, so don't ever think that you can, it is God's grace and our prayers alone that lets God's help us in our time of need, it is not even a coincident as some may think, it's our Lord and our Saviour Jesus Christ our Messiah, Jesus will send into your Holy Spirit what is needed to help overcome your grief and your deepest fears, anxieties ECT.

The Holy Spirit is the power of God, and when the Lord he comes into your life; the way you will feel is an overwhelming calmness within yourself, you will actually feel transformed into a new person, this is how I have felt even though i still have my moments.

But the empowerment enables you to overcome the moments you have by reconnecting with God, and in asking to be touched again in your Holy Spirit; for God he does want you to surrender yourself to him, which is what you do in your deep prayers to him, humbling yourself to him, making room in your heart and life for Jesus the son of God.

Your life beloved readers will become so fulfilled as you release yourself more and more to the Lord, you will become Godly in every area of your life, he will make changes in every aspect, making you think and feel different that even your friends and your family will notice the difference, I know my family and people did, maybe even before I had realized myself that I felt transformed, some didn't even like the change in me, but there was no way I was going to give up my life with my beloved Lord and saviour, Jesus Christ.

Your Holy Spirit it will speak to you and remind you that you have to act the way God would want you to act; you may for instants act badly towards someone and talk about that person to your friends over the phone, but when you get of that phone and God talks to your Spirit and your Holy Spirit reminds you saying (well that wasn't God like) that's Jesus reminding you that he isn't happy and that you better get right back on track into your Christian faith, believing.

## SPEAK THE WORDS OF GRACE

My Lord Jesus I ask if you can help me to stay on track with my Holy Spirit, and when I call on you; when I fall I ask of you too please lift me up, I believe in the word of God and I want to be a faithful child of my Father in Heaven, I love and I glorify your Holy name with all of my heart and soul; send me the love, joy, peace and happiness that I need now in my life to give me the head start that I truly need to live in my

# THE HOLY SPIRIT ✝ 107

new found Christian life as a believer in Jesus Christ, as I praise and glorify your Holy name, thank you Oh my gracious Lord for hearing my prayers, **Amen.**

I was talking to my husband this morning about circumstances in our lives and about people that we come across, and conversations that you can get lead into regarding people, I had a phone call regarding someone that we all knew within our family and friends circle; and this person was being hard to contact and family and friends were becoming obviously concerned.

So my family ECT tried to contact this person via other methods like face book, and mobile phone messages for the person to call someone because we were worried ECT but to no success; eventually the person did replied and it wasn't a very pleasant reply.

So I received a phone call regarding what had happened, my point to this is that even though I am relaying all this back to all you readers, this is still a form of gossip, but for you all to understand, I didn't need to be informed about what was going on in this person's life, for the people that were informing me and including myself were in fact more upset than the actual person whom we had been trying to contact.

So as it turned out if this person had just been left alone to live their own life which we are entitled to do, all this would not have happened in the first place and no one would have been upset regardless of just been worried about someone; the other person involved has made so many mistakes and has asked for help so many times and dragging everyone into his problems and cannot see why we were upset and concerned, Myself I have paid the persons bills, gave them a job and it goes on much deeper than that, so how much is too much, when is enough is enough?

However guilt plays a big part in peoples kind emotions and these can be used by people as well, but our God is also a kind and loving God and he knows that we have done all we can in helping, however the person involved does not like a very Godly life, the sins of the flesh have taken hold of this person's life in a huge way; but as great as this persons sins are , I have baptized him, anointed him with the Holy Oil so he has the Holy Spirit in him so he can turn to God and still be saved, repentance is a must to be saved with God and to have the Holy Spirit work in you.

But as long as his obedience to sin is greater than God that has been planted inside of him, he cannot be saved yet until he breaks free from the sins of our world, his willingness to accept sin is greater than his willingness to accept the grace of Gods favour.

But trying to save someone who is not yet willing to make the change not even for the love of God, is not worth upsetting your own life and having your peace taken away from you, which is what all this has brought upon many lives, it is not even worth the upset to the person who has caused many people grief, for as long as he thinks his life and behaviour is great and he says he is happy, than I believe leave him alone and get back to your our own piece of mind, and for me to get mine back on track with the Lord, my God, God would want him to turn to him as well, guidance is fine and the word of God is great, but forced and bullied is not a good thing to try and save one, you would indeed need to look at your own self, and take the speck out of your own eye, before trying to take the speck out of someone else's; amen.

The best thing to do as a Christian is to stay away from people who live in the world with so much sin in their lives regardless of how much you care and love them, living and listening to behaviour puts you into living that kind of lifestyle by hearing it; but if you want to live by Gods word then you cannot live in the sin of our world.

Gods deepest desire is for each of us is to become Christ like in all of our thoughts our words our deeds and our attitudes; and that our mistakes are of being only concerned about what is happening in our circumstances and the circumstances of others, when in fact living in Christ our concerns should always be what is going on in our hearts.

Do you not realize and understand that God is so much more interested in us changing how we act than changing our circumstances; when you become so much closer to God and how much he changes your life around this is when you realize that inviting our lord Jesus into your life is; and can be, the only way of life; it is the Lords way in you

# THE HOLY SPIRIT ✝ 109

and your life, for having the Lord in your life will allow you to have the experience of the increased power of your Holy Spirit, this is a feeling unlike any that you will ever experience in your life.

I believe in all my heart and soul that God can do wondrous works in us if we allow him too, for if there is one thing that I have learned since becoming a minister to My Lord is that you cannot interfere in other people's lives, or allow other people to interfere in yours.

You know I have come to realize that so many people waste much of their happiness wondering about what's going on in someone else's life, that in doing so in general they cause their own lives and their family members so much grief and heart ache; because they are focused on really what is so insignificant; not to mention that 9 out of 10 it's not going to change, but you on the other hand can.

If you do feel that this is an area of your life you need help in; an area of your life that needs change; call on our Lord and Saviour Jesus Christ to help you, the power in you given be God; it's the power also of the words that come out of your mouth,(prayers) readers to possess the power of Christ you must first understand that nothing is impossible in Christ if you believe, the power in believing is the power in the healing, in all areas of your life, remembering also that you are a valuable child in Christ Jesus, Amen.

# Faith Believing

**MANY PEOPLE HAVE A TRUE DESIRE** to succeed at being just ourselves but in doing so we must first absolutely have a good look at what justifies us? To make us right standing in God; The Bible tells us so many stories about so many lives and this is a good start for Christians of the word and truth of God; for them to learn that they are never really alone with our Lord, the Holy Bible also will teach you that we are justified by our faith in Jesus Christ alone, and not by the works that we do.

I have come to believe and know that once we take Jesus into our hearts, our heart and our faith it becomes real in Jesus Christ, it's not just the knowing of taken Jesus into our hearts it now becomes a deep feeling and understanding that he is with you always, not just in your mind, but your body and your soul, and in having all this divine power you are becoming more and more transformed, you will do good works, our works become love, faith, trust and reliance, they are all from the love of God, and our love for our God.

Our obedience to our Lord and Saviour Jesus becomes so important to our every day existence, as we learn and understand that Jesus died for us to save us from all our sins so repentance has become a new way of living in Christ, staying on the right path of righteousness, and that no one can go to the Father without coming to Jesus first, for he is the way the truth and the life; to have everlasting life in Heaven; our obedience is by which we hope to gain right standing and acceptance in Jesus Christ, This is not the works of our flesh either this is a clear acceptance and obedience in you becoming a new creature in Christ, a new law within your Holy Spirit; a new law of justice and trusting in the love and faith of becoming a changed person, in fellowship with the love of Jesus Christ, knowing also that you have someone divinely to turn to and praying to for help, hope and faith, and acceptance through Jesus, in faith and believing in our God.

Why did Jesus die on the cross for us? I will be doing a section of the Cross and why it is important for us to know about the cross, not just that Jesus was nailed to the cross; however when Jesus died on the cross he made us righteous and we should never forget this as a Christian and believer, many do not even understand the significance of the meaning behind the power of the cross, but you will;

Every one of us has sinned, small or large sin is sin, which is why Jesus died and paid the ultimate price for us; so we do not have to live under guilt and condemnation and that there is nothing that can separate us from the love that God has given us, we may not always do what is right that will please God; but as a Christian he will always be pleased with who we are and have become, followers of Christ; because you are in Christ, we cannot do anything to earn or deserve Gods love, but we must learn that this must be only received as a gift from him, learning the truth by reading the Holy Scriptures picking it up is a great start, learning the truth on which faith is built; building the foundations on which is within us.

Many people fail, however we are a creation of Gods, he never had any intentions of any one of us becoming a failure; it is us that have failed God at many things; especially when we are on the path of trying to become something, many give up and become a failure, and they lose confidence in themselves, when in fact it's not God that failed them but themselves.

Many people also think about God when it is good for them and sometimes it arises in the most crucial time of their lives like failing at something that they want to accomplish, and they ask the vital question, God why are you letting me fail all the time, God why can't I be successful like Jim next door, God why, why, why? Many people just continue to ask God these questions of failures; so why can't God help us to become successful; so let's think about why do people of the flesh only think about themselves, why do people ask God for success why can't people ask for their failures to become miracles, miracles of righteousness, wisdom, faith and believing so that your failures can turn to success with all that power, why would God for instance give you money when the money in Gods eyes is the root of all evil.

    Miracles can and will happen in your life, if you put your faith in Jesus and not the flesh of the world, and the desires of your heart, what God wants is for you to put your heart and your trust and faith in him first, don't you think that God actually approved of you long before anyone got the chance to disapprove of you and dislike you, if you love God do you think God would dislike you, how many people of our world always worry about what other people think? If you knew 100% that God would approve of you and accepted you as you are and that you would go into the Kingdom of heaven no matter what, would you even bother to care or worry about what other people said to you or done, so in fact If God is on your side who can really be against

    you? If you are a child of the light, why would you worry about the world in which we now live?

    Darkness is in our lives and all around us and this is such a huge problem in our lives and you better have faith and believe that it is real and it is around us, especially the Children of God his followers, and this comes with trouble for where there is light there is darkness, this also will effects almost all of the people in our world, when you have a lot of turmoil going on in your life, and it will effect what will play out in your thoughts, fighting back and forth within you, and darkness will want you to think that this is from you alone, your thoughts; you will want an escape route out of the darkness, it will confuse you, want you to feel that you are more of darkness than of the light, turn some of your godly thought into negative thoughts; it is and it will indeed; fight you every step of the way, putting ungodly thoughts in your head, just doing all that he can to keep you away from God.

You must become aware of these thoughts and you must dismiss (rebuke)them from yourself in the name and the power of our Lord Jesus Christ, he cannot hurt you, you are the child of God, and he has no power over you, it is only you that is allowing him to interfere in your fellowship with Christ, you have only one to fear and that is God; the question you must ask yourself is are you going to agree with God or darkness, well if you want my opinion I do not even think that is debateable, as a Christian we all know the correct answer, God 100% and Amen to that.

Readers; there are so many people that have beaten themself up over all the things that have gone on in their thoughts especially when your love for God turns real deep, I know that I have ;and I know a few people that have suffered at the hands of the thoughts that darkness puts in them,

However he is the weak one, God is the Power, God is the almighty one, and it wasn't long before I realized that I had the upper hand and I had God on my side to recognize that the word and the truth of the Holy Bible is the ultimate power; it wasn't me that was against me, it was darkness that was against me and you; well that's sad right, you may be thinking; well now that we realize also that it "darkness" comes to play; people are also against you being the same principle, for darkness doesn't always work alone in the spiritual realm, for Satan will also work on people in our world in which we live.

He works on our minds attacking our confidence making us feel unworthy and depressed, turning our feelings on to others, causing conflict because of what others say and do, don't let us forget Judas one of Jesus' disciples who also betrayed him.

Now the next important question to ask ourselves is how important are people's opinions towards us really? Do we start to think for ourselves or are we going to let people think for us? I believe in the word of God, so I will put it to you in another way; if people are very judgemental and opinionated and even worse, and then there is all the evil in the world like rape, murder, drugs, child molesters ECT sometimes these people are inspired by darkness (Devil), but it is time people started to resist and not to listen to what people think and say to us, never mind agreeing with them for argument sake.

If we believe 100% that God is for us and I do; then it should not matter at all what people say and do or what they think about us, for we are now children of God and our God he wants only love, peace, joy and happiness in our lives and for us to acknowledge our thoughts, take control and to then rebuke all evil.

We can all take comfort and have encouragement from our Lord and have the confidence to say that my Lord he is my helper and I need him in my life so that I can freely have the faith, love, the joy and the peace in my life with my Lord and saviour by my side guiding and protecting me, as all of God's children say praise the Lord, and Amen.

If we stay in faith and continue on the right path of righteousness of Christ and stay confident, God he will always accept us even with all of our imperfections, God he will even continue to work in us helping us to become more and more Christ like, so that we do not have to continue to struggle to win his approval or the approval of others, God loves us because he knows our hearts and that we love him with all of our heart and soul.

When the word of God is heard, faith is in the believing for we will then continue to believe, and God will invite us to live from faith to faith, so as believers one of our most important jobs will be to continue to live in the word of God.

Jesus said, believe in me and I will believe in you, live in me and I will live in you, Abide in me and I will Abide in you; believe and rely on me, and you will see the glory of God.

I just love that saying it would have to be one of my favourites, that is just a wow factor for me, how can anyone in my eyes not take in those words and not want to live up to the expectations of Christ Jesus, and have the glory of God live inside of you forever, wanting to rely on God/Jesus forever, I pray for help, for I rely on my Lord, faith believing; for Jesus he is the way the truth and he is the life.

Live in me and I will live in you, that is one of the most beautiful up lifting sayings that Jesus could give to his followers, he is our Lord and he died for us to give us a new start and to follow him in love and faith and to believe that he is the true Messiah, he is the son of God, he is the only way into the kingdom of Heaven, so for me I want to live in the word of God and be a follower of Jesus, I will believe and rely on Jesus Christ, AMEN

# Relationship in Christ "Not Religion"

**I LOVE THIS HEADING** for it is the most profound subject in all of our history; what do people class as religion? What do people class as just faith, believing? Who called and made Religion?

A relationship in Christ, and not to teach the word of God as a religion; I believe this is where most churches have been making their mistakes; for they have turned the word of God into a business as their focus point by giving it to many heavy rules and regulations instead of what was the main focus of what they were there for in the first place, which is teaching the word of our God.

They (the Leaders)have manipulated what can and cannot be preached, they have cut out what is in the bible and not allowed it to be preached, because they do not believe it should be discussed in church, leaving people to not understand the true word of God, and what he has written to teach his believers, darkness is one, God he wants his children to understand this subject, so they can be lead to him and so they have the opportunity to understand what is happening and that their problems are not necessarily their fault; many preachers do not discuss this so not to put fear in the church, and is this not the leaders of the church being manipulative, them not really believing the word of God, if you cannot get up and preach what is in the bible, then why are you there in the first place

# RELATIONSHIP IN CHRIST "NOT RELIGION"

teaching the full word of God, in love faith trust and believing the word of God.

They have turned teachings into a stressful situation with many ministers/pastors in our world today, who have and want to teach the truth of God to the followers, we go to church because either we have the true calling or some because they have fallen into hardship, or they have lost a loved one, or have simply wanting God in their lives, some have turned to God to change their lives around because they have lead a life of crime, many, many reasons why people have turned to God, faith and believing in God is a really good reason to have a need and want of God in our lives.

Many ministers and Pastors of today have suicided, why you ask? When they have God in their lives and no so much about the Holy Scriptures, why would they want to terminate their own lives, I have wanted to understand that as well, but there is so many factors that I found out in research, and believe it or not the suicide rate is extremely high and its sad.

Many have lost followers for many different reasons, churches have become more of a get together and have a cuppa and there is lots of back stabbing instead of being there for the love of God, many have had to go out and preach what they have not believed to be the truth in their hearts because they are not allowed to preach what they believe to be the truth and the word of God in the Bible, so this causes unsettling between the minister and the head of that particular church, it's becoming more of a business about money than off God.

Many have not been able to stay in preaching because of these restrictions in what they can discuss to their service to the church members; so the conflict causes them to either leave or being fired; and either way they have been left without a Job, and a failure to God in there eye's.

Many of these Pastors/ministers really love their work to God; it's what they live for, they feel abandoned, abused and dictated to by the head of the church they were preaching at, many members that pay large sums of money to these churches have too much to say regarding the running of the church; and they want things done there way and about what has to be preached about; "and if not" they threaten to pull out there funds.

Still isn't this turning the church of God into a business not what they are suppose to be there for"**GOD"**. However these days it's also about what suits they are wearing or who can and can't walk into their church because they are not good enough to sit next too, or who did your nails or what kind of expensive dress Debbie was wearing, I think you get the picture; don't get me wrong church is a great place to be in if you need God in your life, but if you go to church and do not feel comfortable and then you hear this is going on; leave that church, it is not in fellowship with God at all, they are all there for the wrong reasons; the word of God is, love, peace and so much more, and no one should be told they are not good enough to be in the house of God, Jesus he healed and he touched Lepers, and did not Jesus turn over the tables of the money changers and said, you have turned the word of God into a den of thieves; **understand readers.**

But today the world has changed so much and churches are becoming fewer and fewer, and the more people hear about these stories the more that are getting turned away because of the church member's behaviour; and another less person going into fellowship with God, so hopefully more will go to another church, but people are unforgiving as well; I have heard people say if this is what church is like then I am never going back, is this what God is all about? **"unfair"** I say to you though it's not the word of God it's the flesh of the world doing and saying these things, not God, these are the words and behaviour of people, God does not teach this in his churches, however he does warn us about people's behaviour in the Bible, for the children of God, he will always lead you in the right direction.

There are still many good churches out there, churches that focus a lot on feeding many of Gods people who are not as well of as us, the children in the worlds underprivileged countries around the world, God has said to me it's all about his little one's; children who are brought into our world starving, many have lost a parent and many have lost

# RELATIONSHIP IN CHRIST "NOT RELIGION" ✝ 119

both parents and have to feed and defend for themselves, some are all under the age of 8, who are feeding and raising their younger brothers and sisters; many of these children die before they get to the age of 10.

Our Lord he doesn't talk about our Government funded organizations, he talks about our Churches, the money that is collected by its members to feed his beloved children, it has never really been up to our government to feed his children like many think, its Gods people, the church; if you think about it many years ago you could walk in to a church when their where wearing the priest outfits and the nuns were wearing what people called the penguin suits, it was those days they would give you their last $5 if you needed it, and there was plenty of soup kitchens around, and Sunday schools, but not today.

Church members tithe to help the churches to grow and to feed the poor, it says in the word of God; but if all the tithing by the churches were run properly then none of Gods people would be hungry? Many of the authority church members get wages out of the member's tithings which of cause is legal and fair, we all need to be paid for our work and to survive;

Unfortunately many of the bigger churches become extremely wealthy and do not distribute the money from tithing fairly and many people including in their own country are starving, many families and their children are homeless; living on the streets and in their cars, some live in very poor conditions, and the tithing from very large churches can show that they are giving large percentages of the tithing to feed starving children around the world and many are doing a marvellous job, but the millions that are tithing and the 10% that they are entitled to keep for their services is millions of dollars over the years making them millionaires and this is a fact; this is why Jesus has said that if the tithing was done correctly not just about what you think you are worth and keep, no one would be hungry.

When you think about it, how wealthy is wealthy, I understand why God said that money is the root of all evil, and Jesus kicked over the money tables and said you are making this the den of thieves, because church leaders do still want to live a high lifestyle even with the good works of the Lord, they want the very best for their children giving them the world on the tithings, the best of houses, the best of cars, the best of education, the best of clothes, the highest social lifestyle, the life style of the rich and famous, the list goes on, even all their other businesses are because of the riches of the churches, the word of God, and all of them still put people down who do not live up to their world of their expectations.

I am actually myself partnered with churches in the world and these are very large churches, however I still feel no different with what I have written, I do this to feed the starving and because I still do know that the money that I have given does go to feeding many families, I do this because of my faith just like the other thousands who tithe in faith and the love of God, and this is where the frustration does come in to how you feel, yes I can stop tithing and try to send the money myself, but all of them do this very same thing 99% of the foundations to feed the poor, who use the word of God to make money and profit on tithing, so you are the middle person, however not getting overly negative, there are still thousands getting fed through these churches, people and their children that would not have any food or clothing or housing, medicines, or education without them, so what my point is with the word of God and the tithing so much more could be done with the tithed money; thousand more could be fed and thousands more could be saved from hunger and death, not just making these church leaders and their families over the top wealthy which is not what God wants, he can see what is happening and he knows that if the tithing was done to his standards not theirs, not one person or child would be hungry in the whole world, and God states this in the word of God.

The Churches that do help feed the poor do so because they feel for the needy and because they still understand that they are taking from people like yourself and me to feed the poor, and the love of God, and doing what is suppose to be right standing with the laws of God and the tithing needs of the less fortunate that us; with so many thousands and thousands of people that are suffering all over the world; religious beliefs in the church and their rules and regulations have come of track

# RELATIONSHIP IN CHRIST "NOT RELIGION"

when it has come to where the funds go this has become a business of tithing all on its own, I say who's money is it really, **Gods** for his little ones? AMEN

It's important for all of us to understand the love that God and Jesus has for the needy; People do also think that they don't have much so I am the one that is poor so I cannot give any of what I have away, people in our world have become selfish and have become to materialistic, and love of their social life gatherings, their holidays and their parties,

However with God it's about the caring for others, Love thee neighbour, love me as I love you, does this ring a bell to people; a little can go a long way; give up a little of what you have, can not only give peace to someone in need but may also make you feel a sense of being knowing that you have saved a child from starving or worse dying.

You caring about someone else apart from yourself will also give you right standing in Christ Jesus There are still some amazing loving caring people in our world who will give their heart to someone else in need, who love God and want to do what God would want them to do, and how could you not want a good relationship with Christ; believing that God is leading you on the right path to care and love people that are in need, isn't that what God gave you a great heart for, the Holy Spirit working in you, from the grace of God. Amen

God he wants his followers to be loyal to him, to have insight in the word of God, your church in you; your faith that is inside your heart, Apostle Paul; was a great writer for God, he said that a true believer in Jesus Christ is a new creation, and one who has right standing with God and an ambassador for him, how good does that make you feel to know that Jesus can love you that much and feels that way about you, gave you these feelings from your Holy Spirit, now you get what Jesus said when he said Abide in me and I will abide in you, live in me and I will live in you, beautiful right people, your Holy Spirit should be making you feel really good about now, empowered.

When we receive Jesus as our Lord and Saviour, our pasts are completely washed away, we do not have to feel guilty about what we have done in the past anymore because we have been completely forgiven, (washed clean) we have been given a renewal in our hearts, and we are continually renewing our minds, in the word of God, this will further strengthen us and ground us in the realities of our faith believing in the word and truth of God, keeping us loyal and steadfast.

## CHRISTIANITY IS A RELATIONSHIP IN HEAVEN, BUT OUR LORD JESUS, HE IS OUR REALITY

So many Christians in our world love and trust and believe in our Lord Jesus Christ, we believe that he died on the cross, we believe that he died to save us of all of our sins, we believe that God sent his son to save us, we believe that he is the son of God; he is our redeemer who paid the ransom for our sins, we believe he is our Saviour, he is our hope, he is our reality, we need our Lord to seek a relationship with him and our Father in heaven.

So what is Religion in our society and in our Churches of today? There are so many wonderful people who really love Jesus, and many who are desperate to find and have a relationship with him, and I have been there and you reading this then you too also are looking for the truth and the true meaning of Christ Jesus and what he can give you, the religious communities however continue to this day and age are still telling people they need to do something else in order to be accepted by God.

I need to explain for I do not want you to be put off with the word "religion" nor the "Church" for Jesus he started up the church and his preaching's of the word of God, as explained in previous pages, it's the rules and the regulations of the churches, I could say off today, however it was all back in the day of Jesus as well.

Many churches have become too personal in whom they want in their church fellowship, when in fact they should be having a personal relationship with the one who they are suppose to be there for, our Lord Jesus Christ; If they followed and learned what they were in Church for they should not miss the important words of Jesus, for he mentions and talks about his personal relationship with his (our)

# RELATIONSHIP IN CHRIST "NOT RELIGION"  ✝  123

heavenly Father; and the religious leaders of his day, they persecuted him and had him put to death on the cross.

So in today's society also what has really changed? I had come across people from churches and members that are no different, who try to force people to go to their church, and if the person refuses, they tell that person, then ok I will pray for you; so, so wrong, God wants you to go to church when you are ready not forced against your will, If you God to God then he knows that you are in complete fellowship with him, and who made someone else the judge, God is the ultimate Judge, a Judge to fear.

God is a loving God and he already knows who loves him; he knows your true heart and there is no fooling him, he doesn't want anyone forced into anything and that is including his church, only for you to go in your own appointed time, if God has you go when you are ready he then has you 100%, of your heart, your mind, and your Holy Spirit.

In today's society and back in the time of Jesus many are looked down at just by the mere mention of God; never mind talking about the subject over a cuppa; and if you said you talked to God and he talks to you personally, you would be judged and criticized.

I feel empowered by God, and I love talking to people about God, my Lord; and I am personally glad to be a writer of this book and the prayer book and your minister in helping you to become closer to God, a true believer in the word of the lord.

The people who are opposed to listen to God or about having anything to do regarding God are the one's driven by darkness, for it is darkness that opposes a personal relationship with God, the power of God will work continuously in the believer and have an impact on your life and your Holy Spirit.

So what we do need to look seriously at is do we need to keep the focus on religion? Or do we push the emphases' of that aside and focus on the true fact which is the law of God and what Jesus did die on the cross for which is our sins; so do we continue to let the religion side of it continue to destroy our faith when we come across someone who is negative about our Lord? Or as devout Christians do we keep our faith believing and have the eternal love, peace, joy and happiness in our Lord Jesus Christ forever more.

You can have many conversations with different people and people's religious beliefs and you will be surprised at what they class as religious nonsense; I have a book of reflections on my counter next to the donation for children tin next to it, and a man made a comment about not putting his 5cents change into the tin because he didn't believe in the bible bashing book as he called it, I was really shocked, I told him the tin is to feed starving children and has nothing to do with the so called bible bashing book, there was no reference or link to them they were there for two different reasons, the book was not there to make a donation to any church; so I had a chat with him and said why would you think that that the word of God was a bible bashing religion, do you have love, faith and believing in your life do you not want for these things to get you through life, and he said well of cause I do, and I said to him, well did you know that with the word of God that is all he wants for your life, that is what his teaching is about, not a bible bashing religious nonsense that you consider it to be, because people go door knocking and force religion onto people and turn them off the true meaning of what God wants for us; he turned to me and said, you have given me something to think about, plus yes I got his 5 cents.

# The Fruits of the Spirit

**READERS ONE OF THE VERY FIRST** sermons that I heard was about the fruit of the vine, I was really unsure what it all meant, and what are they on about? Yeah I know what fruit is yes it grew on trees and yeah grapes did grow on vines, yes Lord I think I have got it?

Not quiet: Apostle John has quite a different approach than the other apostles, he tells us about Jesus Christ in real depth in words, themes and topics, like the love that he has for God and his deep love for others; Jesus says; "I give you a new commandment: that you should love one another, just as I have loved you, so you too should love one another, so readers as Christians this is and should be one of the most important Jesus sayings in our faith; and it is vital to our lives as believers in our Lord Jesus Christ.

John is also explaining to us believers of the importance of abiding in Jesus; that apart from me you can do nothing, for we must stay as close to Jesus as possible, for we are blessed and our lives as devout Christian believers will bear much fruit, abide in me and I will abide in you, live in me and I will live in you, Is one of my most loved Jesus' sayings, it will lift your spirits in no time if you say this saying when you are feeling down, putting much depth into what it truly means.

John gives us great insight into the ministry of the Holy Spirit, who is our teacher, our comforter, our helper, our counsellor, and the spirit of the truth, so as you read about John keep in mind the love of God has for you, and the connection between yourself and Jesus and the importance of the closeness we need to have with our Lord, allowing the Holy Spirit to minister to you in every area of your life.

If everybody kept a good heart and kept their minds open, what a wonderful world we would be living in, but do you know even Jesus had it rough, much more than we can even try to comprehend.

A perfect example is in John 1-45-47; when Jesus had gone to Galilee and he found Philip who was from Bethsaida and Philip found Nathanael, Philip said to Nathanael we have discovered the one named Moses in the law and also the prophets whom wrote about Jesus from Nazareth, the legal son of Joseph.

Nathanael answered him, Nazareth? What good can anything can from out of there; and Philip replied with a "well? Come for yourself and see; Jesus he saw Nathanael coming towards him and said concerning him, see! Here is an Israelite indeed a true descendent of Jacob, in whom there is no deceit, nor falsehood.

Nathanael said to Jesus, how do you know me, before Philip had even called you, and you were still under the fig tree, I saw you. Nathanael answered Teacher; you are the true son of God! You are the king of Israel; and Jesus he replied, because I said to you, I saw the fig tree, do you believe in and rely on and trust in me? You shall see greater things than this; then he said to him, I assure you, most solemnly I tell you, that you shall see heaven opened, and the Angels of God ascending and descending upon the son of man.

Readers Nathanael seemed to have had a negative attitude towards Jesus and the fact that he came from Nazareth? Saying that nothing ever good come from Nazareth, but in the very next verse Jesus he complimented Nathanael saying; here is an Israelite indeed a true descendent of Jacob, in whom there is no deceit nor falsehood.

Nathanael had a very negative opinion of Nazareth, but just the same as people today really, nothing ever good come out of that person and from where they come from, (heard that from someone before) so when Nathanael heard that Jesus was from Nazareth, Nathanael was very closed minded to the fact that Jesus was the true Messiah simply because of where Jesus came from.

So in fact people are very much the same today as over 2000 years ago, because people of today are very judgemental, opinionated, and would have no problem judging you just from where you came from, are people prejudice? (you bet) people learn by listening to what others have to say about someone else; this is why the Lord wants us to examine our own hearts and to learn by our mistakes about others, to take the beam out of our own eye before we judge someone else; (is your heart open, to listen)

When reading about the story of Nathanael you get the strong feeling that Jesus liked Nathanael even though Nathanael was very negative about Jesus coming from Nazareth, Jesus kept an open heart, and this is what we all need to learn, to walk in Jesus' steps and to also keep an open heart when we find ourselves in similar situations of negativeness from people, people can put you in this frame of mind instantly, myself I understand for I am dealing with people on a day to day basis, I can get up in a great mood and the very first customer can change your mood instantly ruining your whole day.

For an example yesterday I had a local customer come in which I hadn't seen for almost a year, because he owed me money he came in angry and accusing me of spreading rumours about him doing something against the law, well I was shocked and told him that I don't have time for this kind of rubbish, never mind having the time to even associate with anyone in town, and that I would not say this kind of thing regardless of the fact that whether you owed me money or not, I actually said to him I wouldn't know what is going on in our town regarding anything that has been going on illegally.

So as you can imagine I wasn't highly impressed at all, and I tried to explain to this long lost customer of mine that I truly had no idea what he was on about; and said again I just would not do that, and reminded him that he should already know that it's not my kind of behaviour, I don't get out enough to know anyone's business; I explained to him that regardless of the fact that you owe me money, I was no longer interested in the money that you owed because it had been a long time since I had seen you, and regarded it as a bad debt unpaid,

He then changed his attitude and said that he did care that he owed me the money; and that he did wonder how I could know about anything that was illegal going on around the area, that he did know that we do not associate with anyone because we do not have the time, working 7 days a week, he knew that he was accusing me unfairly, but the people were also accusing him unfairly because of the rumours about him; (vicious circle) so in fact we are both innocent victims.

Strange how negativeness can cause so much chaos in people's lives, it ended up that he came back later on and paid of some of his debt that he owed me and he apologised, I never lost my temper with him, although tempted, out of total shock, and I was very upset mind you; upset about the whole situation.

However I did think about my Lord and how he would want me to behave/ act, I actually felt pity and sorrow for this man even though he was accusing me of doing wrong against him; I felt that it just wasn't worth it, yelling back at him for accusing me of spreading rumours it wouldn't change a thing; I felt that it was more important for me to stay calm, to stay in God's grace and just please my Lord.

Jesus worked in both myself and the long lost customer working on him and myself, myself staying in control; because before I found God I would have given him his money's worth in an argument, I would not have taken his behaviour and would have stood up for myself and my tongue would not have been pleasant at all, so I thank you my Lord, and the customer he apologised and that actually meant more to me than his behaviour or the money.

I feel that Jesus being the son of God, he also knew Nathanael's thoughts; for what would have been the point of Jesus acting any differently, because of Nathanael's reactions towards him; how Nathanael he was also judgemental, I felt the same way regarding my customer, in both circumstances we all opened up our hearts to change the circumstances for the better, a reversed situation so that we could all move forward and feeling better in ourselves, God's blessings working through us all.

Having unrealistic expectations about people will almost always set us up for a huge fall and disappointment, you may be saying to yourself, am I saying that we should not be expectant? Of course not! We should always expect the best from people and to not be judgemental; but on the other hand we must also remember that people are of flesh and have imperfections, and remember that this is also why Jesus died for us for God sent Jesus to die for us because of these imperfections, and to change us and to repent for the imperfections brought out by our flesh.

Jesus he went through most of his life here on Earth with many situations with his disciples as also with Nathanael, but he was never devastated; Why? Because Jesus he already knew about our weak nature, and he fully understood, Jesus he could read people's hearts, he never needed anyone to bear witness, and he needed no man, for he knew man; Jesus he expected his disciples to do their best, but Jesus also knew that their best would indeed have imperfections.

What our world has become though is the expectations everyone wants, bigger houses, perfect jobs, and better wages, (but many don't want to work for this money) perfect spouses, better friends, well behaved neighbours, best holidays (even if they cannot really afford one) better cars, perfect church members, and the list does go on, but when you really think about it and put some truth to it, does it really exist? Because as long as we live in our Earthly bodies all we have really achieved is more imperfections which is ill behaviour, many do not care whether they can afford things and credit debt gets out of control; causing many pressures on families, which causes grief and divorce rates become on the increase.

Realistically God knows all about us (right) but our Lord has given us instructions to follow all long and this is the Ten Commandments and the Holy Bible; these also give us insight to learn how to handle our lives our emotions and people, so as children of our father in heaven isn't it about time we listened to our father and be faithful children, loyal children, by being obedient, and living in the will and the law of God.

We are not perfect but we all must learn to have good hearts and how this is important in being a new devout Christian believer, being generous and having mercy by sowing good seeds, so that we can reap more when we do

need it; do you realize so many people expect more out of someone and usually much more than the person can actually give, "why" because everyone expects people to think and even have work ethics like them, we want as people, every situation to go exactly how we plan it; but this will rarely happen, we are creatures of habit and unfortunately some habits are far too hard to change.

This isn't negative thinking either; it's the truth, now as believers we do have the power of the Holy Spirit to help us, to achieve positive situations out of negative imperfections when dealing with people, and this is going to be a battle just in itself; because we cannot make it too easy that we do not need to use our faith in Christ, we will always need him, we have to be extremely careful how we go about it, thoughts are going to be one of the most challenging between yourself, God and darkness and because we all have different ideas and problems you will have to sift carefully through your thoughts and disregard all negative (imperfect thoughts) ask Lord God for help and rebuke darkness (capture them) and ask God to cast them away.

We all expect to want good things to happen in our lives, but you have to be realistic and to realize that we do all have to deal with people who are going to be difficult and unrealistic and we have probably all at some stage in our lives been a little like that for we are not perfect, keeping in mind that although these situations are trying on your mind and emotions, do not allow them to make your life lose its enjoyment; live your life by walking in truth and faith in our Lord and Saviour Jesus Christ, and keep a positive attitude.

I try real hard to keep a positive attitude and I mean real hard, dealing on a day to day basis with the public is very difficult and this is not just my business it's my home I live on the property so I have no escape, these difficult people are walking in my space so it's very trying and I'm being positive, I'm saying that I need Jesus to help me get through my Job much more than you can imagine I sometimes class this as a test of faith between me and Jesus to see how many times I can bring myself back to him and how quickly, yes I call on my Lord every day, you may be laughing but I am still flesh (imperfect) like you and a sense of humour you will need just like me; Ok I may need it more who am I kidding? Anyway without Jesus I could not get through my days, actually without Jesus we are all nothing.

There is so much learning in the word of God and let me tell you he has all the answers to our problems, he tells us how to get through our lives and to help us to overcome the self pity that people feel, (yes including me and what I just wrote) but Jesus he already knew the self pity of man, but Jesus he will not give you pity.

Jesus he will be firm with you and he will do so for many reasons, we have all heard the words tough love right, and this is Jesus' way, he wants us to be happy and content if we are feeling this way it is much easier for us to call for the Lord when we are struggling "Right" if not we are a perfect target for Darkness to creep in, so Jesus refuses for us to wallow in this self centred pity pot state.

Now you are all aware that I myself have suffered this self pity syndrome and my Lord would not allow me to stay in this self pity life that I once lived in, for Jesus he tells me to stop and start walking back into faith, reject the pity pot syndrome, my Lord he gave me the turning point to take hold of these emotions and thoughts, and to help you the reader to listen and learn how you too can control and walk always by the faith and the love of Jesus Christ, you too need to look at Jesus' instructions and what he instructs you to do, and you also can live a better life, through Jesus Christ, because living a life of self pity is no life at all, so I am glad I believe and trust in our Lord.

I know in Spirit that Jesus reached out and pulled me up to bring me closer to my Father, and to put me on the path of the word of God and to spread the word to help others that are not in the word, bringing them closer to trust and cling to Jesus and his word, to keep the word alive in the hearts of fathers children.

This is all accomplished by studying the word of God through the Holy Bible and by meditation on the word, for God's word is his thoughts, for when we give his word first place in our hearts and in our lives, Gods thoughts will become our thoughts, and its only then that we will experience the great plans that he has for us.

So now you are wondering how I can be sure that I am hearing from God "right" When you are born you are the Sheep of your parents and your parents are the shepherds, God says he who enters by the door is the Shepherd of the sheep, the watchman opens the door for the man, and the sheep listen to the voice and hear it, and he calls his sheep by name and leads them out.

When he has brought his own sheep outside, he walks on before them and the sheep follow him because they know his voice, for the sheep would never on no account follow a stranger; but would surely run away from him because they do not know the voice of the stranger or recognize their call.

Let me explain more to you; Jesus is the door for the sheep, and we are his sheep, your children are your sheep and they know your voice, you would not expect your children to "not know" your voice and you would not expect your children to go off with any stranger, neither would Jesus expect you to turn to the voice of deception.

Deception will only come in to destroy you, but Jesus is the good shepherd and he will save you, just as you want to save your children, god wants your life to be abundant and to be enjoyed; just as you want your children's life to be enjoyed and to be abundant, Jesus is the door, anyone who enters in through this door will be a love child of Christ Jesus "God" and they are saved, "will live" he will come to you and you will find the pasture in Heaven; he will not abandon you, all you need to do is to listen to him, trust in him and have faith, rely on him and he will rely on you, trust in him and he will trust in you, live in him and he will live in you, readers I recon this is a fair deal, aren't you glad you have found our Lord Jesus Christ. **AMEN**

Jesus he also says that I am the good shepherd and I do know my own, and my own know and recognize me; even as truly as the Father

# THE FRUITS OF THE SPIRIT ✝ 133

knows me and I know my Father and I am giving my very own life and laying it down on behalf of my sheep; I do have other sheep besides these that are not of my fold (flock) I must bring and look after these as well; and they will listen to my voice and heed my call, and so they will become one flock under one shepherd.

So we can know the difference of Gods voice, and we can know the difference of the voice of deception, if we truly know Gods character and by learning, reading and knowing the bible you will understand how God has lead others out of deception and led them to safety, to know and understand our Lord is to understand and know that what we have heard is something that God would say, for God would not contradict his word, and our wisdom and common sense should prevail, (as we know our children and our children know us).

As children of God and If you believe; truly belong to God, he will give us the knowledge to know his voice, from the voices of deception so not to be deceived, so you can feel safe and have confidence by believing that our Father in Heaven is guiding us to follow him in the right direction; for our Lord will let us know either to go forward or to wait.

God has no intentions to let his children down or to even allow deception to interfere in what he wants for his children, however we do need to put in more of an effort for our beloved Lord God and to listen and follow in his word, so that we can stay on the right path of righteousness and not stray, like the shepherds sheep, for the shepherd wants them also on the right pathway to not get into trouble or to be deceived.

The more time that you spend with God's word, the more closer you will become to him and the more you will become familiar to what God would and wouldn't want from you in your behaviour, and your daily life. It is so important to become closer to our Lord God and spend time with him, for we desperately need his power flowing through us, his love and his grace in our lives for in doing so you will be able to hear the voice of our beloved Lord and obey him.

I have discussed a lot about personal feelings, however the bible really is about our personal feelings, peoples personal feelings from the beginning of time, from the time our Lord God created our world; our relationship with the Lord and in general; people, Jesus he also had to deal with many people especially in ministry, Jesus he came from a royal background (King David) but many people do not stop to think about his family tree, and he was condemned to death for their belief in their Christian faith.

But we love our Lord and our saviour, do you realize that when you accepted our beloved Lord that you are set apart from others and a seed was planted, let me explain; I am the true vine, and the father is the vine dresser, any branch in me that does not bear fruit, (that stops bearing) the father cuts away; and he cleanses and repeatedly prunes every branch that continues to bear fruit, to make it bear more richer and excellent fruit.

For you are cleansed and pruned already, because of the word which I have given you, the teachings that I have discussed with you; dwell in me and I will dwell in you, live in me and I will live in you, just as no branch can bear fruit unless you abide in me.

For I am the vine, and you are the branches, whoever lives in me and I in him bears much abundant fruit, however, apart from me cut off from vital union with me, can do nothing, If a person does not dwell in me, he is thrown out like a broken of branch and it will wither; such branches are gathered up and thrown into the fire, and they are burned; but if you live in me; abide vitally united to me and my words they will remain in you and they will continually live in your heart, and this I promise it shall be done for you.

Reader when you bear and produce much fruit, our father in heaven is honoured and glorified, you must prove yourselves to be true followers of our lords, I love you just as the father has loved me; abide in my love with me.

Our Lord Jesus says; for if you keep my commandments if you continue to obey my instructions you will abide in my love and live on in it, just as I have obeyed my father's commandments and live on in his love,

# THE FRUITS OF THE SPIRIT ✝ 135

for I have told you these things that my joy and gladness may be of full measure, complete and overflowing, this is my commandment, that you love one another just as I have loved you.

The fruits of the spirit attributes are peace, joy, happiness, love, patience, kindness, goodness, gentleness, self control, faithfulness, all the greatness that words can express in our thoughts and attitudes and the way you interact with people.

How many people are out there that think they don't have any of these attributes, maybe you don't think you have many yourself, but let me tell you that you do, they are in you by the seed that has been planted, God is waiting on you, putting the word into your Spirit, it's your willingness to let God in, to let the seed planted grow.

How much are you willing to put the time into the word of God, the depth of your words by your mouth in prayers, to become a beloved child of Christ, how much time and patience do you have, to be able to change the old you into the new you.

Your old behaviour isn't going to be easy to change, for sometimes you think you are on the right path and you say to God, my Lord, thank you so much for the change in me, it is so overwhelming; then something goes wrong and you find yourself right back into the old you in an instant.

But let me tell you it is going to happen as it has with me, but I am more than willing to keep my faith and my love in my Lord to continue to love me; and to keep me right standing in Christ Jesus, for I believe in God and I believe that Jesus Died on the cross to save us.

I know in my heart and my soul that they love me and that I am a daughter of God and I do believe that I will see my Father one day through Jesus Christ for the only way I can see my father is through Jesus Christ.

I am not willing to throw away what I have been given by God, for the flesh that my body is in; for the sins of the flesh are too great, but the love that I have for my Lord is much greater than the flesh and the sins of the world that I am now living in, do you understand the importance.

I know God has planted the seed; and I know that the seed has still a lot of growing to do, for I am not a perfect child of my father in heaven,

I have been forgiven of all my sins for I believe, and God has sent me in the comforter on more than one occasion, because he knows that I believe, I want a relationship for eternity with God, Amen

Reader how do you truly feel, do you want what I have written and said or do you want something completely different, do you love our father in heaven, do you believe and love Jesus?

Do you love this world, for let me tell you that in 2 Timothy 3:1:5 it is written, there will be terrible times in the Last days, people will be lovers of themselves, lovers of money, boastful, proud, abusive, disobedient to their parents, ungrateful, unholy, without love, unforgiving, slanderous, without self control, brutal, not lovers of the good, treacherous, rash, conceited, lovers of pleasure rather than lovers of God or having a form of Godliness but denying the power in which Jesus and the Father have, The seed is the seed of love and faith believing, for against such things there is no law.

I feel excited to know and to understand that as a devout Christian all of these things have been granted to us which is living inside of us, Residing within us, OUR HOLY SPIRIT; now I guess the big question is that we need to ask ourselves is how and what do we do with these wonderful gifts that has been given to us by God; all this fruit for example the fruit of love the first and most important fruit from God.

Now there are always many questions that people do ask about the love of the Holy Spirit given by God and how do I get God to keep loving me and how do I stay in love with this love; how can I keep and feel this experience, the fruit of this love when I have been really hurt and my heart is breaking? How can I get this to continue to work for me, because I do not want to lose it or worse lose favour with God? Can these all be found in scriptures (the Holy Bible); can I learn to have all of the fruits of the vine and if so what results will I get? And If God has given me all of these wonders can I still please God by making them work in my everyday life challenges?

These are question that are very important to a devout Christian of Jesus Christ, because all of these question arise to many, many

# THE FRUITS OF THE SPIRIT ✝ 137

who do worry that God will walk and turn his head on you, never to believe and trust in you again because you have fallen short, but this is not the case, we are all going to fall short at some stage, but the faith and the trust comes with never ever not turn to God for forgiveness for everything that you do wrong, repent, and God will understand, remember that he is your Father and he loves you, even your little shortfalls, he does not like you being upset and he will help you get through your troubled times, he is a healer and he will give you the power to heal as well.

I am devoted to Jesus and I am working hard as well to be like Christ and the answer is to live and think like Jesus, walk in his ways and paths, what would Jesus do in these kinds of circumstances, would he just curse you and walk away? Of course not Jesus was sinless, he wouldn't do anything wrong in his father's name; remember Jesus spent 40 days and nights being tempted by the Devil and of course Jesus passed with flying colours, so much so that Satan left and was very annoyed at Jesus' loyalty to the Father.

Walk in his way and lead as an example, then the Lord can see that you are trying not just giving up, obey and live in the Law to fulfil mine and your purpose as Christians, to be in fellowship, setting an example, to all who will listen, this is the fruit of devoted love for God.

As I have explained Gods love, and truth, the true meaning of the fruits of the Spirit living your life in love (the greatest of the fruit) Joy, peace, happiness, trust and faith, these are power and harmonizing qualities released to us to be in unity in the body of our beloved Lord Jesus Christ.

These qualities deepens our love for our Lord to obey and to stay in righteousness, peace also within our lives and within ourselves, our Holy Spirit alive as we change, staying steadfast in Christ, praying each day for God's word as we hunger for God's love in our lives, because God is love his loving kindness fulfils your every being he draws you close to him every day, your faith and trust in Jesus is so important to him, for he wants you to call on him when you need him in your life and when you truly have Jesus in your heart your love and faith in him is ever so deep and you will find that he is in your mind every waking moment, you will have conversations with the Lord especially when you need him, the power of all the fruits of the spirit are going to be important in your life and your life as a devout Christian, your spirit your God within.

Many of these are based on feelings that we have however many of these feelings all work with the greatest of these feelings which is love, remembering that God is pure love, and if we keep love deep in our hearts we stay more in faith and we believe more; all the other feelings that we have they cannot work without love;

Let me give you an example; God speaks more in the bible about love many times and about Faith, trust and believing, "Why" because you cannot find peace or joy, happiness or trust, gentleness, mercy and kindness because you have to have love in your heart for these feelings to work, and without these working in your heart your heart can become hardened then darkness will start to interfere in your life and the work of the Lord in you, so what can the Scripture say about the fruits of the Spirit, "Love - God" and the different meanings of the fruit.

## JOHN 17:23

I am in them and they are in me, that they may be made perfect in one, and that the world may know that thou have sent me, and has loved them as they have loved me.

## 1 JOHN 3:18

My little children let us not love in word, neither in tongue, but in deed nor in truth.

## 1 JOHN 4:11

Beloved; if God so loved us, we should also love one another.

## 1 JOHN 4:7:8

Beloved; let us love one another for love is of God and every one that loves is born of God and knows God; he that loves not, knows not God, for God is love.

## JOHN 3:16

For God so loved the world that he gave his only begotten son, that whosoever believeth in him should not perish.

## JOHN 13:34:35

A new commandment I give unto you that you love one another as I have loved you; that you also love one another; by this shall all men know that you are my disciples, if you have love one another.

## DEUTERONOMY 7:13

He will love thee and bless thee, and multiply thee he will also bless the fruit of thy womb, and the fruit of the land, the corn, the wine; and the oil and the flocks of the sheep in the land which was unto thy fathers to give thee.

## PROVERBS 15:9

The way of the wicked is an abomination unto the Lord, but he loves those that follow after righteousness.

## COLOSSIANS 3:12:13

Put on therefore as the elect of God, Holy and beloved, bowels of mercies, kindness and humbleness of mind, meekness, longsuffering, fore bearing one another, and forgiveness of one another, if any man has a quarrel against anyone, even as Christ forgave you, so also should you forgive them.

You can see in these verses of scripture how important love is to the Lord loving one another, forgiveness, being made perfect in one; we are made in the image of God, we need to live and behave in a Godly manner, we all have our problems and we make mistakes sometimes very bad mistakes, however we need to deal with them the best way we can, and in dealing with them if unsure that you may have made a bigger one, in dealing with the one you tried to fix; ask God for forgiveness anyway, for he knows your true heart he knows that you are struggling and are unsure, as long as you stay in faith and love with God he will forgive you and not leave you.

God is Mercy and merciful, and he does promise to deliver, the scriptures give us hope and encouraging words from the Lord, he will never let you down it is us that lets us down by giving up when you feel there is no hope, the Lord he will wait patiently to fulfil what he has promises, stay steadfast in his love and stay focused the best you can and loyal to the one who will bring you out of every situation that causes you difficulties and heartache.

The scripture writes in **Isaiah 30:18**

Therefore will the Lord wait, that he may be gracious to you and therefore will he be exalted, that he may have mercy upon you for the Lord is a God of Judgement, blessed are all that wait for him.

**Psalm 103:13** The Lord has loving pity on those who fear him, as a father has loving pity on his children.

As parent we try hard to forgive our children no matter what they have done especially when they get older, but many do forgive their children as our parents did forgive us for all of our mistakes, "why" simple "love" many of us say we are sorry and some will refuse to, but as Christians we must forgive and move on, get over it so to speak, do not hold a grudge, the forgiveness is repentance for what we have done wrong, can you see where I am going, repentance and forgiveness is from God and God forgiving his beloved children for all that they had done "sins" If God can forgive us of our sins who are we not to forgive someone else, Judging, we do not want God to Judge us our fear for God in judging it should be enough if we truly love him to forgive and repent and to stay in righteousness with God.

I know when someone has really upset me, I might have my say but I try to keep as pleasant as possible and being still in flesh that is difficult, however I find myself sifting through my thoughts with the Lords help, in meditation with the Lord, going through what was right and talking to the Lord and saying to him Lord maybe I could have handled that better,

But sometimes you do get short and know that it is wrong, but keeping God as close as possible does help you to get back in the right frame of mind a lot quicker because I know that before I found God

I would have gone ballistic when a Good argument could have been fought especially if I believed I was right, and I am sure many of you that read this can verify my truth and yours in that, but it is not what the Lord would truly want,

Jesus may have thrown the money tables upside down because he was angry as well but we must learn as Christians that it's not right, Jesus was teaching that the money been handed around was becoming a den of thieves, that money was the root of all evil; Jesus is a teacher a messiah of Good intensions not of evil intentions; money should be given to help the needy as well, not for greed, Jesus is love, compassion, forgiveness and of peace believing.

The Lords compassion for love and fairness and what is right is what he was clearly trying to demonstrate and this is what we should be teaching ourselves and our children; by walking in the Lords footsteps living his life of righteousness, faith believing and his deep love for his Father in Heaven.

The fruit of the spirit can teach us so much about our behaviour and feelings; these are traits of all of Gods children good and bad, and weather we are good or bad our Lord God he does not give up on anyone of us, that's what I love about God our God his love and compassion; to forgive, repent and to turn to him with all of our problems and to change our ways and to acknowledge him; that he exists and that you love him with all your heart and soul; for he gave up his only begotten son for us, who died for us taking all of our sins and suffered a terrible death and for us which was done out of love,

When Jesus was dying he said to his father because of what they were doing to him (Forgive them Father for they know not what they do) Jesus was suffering but he still had compassion for us; to ask his father and our father for forgiveness of us all, and this was not just about the people who were there at the time this was about the past, the present (his time over 2000yrs ago) and the future (us) for all of our sins that we have done against God.

Many have heard about the wrath of God, the fear of God; and this is a good thing; for us to fear God and rightly so, Our God is a mighty

God and we must fear him to stay on the right path of righteousness and to have life for eternity in the kingdom of heaven, more people need to fear God because not one of us is going to miss out on judgement and that alone is fear, no matter how righteous we think we are God just might not think the same.

   I quiet often think about God and what I am doing especially when I am really upset, for one I doubt very much that God would want me to feel upset, he would only want me to have peace, it's my emotions that lead me to feeling this way, sometimes emotion can get out of hand, your Holy Spirit it grieves, and when you love God all you do want is peace, and how do you get that peace when your emotions are out of whack; when you cannot make a decision because of the fear that you will might make the wrong one and because of the people it will involve in the decision you make, does God allow you to make these mistakes because he is leading you into another direction of your life regardless, is God leading you regardless of the effects because it is your destiny, everyone that is around you in the decision will have their own destiny as well, the decision needs to be made and not changed, the fear of making the mistake needs to change because God knows your true heart and that you do fear him in making the wrong decision, he is only leading you by your Holy Spirit, if there is children involved then you need to follow your Holy Spirit and stop fighting it, especially if things are not right within your life, is it a warning, to follow your Holy Spirit? What is it, that God trying to tell you?

   Your fear of upsetting God and making mistakes is what God is doing for your life, think about the path your life has been on; past mistakes are they really mistakes or are they lessons that you have to learn and he is teaching you to correct them, and yes darkness and his influences are to blame as well, but do we blame too much on darkness and not the journey that God is teaching us in our Holy Spirits, for fighting is darkness, stealing, drugs, murder ECT these things must not be confused with the path that God is leading us on,

   Happiness and faith believing is of God, unhappiness needs to be tested and corrected, to many of us struggle with making decisions, we

# THE FRUITS OF THE SPIRIT ✝ 143

need to find strength and get on the right path for God loves us and only wants happiness for our lives, do we miss out on all the beauty that he has given us to see; I say absolutely and "Why" is that; could it be because we are all too wrapped up in the new age "technology" are we just to wrapped up in ourselves and what we want especially with the material things that the world has to offer us, children sit around before and after school and play games, TV ect and the beauty God created just passes them by, not enough parents stop it before it is too late, not enough people lead their children to God.

If you really love God and you fear making the wrong decisions understand this; that your faith and love in God regardless of the outcome will get you through your failures, you might fail but God he will not fail you, he will always love you just never give up on God, keep your love and faith your trust and your believing in God, he has already forgiven your mistakes and your failures past, present and future, he actually expects you to make them, all he wants is you to not lose your love and trust in him, trust and ask him to guide you listen to your gift that God has given you which is your intuition, your Holy Spirit, the fruit of the Spirit.

# Page of Prayers and Promises

**GOD'S PROMISE TO US** is that if we would keep our minds fixed on him always that he will keep us in perfect peace, sometimes this can be very challenging, especially when we let our guard down' and are not intentionally focusing on him, allowing all kinds of things to intrude upon our minds, I ask of all readers to pray that even when our minds are in a passive state, that the Holy Spirit would strengthen our minds to stay focused on him,

# PAGE OF PRAYERS AND PROMISES ✝ 145

My Heavenly father, I pray that you help to keep me on the right path, I do struggle at times and I do know that I cannot stay right standing without your help; I promise I will try and keep more focused on you and the word and truth of God, because one thing that I do know in my heart and soul, the one thing in my life that I am sure of, is my love and belief in you, help me my Lord to keep my mind focused on what is right and teach me every day; I pray in your Holy name, in the name of my Lord Jesus Christ, **AMEN.**

> GOD always has something for you, a key for every problem, a light for every shadow, a relief for every sorrow and a plan for every tomorrow.

## Dear God

**WORK ON MY ATTITUDE. TEACH ME TO BE MORE LOVING, COMPASSIONATE, PATIENT, OBEDIENT, AND HUMBLE. STRIP AWAY THE ANGER, THE BITTERNESS, THE STUBBORNNESS, LAZINESS, PRIDE, AND COMPLACENCY. HELP ME TO BECOME MORE LIKE YOU AND TO PRACTICE WHAT I PREACH.**

*In Jesus' name, amen!*

My gracious and beloved Lord for all that you've done, and I will thank you, for all the things you're going to do, I thank you, my Lord for all that you have promised and all that you are, Its all that has carried me through, in my everyday living in your word, you are my strength and I thank you, you are my shield of protection and my Lord I thank you, my Lord I love you.

**MY LORD JESUS CHRIST I THANK YOU, AMEN**

# Promises of God

**GOD HE PROMISES US** so much in the scripture so much so that it can actually help us in so many areas of our lives, sometimes the only answer for our problems can only be sought from the word of God, he is the key to happiness, love, joy and peace, sometimes we try to solve our problems all on our own because we have no one else to turn to, not in this world anyway,

Then one person you feel you need to open up to, you finally; and sadly realize it's not always the best option, this could be a partner, a parent, a friend or someone else is doesn't really matter it happens to us all; people become frustrated and they feel totally lost and nowhere to turn, however becoming a Christian can take time to get away from our old thinking, when realistically the one that you should have turned to right from the beginning of becoming a new child of Christ, is Christ himself, our Lord and our saviour,

He is the only one to turn to and to help us in our most difficult times; fear can overcome you, depending on the situation that you are in, and being a Christian that is a normal process that you will go through, it has taken me time to overcome the stress and worry about upsetting the love that you have for God, which is offending him, disappointing him because of your behaviour when upset, however he is our teacher and our guide to the kingdom of eternal peace and happiness, not like the world in which we live, that throws at you every obstacle imaginable, testing us,

In our faith, our personal situations in which we live our daily life, it can test your strength to push us to our very limits, to see how long it takes for us to realize what is going wrong and to turn our faith back to God, to ask him for our help, to give us strength; to get us through what you are going through, sometimes it isn't darkness that causes our problems, he isn't always to blame, sometimes it is God, testing our love and faith in him, testing to see which way we are going to go when pushed too far.

Let me explain the pushed too far, when people are pushed to far we have a certain breaking point regardless of how strong you think that you are, many think that they can handle all situations, when in fact unless you have a severely hardened heart, everyone sheds tears and everyone can be broken.

Everyone has weaknesses, in a death of a loved one, sicknesses, diseases' that are incurable, a marriage breakdown leading to divorce, loss of income from losing your job, pressure at work, at school, even children become under pressure from situations like being bullied, molestation, rape, dysfunctional family issues like alcohol ECT, drug abuse this is even in adults and the list goes on and on, I believe you have the picture of what I am getting at; everyone can be broken, family issues are climbing, the best marriages can fail no matter how hard you think you have tried, but two people need to communicate to fix problems not just one, and this is very common, one always believes that there isn't a problem, even when there isn't communication happening, this is a perfect example of being blind and a closed book syndrome.

This is when you call on the most professional practitioner of all time God, Our Lord and Saviour Jesus Christ, his miracles on Earth were outstanding from the beginning of creation and right up to his crucifixion that many know about; who are new at scripture, the miracles after his resurrection and his miracles that he has performs today our outstanding, however many people do not recognise the miracles that he has done in their lives; their prayers answered and they have even forgotten that they had even asked the Lord for their miracle either for themselves or for someone they love, know or care about; and Jesus never gets the recognition that he rightly deserves, because being in flesh we so easily forget because we only see what we want to see in this world.

One of the Lord gods promises are that if you love me with all your heart and soul and you believe in me and the word, and you continue in prayer, and if you call on me and ask me in prayer for anything, I will give you what you want.

Is this not a loving caring God who loves his children, who sent his beloved son to save us from all of our sins to have the choice to repent and have everlasting life in heaven to never die again, to never be unhappy, to have joy and peace, to see for the first time what real love truly is all about, in scripture it talks about so many promises that God is willing to give you.

The promises of God; for the believer in Christ is one of the most uplifting feelings of hope that we can hold onto in our Good times and our bad; that our Lord God he knows what we want and need and knowing that he is there is a great comfort.

God says to us that if we continue to live in the light as our Lord God he is the light, we will share what we have in God with each other, and the blood of Jesus Christ, Gods beloved son, makes our lives clean from all sin, but the saving of those who are right standing with God is from the Lord, he is there strength especially in times of trouble, this is a promise from God.

The Lord he will open the eyes of the blind, the Lord he will raise up those who are brought down, the Lord he loves those who are right and are good, for the Lord he is good, being with the Lord is a safe place to be and in times of your life when you are struggling, and he does know those who come to him to be safe, The Lord he will show you many troubles of all kinds, but he will make you strong again, and he will bring you up again from the deep in the Earth.

The Lord will say unto you, why are you sad, Oh my soul? Why have you become troubled with me? Put all your hope in God; how wonderful it is to have the Lord on your side to place all your cares and worried in him to heal you, to give you strength and this is his promise for you, the Lord also says' nothing will hurt you, no trouble will come near your dwelling place (your home) and I will tell all your Angels to care for you, and keep you in all your ways building your strength.

And I say unto you those who plant with tears will gather fruit with songs of joy, and the one who goes out crying as they carry their bags of seed will return with songs of Joy; For I have brought you with a price, and I have made you free, I have called you by name, you are mine, a promise that I will keep, and I say to you again, do not be afraid; for it is those who are with us that trust in the Lord, and do good; so you will live in the land and will be fed, and I will give strength to the weak and give power to the one will little strength, so be strong, be strong in heart, all who have hope, trust and faith in the Lord and the promises of which I give, for I your Lord God is with you anywhere that you will go.

Trust in me, For I the Lord your God is good to those who wait for him, to the soul who seeks me, For the Christians who are devout believers this is very real in their hearts trusting in our Lord God and seeking him, the faith and the love that you have as a believer is very strong and you can receive so much from God to help you in difficult times, God is good to the ones who seek him, who believe in him and have faith and trust, his promises are true, and he does deliver.

Wait on the Lord and keep his ways and he will exalt you, wait for the Lord; be strong and let your heart take courage and may the Lord your God answer you when you are in distress, waiting patiently for our Lord to act; the ones who put hope in the Lord will renew their strength, they will soar on wings like an eagle, they will run and not grow weary, they will walk and not grow faint, and blessed are those whose hope is in the Lord their God.

I pray that God, who is the source of all hope, will fill you completely with joy and peace, and this is because you trust in him, all things are made possible with God and this is a promise of his, believe this and then you will overflow with confidence and hope through the power of the Holy Spirit.

We have this hope as an anchor for the soul, its firm and it's secure; it enters the inner sanctuary behind the curtain, where our forerunner, Jesus Christ our Lord and Saviour has entered on our behalf, his trust must be strong in our hearts and that is because faith and believing can conquer so much in our life as a Christian believer, that Jesus he died for us and he rose from the dead taking with him all of our sins, so our faith and believing to have eternal life in the kingdom of God is important to God and the believer; hope will also not lead to disappointment, for we know how dearly God loves us, because he has given us the Holy Spirit to fill our hearts with his love, and I can promise you the reader that you can feel God deeply in your Holy Spirit his presence he lets you feel it/him, search for him and you will find him and people who search for him have the seed planted and it will grow inside of you every day, those who have ears let them hear.

The Lord our God has called us for a reason, he has a purpose for our lives; many believers know this calling deep down inside, and it is the Holy Spirit leading us to the path of righteousness, turning us back to where we belong and that is with our true family in heaven, its being saved from the world in which we live, one might say it is a wakeup call from the divine, I know for me it was a wakeup call, I was given for years divine warning, but I just didn't listen or maybe it just wasn't the right time, although I wondered? This wondering was my Holy Spirit trying to awaken my inner calling to turn my life around and search for Jesus in my heart to bring me back on the path of righteousness.

You can search your mind and your heart over and over wondering why didn't I find my Lord years ago, how much different would my life had been? Oh how I have prayed about all my sins, the ones you know about and the ones you just would not have even thought was a sin, pray and repent for all because god has different ideas about the sins you would not have expected to be a sin.

# The 10 Commandments

**I PRAY THAT THE EYES** of your heart may be enlightened in order that you may know the hope to which the Lord your God has called you; for we were saved in this hope in the Lord, believing in Gods promises for your life eternal; the Lord your God says If you obey me and keep my covenant, you will be my own special treasure; for all the Earth belongs to me, serve only me and you shall spend your days in prosperity, and your years in pleasure, for if you love me you will keep my commandments.

I am the light of the world; whoever follows me will not walk in darkness, but will have the light of life, you shall walk after the Lord your God and fear him, and keep his commandments and obey his voice, you shall serve him and hold fast to him.

The commandments of the Lord our God have been known to many Christian believers and even non believers, many still learnt about scriptures as young children, although today Christianity has been taken out of schools because of the many different cultures in our countries, changing religion and faith; there are many scriptures in many countries bringing with it many disagreements in the believing of which bibles is the right bible, my answer to this is that there is only one bible and there is only one true God.

So what is the arguments all about why do not all believers keep to their faith and not interfere with anyone else's and do what they feel is right in there love for God the God in heaven, not turning away from the church of their nomination and their faith in God, does not God say do not judge, for he is the only judge, and yet many read the bible, it is a known fact that even today it is the most sort after book in the world.

Many tried to destroy the Holy book, but it was hidden and it was republished this is the work of God to keep his word alive, many tried to destroy Israel and many times Gods people were driven out for hundreds of years but God said in the word that his people will return and this happened, God will fight for his chosen people, and rightly so.

We fight for our beloved ones, god he loves his children, as we love our children; we fight for what we believe in but this should not be done in any physical way, but done with faith, love and believing in God, thinking and living in the law of God, to the best as we possibly can and repenting for what we have done wrong, past, present and future.

Many people know about Moses and that God gave Moses the commandments for us to keep but what people do not realize is that there are about 600 other commandment that like you and me we do not know them and this is the other good reason for repentance for all the laws that we have broken that we are unaware off; many people may also think that this is totally unfair and that we are already condemned and are at a disadvantage in breaking Gods commandments, and I agree, however many also already know the 10 commandments of Gods laws and If not they do know it exists, written for us in the Holy Bible so that they can learn them, and the ones that do know the 10 commandments of God, do not stick to them anyway; nor would the people who would look for the commandments follow them, so my point is are we at that much of a disadvantage with the other laws if we cannot stick with the 10 laws given to Moses by God, so who is really being unfair God or his children.

## DEUTERONOMY 5:6:21

Moses he called all Israel, and he said to them, hear me oh Israel, the statues and ordinance which speak in you hearing this day, that you may learn them and take heed and do them.

The Lord our God has made a covenant with us in Horeb, The Lord has made this Covenant, not with our Fathers but with us, which is all of us here alive today, the Lord has spoken to you face to face at the mount out of the midst of the fire.

## EXODUS 19:20

And the Lord came down upon Mount Sinai, on the top of the mount: and the Lord called Moses up to the top of the mount; and Moses went up

## EXODUS 20:1

And God spoke all these words saying,

I stood between the Lord and you at the time to show you the word of the Lord, for you were afraid because of the fire and went not up into the mount, he said; I am the Lord your God, who brought you out of the land of Egypt, from the house of bondage.

## THE COMMANDMENTS

*Thou shalt have no other Gods before me;

*Thou shalt not make yourself (to worship) a graven image or any likeness of anything that is in Heavens above or that is in the Earth beneath or that is in the waters under the Earth.

*Thou shalt not bow down to them or serve them; for I, the Lord your God; am a jealous God.

*You shall not take the name of the Lord your God in vain, for the Lord will not hold him guiltless who takes his name in falsehood or without purpose.

*God says observe the Sabbath day (7th) day being a Saturday; and keep it Holy, as the Lord your God has commanded you; remember readers that although many God to church on a Sunday in respect of the Sunday being a biblical Lords Day; many think that Sunday is the Sabbath, but it actually is Saturday.

I want you to also understand that Jesus he died on the cross and gave a new Covenant to release us from the Old Laws because we were

# THE 10 COMMANDMENTS ✝ 155

sinning and could not live under these Laws, not that we should forget these commandments, but Jesus gave his life to release us from the Law; manmade rules and regulation was condemning us even further into sin, Jesus came to forgive us of all our sins through repentance.

*And for 6 days you shall Labour and do all your works; but the 7th day is a Sabbath day to the Lord your God; in it you shall not do any work, you or your sons or daughters or your maidservants, or menservants' neither your ox or your donkeys or any of your livestock, neither any stranger who is within your gates, for your servants they may also rest as well as you.

For I say unto you; to earnestly remember that you were a servant in the land of Egypt and that the Lord your God brought you out from there with the mighty hand and a loving outstretched arm; therefore the Lord your God commanded you to observe and take heed to the Sabbath day.

*Honour your Father and your Mother, as the Lord your God commands you; so that your days may be prolonged and that it may go well with you in the land which the Lord your God gives you.

*You shall not murder.

*Neither shall you commit adultery.

* Neither shall you act slyly or steal.

*Neither shall you witness falsely against your neighbour.

*Neither shall you covet your neighbour's wife, nor desire your neighbour's house, his field, his servants, his ox or his donkey, or anything that is of your neighbour's.

I say unto you these words your Lord has spoken and to all your assembly at the mountain out of the midst of the fire, the cloud, and the thick darkness, with a loud voice, and he spoke not again he added not one more word, the Lord God wrote on the two tablets of stone the words written with the finger of God, and he handed them to Moses, I command you to teach, so that they might fear the Lord their God.

# The Power of God Almighty

**THE HEADING OF THIS TOPIC** says it all; the power of our Lord and Saviour, Jesus Christ; however this topic could be ever so long, for god's power is everlasting; how great can our God get; for the power of God is unimaginable; the size of God is unimaginable; because we have no idea of the extent of God's creation.

The scientists of today have no idea they live their lives on theories, and if it makes sense to someone then they except it; for most people are gullible; many except the big bang theory because the scientist said so; however something had to create the energy of the big bang theory to start from, where and what created that energy which would have been astronomical to begin with, that power had to have a creator?

I have seen a scientist interviewed and he walked away from the camera and the interview because he could not give a valid explanation of what created the big bang; he could not deny that God truly exists, which debunked his theory of the big bang creating all, not God.

I however believe in God, that he is the creator of all, there never was a big bang theory; it's a cover up theory so that people will not believe in God or the word of God; regardless of their overrated imaginations let them find out when they meet their true maker when one day he will be standing before them and God says; explain your theory to me.

Mean while it is still every ones free will to believe what they like just like me, because many are not going to believe what I have to say either, and this is the reason God gave us a choice to believe who and what we want; and people do need to understand this; there is only one judge; one who will all come before him and that is God.

The word of God is the most important book in the world's history and the most debated; however it is still the most sought after book in the world; but many people do not know how much was deliberately taken out of the bible; many of these books can be found they are called the forbidden books; the book of Adam and Eve; the books of Enoch; the ancient book of Jasher; the book of caves; the book of Elijah and Elijah; the book of Giants and many more; these books have been removed by religious leader over centuries; to deceive people from knowing the true; however this is the deception of man to keep for themselves; but it is unfair to the children of God; but God has said to his children seek and you will find, and the truth will set you free.

It was a huge sin for man to tamper with the word of God; this is a clear message in Revelations 22:19 by our saviour Jesus Christ that no one shall distort the work of God; but man does what man does best, I will do what I want; I will control and I will manipulate: however all is not lost from the children of God, for God had many faithful believers to continue to keep the word of God alive.

These lost books are an eye opener for the believers of God his followers and you will be able to see why we were lied to and manipulated; it was in the best interests of the higher authorities to keep the believers under the control of them and their laws, the law of man not the laws of God; and Jesus calls, it man made rules; so man was being manipulative right back in the times of Jesus when the high Priest were manipulating the word of God to make themselves look highly important.

They never had the best interests in the word of God nor the truth, they even had Jesus murdered because they did not believe he was the son of God, even though it was stated in the Holy scriptures they had that there was going to be a great king born, the son of God; they only believed after he was sentenced to death, many then believed and became the followers and the word of God spread, even today the word is powerful and the truth is coming to light; more people believe in the power of God, Gods power is in the believers of God, the truth and faith.

In the days of Jesus Christ many Roman leaders and the high Priests covered the truth but they certainly knew the truth; they did not want to lose what man treasures more, living in the world of power and manipulation, the power of money and the greed to stay in power and control, and they did kill for it.

Much like today, what has really changed; we have free will God did give us that; but he also said thine shall not kill; from the beginning of creation until end times, the amazing power of God will reign over all mankind, God will always be God almighty and it is God who has all control; including over man, believe it or not, it's your choice.

The reasons why Jesus came to Earth in the flesh, and the connection between Adam and Jesus, the full comprehension of why Jesus was called the second Adam is a startling revelation in these missing books and what we never knew and the depth, these as Christians are a must to be read to understand the depths of creation, the full comprehension of how God works is a masterpiece, and the connection of dates, years and numbers from creation to end times.

Let's have a small rundown together from beginning of creation of Adam, and fall in love deeper with our God, Jesus Christ on an intimate journey of power and strength.

We all know that God created in 7 days, but we do not know all and the depth of these creations; what did God create first on that very first day; the first Holy day of creation was Sunday; God made Heaven and Earth, all the waters and the air that we breathe; God made fire and then all the Angels; the archangels, the cherubim and the Seraphims; and all the invisible (winds).

This was done on the first day, on the first day of the week again a Sunday; God created the seven wonders of the nature, Heaven and Earth, water, air, fire, the Angels and the Archangels and Darkness.

Then by the mighty hands of God he plunged into the midst of the depths of all the waters; Earth, the waters were above and below the firmament, now how great is our creator to hold Earth in his hands and throw Earth into the waters he has created, hard to fathom the power and the size of our almighty Father God.

Our almighty God who sits upon his throne has many who watch over him and these are in the highest heavenly realm, now the kingdom of God has more than one level, the Highest is where God sits upon his throne; the ones who protect and watch over God are the Cherubim's and the Seraphims; wherever God moves these protectors move with God; their eyes are many, and they can see in all directions; side to side; above and below; and they worship God singing; Holy, Holy, Holy Lord God almighty, worthy to be praised.

The Heavenly Realm below God contains the realm of the Lords rulers these are the Angels and the Archangels; the Archangels have swiftness, the Angels have strong spiritual knowledge; these Angels have many Jobs to do in the Heavenly realm and on Earth and dealing with evil forces; and keeping both realms in balance.

The second day of God's creation was the firmament, the firmament is a fixed and solid foundation, and God also separated the waters from above and below; the below firmament was separated and used for the good of man and all creatures great and small; and all the seas the lakes and the rivers.

On the third day God commanded that the waters be gathered together in places to create all dry lands; the dry lands and the mountains could then produce nature, life as we know it for all living things, these could balance with the winds the channels flowing; including the oceans producing the heat and the cold; dews and mists, storms which will service all Earths resources in foods and all plant life, and to finish off from the third days creation our Lord God wanted more to perfect the three days work so he spoke the word and created the sun, the moon and the stars; for the heat and the light and darkness; the heat of the sun was to spread all over the Earth which was to cause dryness, humidity and dampness all because of the waters; the sun and the moon and the stars they were created to bring forth all light and life to the planet Earth for all the living.

On the fifth day of creation our almighty God brought forth with the spoken word all creatures great and small in the waters, and all that was in the air, all that walked and crept upon the Earth all that could see in the day and of the night.

On creation day sixth was the eve of the Sabbath now this was the creation day of Father Adam the first man; for all now had been created and God was well pleased and all was quiet; God wanted to create man in his own image, so he called forward all his Angels and he told them his plan to create in his own image man; "the trinity" the father, the Son and the Holy Spirit" now this sent fear and happiness in the Heavenly Realm, that God was going to manifest another being in his image, his likeness.

God then held out his hand over the centre of Earth which is "Jerusalem" over the mountain of Golgotha, the mountain of the skull, as God stretched out his hands he gathered from the Earth (1) grain dust (2) and from the water he collected 1 drop of water; (3) he collected from the air 1 puff of wind, (4) from the element of fire only a little of warmth was needed for the creation of Adam.

From the four elements that God held in his hands he could now create Adam for he had, cold, heat, dryness, and moisture, all these to create the human form, why has it been said the Adam was create by dust; The grain was from earth the nature formed from the Earth; which was subject unto him, the water was all earths seas and rivers which are also his; the air was all the flying creatures of the air given unto him; and the heat is of all the fiery in nature, and the Angel that will be his helpers in the garden of Eden.

Now God had a perfectly formed Adam in his mighty hands, in his own image and likeness; now all who looked upon Adam were in awe of this beautiful creation; for his glowing appearance was like the sun; his eyes were as bright as the stars; his nakedness was like the most sparkling bright crystal.

# THE POWER OF GOD ALMIGHTY ✝ 161

God looked upon Adam and his splendour and was well pleased at his perfect creation and God loved him very much; God placed Adam down and he stood very high as high as a giant, like all the heavenly Angels; his feet were planted on the same spot that the cross of our Lord Jesus Christs cross was to be place in Over 5,500 years time; and in all Adams splendour God placed a crown upon Adams head, then he was placed in Heaven upon a throne; as a King, and the first priest and prophet, who was given reign over all creatures great and small; and he had the authority to name all the creature created by God; and they bowed down before Adam, and this included all the Angels in Heaven; they honoured and worshipped Adam on their knees, in all his splendour; and God saw that what he had created was good; like Adam our Messiah Jesus Christ is the exact expression of Gods true nature, like a perfect photo copy.

Jesus Christ is the great I am; he who never changes, he is never ending; he is our Lord God who holds all together by his words spoken; he was the one who formed the Earth in the beginning, he crafted the universe and all with his hands, and they will all disappear one day, but God said all my children will last forever; fiery flames are my ministers for they are my witnesses, all who speak and read the word of God, all who spread the good news, all who trust and have faith in the church of Jesus Christ, the great I am.

In all of God's creations there was one Angel who was displeased with the creation of Adam and all the attention placed on him; never mind the crown placed upon his head, that was just another insult; "yes" Satan; he wasn't pleased about all who were worshiping Adam on bowed knees; he was becoming hostile; and he was demanding the Angels to stop, and that they should not be on their knees worshiping this creation of Gods that came from just mere dust.

Satan was becoming more and more rebellious towards Adam and God every day, and the more he became jealous of God and the Angels love for Adam; the more distant he was becoming towards God; he believed that he should have been worshiped not Adam, he was before

Adam; so after a short time Satan began to plan a Heavenly war on God and all the Heavenly realms of Angels.

God was becoming concerned regarding Satan's rebellious behaviour, God had given Satan the best of everything, beauty, finely dressed, every precious jewels, commands over Angels, and much more he had power; but he wanted to be God and he wanted to be worshiped; he wanted a throne and all the glory that came with Gods higher power.

God commanded Archangel Michael to gather forces against Satan and his armies; Michael's army size was unimaginable to our comprehension; in full total of all God's Angels the army was a staggering 4 million in warriors; however the first battle Satan did win the first fight; all Archangels Michael's Army scattered; then God commanded the Angels to carry as weapons the flaming cross of light to battle against the armies of Satan; the flaming cross which is "trinity" is the Father and the son, and the Holy Spirit; this powerful sign had defeated Satan's darkness and he retreated along with his army.

God then commanded his Archangel leader Michael to cast Satan into hell; now this fight between the powers of light and darkness still exists today between the children of God and the forces of spiritual darkness; and many are unaware that this has been going on since the beginning of creation; they find it hard to fathom, but it is a fact, and this battle continues all the time, and the greatest battle it still yet to unfold between the forces of good and evil, and this is when our Lord Jesus returns to Earth to rid Satan; defeating him and his Army once and for all; they will be cast into the pit of hell, for one thousand years, then released; because God is merciful; then he causes battles against Jesus again and Gods children, he is then called up for final judgement and cast forever in the fiery pit of hell; never to be released; and the new Earth and the New Jerusalem will be the new home of love, peace, no pain or sicknesses, nor tears, for God's children.

Now let's take a few steps back to Adam creation; the size of God and his Angels are unknown but to give you some idea, legendary scriptures written from the lost books have put Satan's size as 2833 feet tall; his hands were 117 feet long; his feet were 11,666.62 feet long; his mouth was 66.7 feet wide; his face was a day's journey for us to walk; and his eyebrows were 3 days journey long; now as mere humans this is very hard to comprehend, now God is mightier than Satan he is the most high; so try and comprehend the size of God almighty, then you have Lord God Jesus Christ, how really powerful he is and his size then there is all God's mighty Angel armies, this is the almighty forces and the power of Heaven.

When Satan's behaviour was becoming out of control in Heaven and Satan's outbursts of his bitterness was apparent towards Adam; his arrogance and his lack of discipline was becoming clear to God that he was seeing Satan for his true wickedness; and the raging war in Heaven because of Satan's rebellious behaviour.

God almighty called his Angels to strip him of his authority and his armour, however when the Angels went to do what God had ordered they hesitated so God called Archangel Michael to piece Satan through his side to the backbone and shoulder blade; then a Cherub broke his wings and his ribs rendering Satan helpless and vulnerable against God's almighty armies strength; then Satan along with his rebellious army were cast out of Heaven and cast to Earth, Satan and his followers became Devils with Satan as their leader.

Adam now being in paradise and God seeing that all was good he said to his Angels I am going to create a helper for Adam a companion; so he put Adam into a deep sleep; and he took from him a rib; and he created Eve; when Adam awoke he saw Eve and he called her woman, because she was made from man.

Now there has been much speculation from where Eden was actually located; many say that Eden was located in the middle of the sea on an island, many say it is just below Heaven, in all the books God does give clues, however I believe we are not meant to know everything; however he does clearly state that he placed Adam on the spot where Jesus cross is to be placed and that Adams body was to be placed in the Ark of Noah; and his body was to be placed in the centre of the Earth being (Golgotha) where Jesus is to be crucified.

The cave of treasures I believe is either the cave of the Holy Mountain of God's; which is Mount Sinai or Golgotha (the garden tomb) where God placed Adam, where the cross of Jesus stood; and to me this makes perfect sense for one God chose Israel to do all his work it was also were he resided; it was his chosen place to be; and Adam was given the authority by God to minister in this cave when he was expelled from Eden, he was the first priest, prophet and king, so to all his family members that lived in this cave he taught the word of God, this cave become the first church of God and also it become the burial place of all his family members; God planned everything perfectly and everything was to be exact and to coincide will the coming of his son Jesus Christ.

Many might disagree at what I have written and fair enough; but you have to understand God and how he thinks and what he has written to see that it can only be in these two places, the first was where he took Moses and where he resided; this was also the place of where

# THE POWER OF GOD ALMIGHTY ✝ 165

Abraham took his son Isaac to be the first sacrifice, where God showed himself as the burning bush, and gave Abraham the Lamb as in place of his son as a sacrifice, the burning bush represented the cross off Jesus, the lamb represented (the Lamb of God).

The second is where his only son died the mountain of Golgotha or the garden tomb grounds as many would know it as today; and his first creation Adam was placed not only where he was created but also the exact spot where Jesus cross was to be placed and where his son died, but also it was where he gave instructions to Adam; to teach his family line right up to the generation of Noah that he (Adam) was to be place in the cave of Golgotha by Noah's son Shem to place Adam in the exact spot above the cross of Jesus; "why" so that the blood of his son (Jesus)can flow into the scull of Adam in the "mouth; to be baptised by the water that flowed from the blood of Jesus and the blood from Jesus was to give Adam life; The first resurrection.

Now why would God if he is going to be exact on all his works choose another place to have the mountain of caves, or the Garden of Eden for that fact; except these two choices of God's? He is a perfectionist in all he does; the bible the word of God proves this from creation until the return of Jesus; these are the two perfect locations of the cave of treasures.

Now many will look at Golgotha or the garden tombs grounds today and say; how can this be a huge mountain and a cave underneath it's not high enough? The fact is there has already been done excavations underneath this mountain which was done by a man called Ron Wyatt in 1979- 1982; Ron found a cave underneath the exact spot where the cross of our Messiah stood; now you can do the research on line and type in his name; but Ron he found blood in the cave underneath where the blood flowed from Jesus and he took samples, he had the blood tested professionally; and the tests came back by the experts saying this blood is alive; however the scientists they where dumb founded because they said the chromosomes were only 24, 23 which would have come from the virgin Mary and one "y" sex determinant chromosome which was from "GOD" now we all know that each of us has 46 chromosomes 23 from a mother and 23 from a father; however Jesus never had a human father did he; but his mother Mary was indeed human, that's the 23 from the tests and God was the one chromosome making up the 24; the experts said to Ron this blood does not have no human Father, who's blood does this belong to, and Ron said this is the blood from our Messiah, the son of God.

Ron also has found much more including the discovery of Noah's ark 15 miles south east of Mount Ararat in 1977; in 1987 the government of Turkey declared this to be the site of Noah's ark and labelled it also as a national park; a visitors centre was constructed and visitors are today still welcomed; now the length of the Ark Ron measured was 515 feet, which is 300 Egyptian cubits the exact measurements that God told Noah to build it, the exact description in the Bible; now many scientist said this was a natural formation because it was sighted in 1959 from space, so years later God made an earthquake and the Ark split from right in the middle from one end to the other exposing the size of the Ark and exposing all the wood.

Testing was conducted on the Ark in front of Turkish authorities and cypress wood was found and in 3 layers, rivets of metal were discovered and analysed in there labs, they had aluminium metal, titanium metal, iron, and magnesium, now aluminium and titanium are manmade metals and the Ark is a manmade structure; after these testing they declared that it was indeed a ship and manmade; in the Bible in Genesis the tribe of Cain was already using metal works before the flood.

They continued to use scanner radar like what they used over the sea to find the titanic; and they found that the ship of Noah was indeed in three layers in depth and had many separate section in each layer that had collapsed onto each other, but many sections to house many animals; reaching down deep into a hole that was exposed they pulled out dung and cat fur; to completely confirm the Ark was authentic a village about twelve mile away had many stone anchors which kept the Ark afloat; it was discovered near this village it was also named the village of eight, because there were eight in the Ark; this is a very ancient village and today you can still see the remains of the house which Noah had built and the graves of Noah and his wife, these graves were vandalized hundreds of years ago, but it has been told over many years that sold was expensive jewellery that was stolen from the remains of Noahs wife.

God has worked in so many people from creation up to today leading them to the truth and this is including Ron Wyatt who passed away in1999; but he glowed and right up to his death bed he asked to be interviewed to say he would donate all his money to continue in his research after his death in the work for God; he never had donations given to him in any of his expeditions it was done with his own money, he went and worked and his wife and son; and when they had enough money they would go and do more expeditions in finding the truth for Gods children; God spoke and worked in Ron to give all his children the light of the truth, not of the truth of our world but the truth that his children would believe the facts backed by the word and truth of God.

Many unbelieving people will always find a way to discredit the truth to find a way to destroy biblical facts; but you know they cannot deny scientific testing you can only lie to yourself because you do not believe period.

Now back to this amazing cave of treasures where Adam and Eve lived in the days after expulsion from Eden, which god says is in the centre of the Earth, this he has also said is also where he placed Adam after he created him and placed him (where) in Golgotha (the place of the garden tomb) the centre of the Earth, where the cross of our Messiah was placed, this is also where he said the garden of Eden was, the Garden of Eden is the **Church of God**, the hidden treasures are his children; YOU.

The keepers of Eden are Enoch and Elijah; these great prophets are also the same two prophets who return in Revelations; they are killed by the dragon (Satan) who is released out of the abyss and they are left lying in the streets for three and half days in the exact spot where Jesus was crucified; now after these three and a half days they hear God call them and they rise to their feet in front of all who are watching and all who are watching them around the world on their televisions/

computers ECT; and they are terrified and then realization sets in that they are from God almighty.

    These two prophets were commanded by God to come to Earth in the final battle on Earth and for forty two months (3 · yrs); this is the same as Jesus; once again who came to minister on Earth not to be ministered too; Jesus ministered for 3 · years; coincidence; "NO" The bible is Jesus from creation right up till the return of Jesus; and the bible also ends with the return of Jesus; "why" because all will be fulfilled; what Satan destroyed from the creation of Adam with all his lies and deception; all has to be reversed by the son of God, all evil is to be destroyed; all God's children shall live a life of peace, and happiness without the destruction and sin nature of the deceitful Satan; who will be cast along with all evil in the fiery pit of hell on the final judgement; so children of God, repent for all your sins, to live a life forever in the kingdom of God; and anyway why would you not; you do only have the choice of two; I do not want to live a life of torture nor in the company of pure Evil; I have chosen my Messiah Jesus Christ and I give myself to him with all of my heart and my soul; and all God's children pray...AMEN.

    When Adam and Eve first took the fruit there eyes become opened and their spiritual eyes become closed because of their sin; they could no longer see God, they could no longer see the Angels and they could no longer hear the Angels rejoicing; they saw their nakedness and they felt shame and hid themselves when they heard our Lord Jesus walking in the Garden; he then clothed them with the soft bark of the trees in paradise; now this amazing grand tree was so massive that each bunch of fruit contained over 150,000 kinds of fruits, berries and grains; this is unimaginable to our thinking that such a tree could hold a bunch of foods and fruits so large, however in the new Jerusalem when Jesus reigns there will be a tree the same if not the same tree and its leaves are complete in healing of all sicknesses and diseases; it is also described as the cross of our Lord and saviour.

    When they were cast out of Eden their grief was overwhelming; their fear became great and Adam fell to the ground in fear; even his

# THE POWER OF GOD ALMIGHTY ✝ 169

feet touching the rough ground frightened him, the rugged terrain was not like anything that he had seen in paradise; God however still felt much compassion for Adam and Eve; his heart was grieved because of the deception of Satan; God he told them do not be afraid; and he promised Adam that he will come back again after 5 · years, when he will be returned to Eden, now 5 · years is 5.500 years when Jesus returns to Earth to the minute and the second of his resurrection; this is when his promise to Adam is fulfilled and all the dead in the graves of the righteous will also rise.

Meanwhile Adam could not return to Eden for it was well guarded by a Cherub carrying a two edged flaming sword, Adam and Eve had to now fend for themselves in Eden they had available plenty of bread and wine (last supper)and fruit in abundance from the tree of life; now they were at the perils of the rugged terrain; and for a long while they did not eat; God warned them that they now had a fleshly body there new bodies had to be given food for nourishment or they would die, which they did on many occasions, but God brought them back to life to fulfil what was now destroyed by Satan.

When Adam and Eve where shown the cave of treasures to live in by God, Adam knew not Eve for over 30 years; they kept their purity; now Satan still tried to deceive them on many occasions and Satan was warned off By the Angels God sent to protect them commanding Satan to leave them alone; however Satan did not listen and he frightened Adam and Eve on many occasions until God taught them about the deceptions of Satan, for Satan deceived them in a form of a serpent in the garden of Eden; but Satan had many faces of deception which he and his watchers used; so God sent his Angels to teach and make Adam and Eve become aware of all Satan's trickery; and Adam prayed and called on God many times because of Satan Evil.

Adam was given in the cave light because they never had darkness in Eden so the darkness frightened them and Satan used this fear against them, so God gave them light in the form of a lamp stand (made of gold) that never went out; they were also given frankincense and myrrh; now these three gifts are the same gifts that the three kings gave Mary at Jesus' birth and also his death.

Now you are probably aware of the similarities between what has happened from creation to the crucifixion of the son of God; and why Jesus was also called the second Adam; I will give you a few more; the first was Jerusalem where God placed his hands over the centre of the Earth to create Adam; then after his creation God placed him in the exact spot of where the cross off his son Jesus was to be placed, now on the 3rd hour on a Friday God placed on the head of Adam a crown; on the 3rd hour on a Friday Jesus had a crown placed on his head; Satan on a Friday was speared in his side and cast out of heaven; on a Friday Jesus was speared in his side after he had died on the cross; Adam was given the authority to be a king a prophet and a minister; Jesus he is our King a prophet and he ministered for 3 · years; 3 · hour after creation Adam and Eve ascended into Eden by Gods hand; Jesus ascended into Heaven after 3 · hours; Jesus also was 3 · hours in the judgement hall; Adam and Eve felt much shame for 3 · hours in Eden; Jesus son of God for 3 · hours was tortured, mocked and spat on; on a Friday and for 3 · days Adam and Eve were naked in paradise and felt shame; on a Friday for 3 · hours Jesus was stripped of his clothes and was humiliated and naked on the cross; in the garden of Eden Adam and Eve lived on bread and wine; at the table of the last supper with his disciples Jesus gave bread and wine, the bread broken was Jesus body, broken as a remembrance of the son of God; the wine, his shed blood which was shed for us a covering of all our sins, a covenant made to give us life eternal.

In the garden after being deceived by Satan, Eve after 6 hrs gave Adam the gall fruit of death for Adam to eat; after 6 hrs the crowd called to give Jesus something to drink because he said "I thirst" he was given gall and vinegar to drink; now on a Friday Adam and Eve were sent away from the garden of Eden, on a Friday Jesus our Lord and saviour was placed in the cave.

Adam even suicided and shed his blood, when he was given back his life by God, Adam out of love collected his shed blood and he made the first altar to God; and it became the first shed blood; God promised that this will be repeated in his son; Jesus became a sacrifice and his blood was shed; for all of our sins; both incidents took place on a Friday.

It is without saying that the word of God and all that he has planned is a masterpiece of creation and of great power and planning in the word spoken by God; and God has a purpose to change what was destroyed by Satan's deception it must be reversed; from creation of Adam until the return of the son of God; precisely and in the correct timing, by the hour and the seconds, and in the same manner, restored by the word made manifested by God.

Now Adam was taught much in the cave of treasure his knowledge and wisdom had to be given to him he had to continue the church and the word of God to all the future descendants; to keep them in faith and trust and to keep them away from the deceit of Satan's evil; God taught Adam everything from his creation, the flood, the crucifixion of the son of God, Adam was given all knowledge; nothing was kept from him even his own death; and

How he was to be embalmed by his son and later taken and placed in the Ark after the flood.

When Adam died he was 930 years old, he ordered his son Seth to embalm him, now his son Seth was a good loyal son who knew the word of God well; he was to follow the footsteps of his father Adam and to keep the people away from the children of the murderous Cain who was banished by God and Adam from the mountain of the cave.

Adam's body was to be washed and cleansed with Gold, Myrrh, and frankincense, and his body was to be buried in the cave next to the golden lamp which never went out, Adam's body was the first body to return to the Earth in which it came, and they mourned over Adam for 42 days; and they bowed down to Adam and prayed to God in prayer and worship to a God worthy to be praised.

All the generations of Adam were to be buried in the cave of treasures; and all the generations of Adam they were now under the command of Seth, and on his and his father's Adam's commands they were to stay away from the tribe of Cain's people who were below the mountain; all Cain's people were full of sin, they interbred with the fallen Angels of Satan "the watchers" they were full of lust, rape and murder and Satan taught them well; all the shame and sin, that God despised.

Now the body of Adam was to be taken by Noah who lived and dwelt in the cave along with Enoch; and all the generations of Adam; Noah was commanded by God to build an Ark because he was going to bring a great flood upon the Earth to destroy all evil; now God is a merciful God he still gave all his children time to repent with the words of Noah's warnings about the impending great flood which will destroy all on Earth; but nobody listened they laughed and mocked them and God and they kept in their sinful nature; however Noah had 130 years to give everyone enough warning; so Noah started the quest to finish the splendid ship in time for the flood.

Noah had already been given the knowledge from the generations of teachings of the word of God that it was he that had to take father Adam and place his remains in the centre of the Ark; and his son Shem was to remove Adam and place him in the cave of Golgotha in the centre of the Earth; above where the cross of the son of God was to be placed, and an Angel of the Lord was to tell him precisely when this was to take place; in the precise day, and hour and the precise position of the body of Adam was extremely important.

The body of Adam was to be placed in Golgotha; the Earth was to be opened by God to receive Adam and then reseal itself and nobody could reopen it again, however when the son of God's cross was pushed into the Earth a crack would appear and where the Ark of the covenant is in a cave below the cross of Jesus was it become opened.

The crucifixion of our Lord Jesus was to become a baptism and life for Adam, but also a forgiveness of all sins; when Jesus was speared; water and blood run down through the crack and onto the mercy seat of the Ark; it then flowed down the Ark and into the skull and mouth of Adam and they become a baptism; Adam became baptized; when the Earth shook after Jesus died all the dead in Christ rose again and lived; and Adam through the blood of Jesus was given life; and the water from the blood of Jesus- water being baptism and the Blood of Jesus- the blood being life for life is in the blood.

The cross of our Messiah Jesus Christ was made from the Ark of the covenants carrying handles; and after Jesus was taken down from the cross; Joseph from Arimathea took down Jesus' body and had his body embalmed washed and wrapped prepared to be taken to the cave.

Meanwhile the cross by order of Joseph and the Jews was taken washed of all the blood and the handles of the Ark where replaced back in the Ark; these handles were the correct height of Jesus length and width of our Saviour Jesus Christ; when they were taken back to the Ark; the covenant was fulfilled, the failure of Satan's deception to have our saviour put to death; for our God lives; and life in repentance given to the children of God; through his son Jesus Christ is fulfilled; shed by the blood of our Saviour Jesus Christ.

This is the remarkable power Readers of God Almighty the creator of all; for in the supernatural realm of God nothing is impossible; do you believe,

I guess this is one of the most important questions that you will ever have to ask yourselves; because the world of God is supernatural; and he is the almighty great "I am" and with God nothing is impossible, God wants us to whole heartedly believe in him in doing great things in your life; God is love and strength and it's love and strength that he can give to you if you believe.

I believe many people want to know about our God almighty but they just do not know how or where to find the right answers; God has said to me on more than one occasion "it is not for you to know" for life on Earth is full of question's and God of cause is correct; we want proof, we want to pull everything apart to find something wrong so we can dispute it, why is that, I have an answer to this as well; it's the world in which we live in it is full of lies and deceit, we live in a world where Satan rules us not God, God is pure and he is Love; what do I say to this for us all, we are living in this proof everyday; look around you, and listen to what is happening around us; look at all the truth about God and Jesus, look at all the evil, lies and deception in our world; what more proof do you really want.

When you turn to God for whatever your reasons are; it is because you want to know God; isn't that the ultimate question; your personal relationship with our God, and can he really help me; you believe you have tried so many other things and all have failed; well my deepest and heartfelt answer to this question is simple and straight forward; believe in God; trust in him, love him with all your heart and soul; believe that he sent his son to die FOR YOU; and for your sins and mine, how hard can this be for someone who is reaching out to someone as important as your saviour and our Messiah.

You know these questions are all pointless in your relationship with God unless you truly believe, when you finally decide to pick up the cross and except Jesus as the son of God it is only then you will have a living relationship with God that will last forever, "why" because this is Gods promise to his beloved children.

The biggest hurdle for a Christian to try and overcome is people trying to tell you that God does not exist because creation started from the big bang theory, not God; so searching for your God, Good luck; so Christian reader the best answer to that is to say; your certainly right because it is pointless searching and turning to our creator "GOD" if you do not believe that he exists.

A little more on the Big bang theory and God almighty's power, you already have my point of view on this theory, on how and where did all these materials come from to start this massive explosion to create our amazing universe? Do people who believe this theory do they not understand that even our biggest atomic nuclear bomb has materials to get it to work?

Realistically this theory of a massive explosion is extremely as weak as trying to believe what a scientist has to say to explain how something started without our creator "GOD" we are not from a fluke of nature; we were created by God not from something that existed from nothing; we have love from God, compassion, logical thinking; a personality and a conscience, we were made in the image of "GOD" not an explosion.

If we were created by an explosion not from the image of God then also explain how we see, feel, touch, smell, hear; taste, all these god gave us, everything around us including all the animals and nature, water, skies all Gods magnificent beauty; but man is still extremely ignorant to what God has given us including themselves trying to destroy their own creators creation.

Let's not forget readers God's power, his grace, his brilliants, intelligence, and imagination in creating so many things; and yet today people still criticize our Lord God, not understanding that without our father in heaven we are nothing; as Christian believers we must understand that it is the love and the words of God and the faith believing that brings our Holy Spirit into God; we must believe as a Christian that this is not of man but of God alone; for well over many years nobody in any scientific area has ever been able to disprove anything that has even been written in the Holy scriptures or in any of the found scrolls/missing books from the bible; and we ask "why" it's not because they haven't tried; they simply cannot deny the evidence it's that simple; they are the works and the words of our beloved creator.

The Holy Bible gives us all the answers to all our questions and it is how he can generally answer you, the words of the bible change all the time no matter how many times you read scripture in a life time you will find different answers; God speaks to you all the time giving you different insight and knowledge, hope and faith, you get to know and understand father God on a personal level.

What is God to us in a personal level; God is personal, just like we can be personal in every way we live our lives especially around certain people; is not God our creator in everything so we need to understand that God is the word made manifest; he is mighty in every way; and he is "one" we have only one God; there is no other and he is eternal.

God Almighty is the first and the last, the beginning and the end; and he says, apart from me you are nothing; he revealed himself as three persons and this is the trinity; the father, the son and the Holy Spirit; and they are all equally GOD; the holy scriptures speak of the glory of our father God saying that the word Jesus Christ is God incarnate (in flesh) and the Lord as the spirit; our God does not have a physical body like we do, he is of spirit; so as his beloved children we do not worship any other God except God the father in spirit and in truth; amen.

There is nobody in the flesh that has seen God almighty because he is invisible and our fleshly bodies cannot see the spiritual, our eyes are spiritually blind and closed until we lose our fleshly bodies due to our sin; this is also the reason Adam could not see after his expulsion from Heaven (Eden), God is everywhere he knows our thoughts and every detail about you.

We cannot hide nothing from God; but the question is how close do you want to be to God; because he should be everything in your life did God not say that he fills Heaven and Earth is this not God's almighty power; God clearly is everlasting to everlasting; he never changes, God is always the same, it is us that needs to change our lives for God to become more like him and live a life pleasing to God, to repent for all of our sins that we have

Committed not only against ourselves, but also against God; so to have everlasting life that Jesus he promises that he will give us, we need to make changes in our lives and become Reborn into faith

# THE POWER OF GOD ALMIGHTY ✞ 177

and believing in the word and truth of Christ, and living our life in Jesus Christ.

God is not dependant on anyone here on Earth, but we are dependent on him, our Christian faith relies on our Father in Heaven to teach us and to keep us faithful, to keep us on the right path of righteousness, and to forgive us of all of our sins, so we can have life everlasting; so guess what I am saying is who really needs who? We need to stay faithful to God if we want to have life after we leave our fleshly bodies.

Our father wants us to love him with all our heart and soul, for he loved us before we were born he knew us then so he needs us to believe and rely on him and to keep faith in him; what I am saying is that in essence every living thing relies and depends on the father to give us life just like in the beginning of creation.

In the beginning God created with his hands and his word which was made manifest, he spoke and the word created and all was good, he saw it was beautiful; his communication was a clear desire in his heart for us to be fruitful, what he created was fruitful, it grew and produced and it multiplied, he gave life, he took the time to look at what he created; should we not take the time to do the same; he loves us unconditionally, should we not do the same, after all he is our true father, our true creator, he gave us life, should we not return the favour and give ourselves to him, amen.

I love my Lord God with all of my might unconditionally as well, I can clearly see that everything God has done for me; and changing my life around that it is very good also; we were created to rule under God and to be the physical carrier of God's spirit in the Earth.

God puts no demands on us, but he still wants us to love him with all our heart and soul, love him unconditionally and also faithfully; however part of human nature is that we as living beings like Adam we have a free will; but God is a loving Father; God has mapped out our life for us, and there is absolutely nobody that can actually stop him, amen.

God does what he wants he is in control of us and the whole universe; and he is the decision maker; God needs no consent or advice; God states in the bible, I am the God of all mankind; nothing is too hard for me; that is our God almighty readers greatness that is out of our comprehension, however this is the power and strength that we rely on from our Father, the great I am.

> In the beginning was the Word, and the Word was with God, and the Word was God.
>
> John 1:1

# Spiritual Darkness (the Watchers)

**SATAN (HEB. SATAN)** the word means "adversary" Enemy of God, the death of Jesus Christ on the cross is the basis for Satan's defeat in his continuing rebellion against God; Satan only has one goal and that is destruction and misery in the lives of God's children, emotional and mental torment; and he can affect your lives and do it in such a way that you do not even realize that he is there living inside your mind telling you what to do and say; causing havoc in your life, your family and your relationship with your partner, he is longing to destroy and keep you as far away from God as possible.

The more that Satan can get hold of you the better for him he starts on people from a very young age; you are not even aware that he has been with you most of your life; all the years that people have been suffering from mental turmoil they think its them and their thoughts when in fact it is darkness Satan working on you causing your depression, and destroying your life.

Satan comes to steal and destroy everything good that God has in mind for us; Jesus that he has come (Jesus) to give us life and to enjoy our lives, believe and have faith and trust in him; as children of God we have the power in our love and belief in Jesus to stand up to Satan and his evil (watchers); we can turn it over to God and he will take care of it, he loves you; he hears your prayers of help; he is the answer to you being saved by the dark forces of Satan and his dark forces that work for him.

Trust, truth and believing in God are one of the most powerful weapons as a believer in Jesus Christ to have to fight against the kingdom of darkness; he cannot harm you, the power of God is the most powerful weapon to have you must not fear Satan, but God only; this fear God wants you to have for him, the fear of God also gives power because it is this fear that keeps you on the right path of righteousness, you do not want to upset God in any way or form it is this fear that God relies on to keep his children in love, trust and faith, truth is in the light, believing in Jesus Christ who is of the light; the ten commandments are of the light (Gods rules of peace) love, joy, happiness, these are all of the light; the bible says that darkness has never overpowered the light, and it never will.

Have you ever been scared of the dark at a very young age and even as an adult and maybe you actually still are (it is very common) I know I was; God isn't the one that is making his children scared of the darkness, we are not scared when the light is on or during the day for a reason; it's because we feel safe; and in the kingdom of heaven there is no darkness it is full of love and bright light, peaceful comforting light of love, the brightest of light that would blind our Earthly eyes; Adam felt and loved the light of Eden, he felt fear and grief when he was in the cave of treasures; darkness grieved his heart, until Gods compassion and love for Adam sent him the golden lamp that never went out.

This is the same kind of love children feel for the light, because God is light and God wants you to feel comfortable and at peace, and to have no fear of the light; this is a inner spiritual knowing that you are in the presence of God; but when you are a very young child you do not have the understanding or the knowledge about good and evil, you just know you feel safe in the light; so it takes a long time not to fear the darkness; God said let there be light, and the light shines on the darkness, for the darkness has never overpowered the light; the light of men is God, and the life is the light of men; and the darkness is Satan.

# SPIRITUAL DARKNESS (THE WATCHERS) ✝ 181

The fear that Darkness has upon your life is stealing all your peace and joy away from your life, but Satan he wants to steal that from you; Jesus said he came so we can have life and enjoy our lives; but not Satan he has his own ideas and that is to steal your peace and joy that God had planned for us; God created us to learn, to plan, to have joy, trust and faith and to enjoy life abundantly.

Now let me give you an example how Satan can destroy and steal your life away from you; you get up in the morning happy and peaceful looking forward to having a wonderful day and you start your day at work (or you could be home it doesn't matter) and you get a customer who is terribly rude; arrogant, difficult, you cannot do anything to please this person no matter how pleasant and obliging you want to be; you could bend over backwards or do a cartwheel; Nothing helps; then you feel their negativeness rubbing off; you are starting to feel agitated, frustration and becoming quite upset yourself; and all because of this one person, you didn't even get to have one cup of coffee and you are thinking just as well I didn't have that cuppa in my hand when that person was in the shop:

Sound familiar; now you have to ask yourself should that incident have really changed your circumstances and feelings, (think about it) because all Satan wants to do is steal your peace and joy away from you; however you do need Gods help that's what you really need; (you can pray at anytime to God, he is waiting); this is what happens to me all too often in my business sometimes on a day to day basis; and it sent me into a deep emotional state, people are not very nice at all they are miserable and want to cause you upset and the sad thing is they really do not care at all, no respect.

I would feel down for the rest of the day that one person took (stole) my peace away from me; it was not only at my work place but my home because I live on the premises so I have no get away exit to give me time out; yes working at a job 7 days a week every day of the year except Christmas day is the worst job ever dealing with people on a day to day basis; it does make you dislike people; but God says love one another, and bless those who curse and hurt you, amen.

Have you had this in your life; it could be family disagreements or even a phone call you had, your children, partner, parents, siblings, a friend; it doesn't actually matter the circumstances it is anyone who has taken your peace away from you; it is darkness at its best when you are vulnerable; he has his own way to get in and cause you upset; and feeling depressed.

However to God Satan is a defeated foe and this is how you need to treat him; to keep him out of your life, why; because you are a beloved child of God; that's why; and you need to understand and fight because he cannot have no charge over your life unless you allow him and his watchers to do so; you can refuse to allow Satan to upset you; that's now how I see him as a defeated foe; I am not afraid of him anymore, I am a child of Jesus Christ and the only one that I fear Is God almighty, it doesn't mean Satan will give up because he wants to steal you from God, but thank God for Satan still trying to be a hindrance because you know then in your heart God is ever so close to you, because Satan he is wanting to still cause you problems, even amongst your family members; give God the thanks no matter what, because you recognise what Satan is up to and remember to keep your peace, you might still get a little upset, but do not allow it to escalate into a bigger problem, let it smooth itself out by the help of God almighty, amen

The best decision I have ever made was to listen to the calling of God to turn to him for salvation, to start to enjoy my life again and to have peace and happiness back in my life, I am still of flesh so I still have my days; but it's different I find it harder to lose my peace to really get upset never mind out of control and wanting a good all out argument to state my opinion; but the fact is your opinion doesn't matter to God, do not upset anyone if you can help it because you still do not know how the other person will react and this is out of your control, just tread carefully, you do not want your peace taken away so remember to try not to take anyone else's, and this is a tough one but remember to trust always in God's love and help.

The more time I spend with God the closer I feel to him, especially writing for our Lord God; writing this book and my Prayer book My

# SPIRITUAL DARKNESS (THE WATCHERS) ✝ 183

Peace I give unto you; is the most amazing journey with God; to minister to you all and give you what God has shared with me and my own journey of darkness to teach all his children how damaging Satan is to his children; I have actually thanked God for going through all that darkness because with God's loving hand to lift me out off my tough times I have found love and joy in my amazing loving Father I am truly in the best place and time of my life; it lead me to God and all my reader (Gods Readers); the Prayer book still puts me in an awe state, they are not my words but God himself, he is the word made manifest in his children also to get his word across and to save as many of his children as he can, to turn their lives back around and into his loving arms because there is nothing loving or caring or compassionate about God's enemy Satan.

God is an amazing poet and God stunned me with his amazing words and stories of prayers; I cried many times when I read back what I wrote and could not believe how beautiful they are, but with God nothing is impossible; we all who love God say God bless; I say to God thankyou and God bless God himself for he is worthy to be praised; no matter what you are going through and might go through in the future always remember that God's power is always greater; your Holy Spirit will always inform you and put you back on track; and with the power of prayers to your Lord God to help you, he will send you in the comforter, he loves you always, God said seek and you will find.

Jesus said in John14:27 Peace I leave with you; my own peace I now give and bequeath to you; not as this world gives do I give to you; do not let your hearts be troubled, neither let them be afraid, stop allowing yourself to be agitated and disturbed, and do not permit yourself to be fearful and intimidated.

We are partners with God, his part is to provide peace and joy and our part is not to let the devil steal; take away any of what God has given us, so you must decide today to start enjoying everyday life; and live like God wants us to live in love, joy, peace and happiness to live in the word of God with obedience.

I want to take you down the Journey of these dark Angels and there deception; these Watchers are the followers of Satan; another name for these watchers are the fallen Angels, these Angels were cast to Earth along with Satan.

These dark Angels took favour in the daughters of the children of the murderous Cain; Satan and the watchers lived and mated and taught Cains people much Evil; and children were born to these watchers, they took over in spirit in the men of Cain; Gen 6:1:3 and it came to pass when men began to multiply on the face of the Earth, and daughters were born to them; then the sons of God (watchers) saw that the daughters of men that they were fair; and they (watchers) took them as wives of all which they chose; and the Lord said; my spirit shall always strive with men for that he also in flesh yet his days now shall only be a hundred and twenty years.

God was upset that these Angels of Satan's was defiling all sexually and causing great sin among man on Earth; enough that God changed man's life from living over 850 years to 120; this great sin caused these giants to be born in Earth; Gen 6:6 there were giants in the Earth in those days, and also after that; when the sons of God (watchers or fallen Angels) came in unto the daughters of men, and they bear children unto them, the same (these children) become mighty men(giants) which were of old, men of renown (they were from heaven and were of old or Ancient age).

These Giants born to these women were so large that they were taken from these women before their due date a surgery done by these ancient ones; these giants were of status of 5,000ft in height or 1 · km high, unimaginable but the truth; they were evil and taught among man all about murder and bloodshed, music, spells, charms, how to make weapons, idol worshipping, adultery, fornication; homosexuality, sexual abuse with animals all that moved on earth, then when a lot of the food was running short these giants started to eat the people there was much bloodshed and they killed one another and drank their blood.

God was becoming unpleased for the wickedness was becoming now great on Earth; every Evil imagination of the thoughts of man's heart was becoming very apparent, God repented that he ever made man on Earth, he was grieved in his heart.

The evil in our world is also much greater than we can ever imagine, and also even from the beginning of creation and up to Sodom and Gomorrah who were destroyed because of their idol worshipping and their depravity in there sin; they would not listen to God's words to repent and change their way of living there life style was great and full of immorality; however they did not want to change their lifestyle of sin, they refused to listen to God's plea to change; and they continued further in their sinful life style; their sinful nature was more important to them than the words of God.

However in the time of Sodom and Gomorrah they never has a Saviour; our Lord Jesus Christ has given us that opportunity; in the days of Sodom and Gomorrah; they knew not of the son of God; not like we do; so the fact is that we were given a Saviour in Jesus to turn to him and turn our lives around and to repent for all of our sins; to have a new life through the death and crucifixion of the son of God.

We know about Jesus and why he died; the people before Jesus birth had no Saviour, they lived by the laws of the commandments and the law of Moses; Jesus he also died to free us from the laws of the commandments and to repent for all of our sins past, present and future; and to have faith, to believe, trust and follow the son of God; to have a life everlasting, through the blood of Jesus Christ.

Will we be judged more severely because of our knowing about Jesus Christ; I believe so, our punishment will be handed down due to our unbelief and ignorance more harshly than the people who lived before our saviour was born; and rightly so; our God gives us free will to change our behaviour to be sorrowful in our hearts and to repent for all we have done wrong; it's not a command or a request; once again we have the knowledge of the son of God, we have no excuse, he gives us a choice.

We know more today than many thousands of years ago, we have scripture knowledge through the Holy Bible, although we have also been deceived through the darkness and deception of man; and these are the lost books of the bible (the forbidden books), but how far does one want to go for the love and truth that God wants us to be aware of how far does an individual want to go for the knowledge written by God.

There is much in scripture that is lost forever and many are aware of this; and this knowledge is lost forever, but we still have the greatest of knowledge we have the ONE who is greater than every single bit of knowledge, and that is our God; "yes" Jesus Christ; our king, our Messiah; the son of God.

We have no excuse whatsoever for our behaviour; I cannot speak for everyone; I cannot judge anyone, I can only give facts; and pray for all my beloved brothers and sisters; I was a sinner, we are all sinners; but I finally woke up to what and where I was heading; where Satan was leading me, and that was permanent death; he was out to destroy my life, and without the calling from my Lord Jesus to take me to my knees and beg for help and to please save me, I need you Lord to come into my life today, I would have been lost, forever dead to my sinful life.

You know even writing this to you fills my heart and eyes with heartfelt tears, mixed with sorrow and joy, sorrow not because the pain is still there because I can still remember how bad it was, but I cannot feel what the pain was like anymore the deep emotions are gone forever; because God has taken it away, especially the pain from losing my mum; it is hard to explain, but the joy is overwhelming how God has healed and taken the pain away; I cannot go back to the way it was I find it hard to comprehend that I was even that I was even the person I am writing about; I know I lived it, but the strength comes more from the love inside given by Jesus and his devotion to his children who will receive and love him; that need is powerfully strong, it's so much more than a longing, it's the willing to never let him go, a wanting to just embrace Jesus even more and more; you will not want to live without him in your life, it is that simple.

Finding Salvation in our Lord Jesus has not only saved my life and my family, but our lord has spiritually opened my eyes more to the truth, he has opened my heart to being careful about what you say to

# SPIRITUAL DARKNESS (THE WATCHERS) ✝ 187

others even if they are being hurtful, just receive it keep your mouth sealed do not offend or grieve them (you just pray for them), I thought that would be hard but not at all, God is a miracle worker; to forgive all hold no malice in your heart even for the ones how are eagerly wanting to knock you down, steal from you, curse you; whatever the situation; (pray for them) and turn the other cheek; it wasn't a problem; as a matter of fact I made phone calls and apologized to a few who I thought I needed to; it didn't matter to me whether they were going to accept it or not because it goes both ways, it always takes two; I wanted to do the right thing in the name of my Lord Jesus my Saviour; I wanted to start of my new life in my Lord with a clear conscience in repentance for all my wrongs; my faith was the most important decision I had ever made; It was a new life a new start in receiving Jesus as my Lord, I gave my life to Jesus, I no longer wanted darkness to be in control, I wanted the light and the faith of Jesus Christ.

What Satan and his workers can do to people is pure evil, they have one goal and that is to turn people's lives upside down; and what truly is sad is that many people believe it is their thoughts controlling them; and they are so wrong, they cannot comprehend how an evil entity can take over and change them in an instant; but it can and it's been around since creation.

There has been enough proof in our world and in scripture that dark forces are at hand; it is up to the individual person to recognise it and to take notice; too many doctors do not recognise and will not recognise the forces of darkness, an injection and a pill cannot heal darkness and deception; you cannot fight what you cannot see; you need the forces of light in your life and that comes with receiving Jesus Christ and become a loyal faithful follower, he is the only way to life everlasting; Jesus he teaches you to rebuke and call on him, and the Angel of righteousness along with you, and along with the power given to you by Jesus; "LISTEN" these dark forces have to leave, they cannot hurt you, there power is not as strong as the power of yourself and the light of Jesus Christ; Satan HE IS OVERPOWERED; **amen**; we have always two Angels around us one is the power of Jesus' Angel the Angel of righteousness and the other is the forces of darkness the Angel of iniquity; now remember that both of these Angels want to fight to win the battle; so who are you going to allow to win, that is the big question.

However the greatest battle is yet to come in the end times, in revelations; this is should be enough to want you to turn your life around to our Lord Jesus; I am for one glad I found the love of Jesus my Lord before I ever knew anything about revelations; Our Lord says the one who loves him and accepts him as Lord and saviour have nothing to fear; for they have life eternal through him, through his shed blood on the cross; you have no fear, believe in him.

Revelations is a full on battle between darkness on Earth and the battle on Goodness in Heaven; the battle of good and Evil; and it's not for the faint hearted I can give you the tip it is scary; but Jesus said his children have nothing to fear; however my flesh says are you kidding Lord; my flesh says fear with a big WOW; and readers it is scary; unimaginable for us to comprehend, then I find myself thinking, "GOD" go kick butt and can I help; Lets rid this world of all Evil and its deception, and if the world won't love and accept you and wants to live in this Evil world, they deserve what they get; we have given it our best effort to turn people around to receive you as Lord and saviour.

Nobody except God knows when this will take place; but with all my heart and soul I really hope us Christians can do much more to get together and change people to receive and accept Jesus as Lord and saviour, everyone is our brothers and sisters and we do not want anyone to go through this terrible battle; we must all get together and rid this planet of Evil, fight the attacks on ourselves from Satan and turn to our Lord Jesus for help, let us all pray together every night to save as many as God's children as we can; for all to repent from all sins, because Jesus he died for us.

All Christians who love our Lord and Saviour should work with our beloved Lord and change people who we come in contact with as a follower a "Saint" of Jesus, and try to save them; if they refuse to listen

# SPIRITUAL DARKNESS (THE WATCHERS) ✝ 189

to you about our Lord and condemn you for it then don't get discouraged because you have done your best in your Lords Holy name, but love them still and pray for them with all of your heart and soul; your reward from God is that you did your best and he loves you, AMEN.

It is our duty as followers of Jesus to work like a church and minister; to honour and love and worship God; but listen to me God does not want you to badger people to cause them grief, guilt and upset, God does not work like that, he is a loving God, and he still has not given up on that person, you have planted the seed in them, you let God do the rest of the work the same as he did for you, they still have a free will to make the choices they want to; God knows people's hearts, he knew you before you were born, so he already knows the ones who still need saving, and the ones who belong to Satan, we as Christians always need to be on guard ourselves, do not think for one minute that Satan has forgotten about you, any chance he can get he will wait for you to fall out of grace; so remember do not bully or push anyone, let them come in with an open heart to receive Jesus.

My beloved brothers and sisters, I want to give you the best advice I possibly can; accept Jesus wholeheartedly, not just for a day or two or now and then; you would not want Jesus seriously to only accept you now and then would you; Jesus he is the only answer for salvation; you need him every day in prayers; especially in the troubled world we are living in; I know in my heart that I was chosen to write to you to give you God's message; I believe God is coming back in the depths of my soul; Jesus will return soon; but as soon as he has saved as many as he can get away from Satan.

Look at what is happening around us; look at our future children's lack of knowledge about our Lord, look at our children's lack of respect for their parents and family members; children are suing their parents for spanking them; and some people are accepting this; (in the Bible it says children will not die from discipline) admittedly some go too far, but we are just talking a spanking not full on abuse; look at the lack of compassion people have towards each other; look at the selfishness and the crime rate; now can you see God in any of this or the work of Satan.

Now ask yourself, can you see any future change of love and respect for all or can you see things getting more out of control, the world getting worse with terrorism increasing, globalism, government getting more control over us; economic failure; lovers of money and themselves; blasphemers; rape, murder, moral corruption, boasters, haters of Christianity becoming more heightened, famine, ethnic violence is ripe; now you are probably thinking yeah we live in this already and yes I agree, but it will increase at an astronomical level in the future of our children, if not when some of us are still around, and let me tell you God is only waiting for it to get to this level before he returns to take control especially when Israel and his Christian believers are under attack.

Are your eyes blind to this worlds darkness; because I was certainly blind, I couldn't see what was wrong either with our world how bad it really is, "Why" because you become complaisant to hearing it all the time, I guess people think like I use to, saying there is good and bad in us all; and that is true, we are all sinners; the good fighting Evil; but we have a choice; however who are you going to pick Good vs. Evil; it is your free will; Jesus said in John 14:27 Peace I leave you, my peace I give unto you; not as the world giveth, give I unto you; Jesus is he not telling you that he has more to offer you than this world does; he is correct, he can give you life, Satan he offers you death; what Jesus has done for my life and can offer thousands; is a miracle, he saved my life, will you let Jesus son of God save you; will you pick up the cross and follow Jesus today; AMEN.

If you have not already read the amazing prayers God wrote, get my prayer book, called "my peace I give unto you" you will truly know and find Gods love for you all; you will walk with him deeply in your heart and soul; Jesus is divine in every sense of the word; he is a poet of divine love; he is the word made manifest; he is our teacher; our Messiah, truly in every way; he lives in us to his name; Jesus the son of God.

# SPIRITUAL DARKNESS (THE WATCHERS) ✝ 191

## SPEAK THE WORDS OF GRACE

Jesus is greater than all, he is infinitely greater than even the Angels; he is the favoured son, and the father God; he fathered him; God will be his father and Jesus is his devoted and loyal, faithful son; and all are to kiss and bow down to him in worship, because he is our sinless Messiah.

All who minister are Gods fiery flames and God called Jesus; oh God who endures forever who rules over all the kingdoms with justice and detests all unrighteousness; but my children who love me, I anoint you with oil of blessings upon your head; this is God with all his love he will give to you, all who follow him faithfully. AMEN

You must understand and be always reminded that our enemy is Satan and there is a spiritual war raging between the forces of God and God's copycat - God's enemy Satan; and this fight is still raging in our world over God's chosen people Israel; understand that God will not allow his chosen land nor his people to be lost to Satan; God does win in the end and Satan and his followers will no longer be a hindrance to God or his children.

The people who choose to never accept Jesus as the son of God; will have the truth given to them one day; Jesus says that all will come before God for Judgement "all" in other words he is saying believe what you want because you will believe one day "like it or not" you will bow before me.

The greatest door is open for all; you have an invitation to receive the greatest gift that no one can ever give you; "come to me" so your response to our Lord could be the best and the greatest decision that you could ever make in your life for yourself or anyone you can change to the faith of Jesus the son of God.

Let God write your name in the Lambs book of life; for God's door of mercy and love and patience is open for all who receive him; receive the word and the truth; the truth will indeed set you free; blessings of grace from our Lord Jesus Christ will be placed upon all who have opened their hearts to the marvellous prophesies of the Holy Bible; Jesus says come all who are thirsty; and I will give you the water of Life.

## SPEAK THE WORDS OF GRACE

My confidence rests in my almighty God; my God I call unto you, and you say unto me "here I am" My Lord Jesus, the destiny is you for all your believers; you are our hope and our eternal future; our faith rests in life everlasting with our Lord God; our compassionate king Jesus; I will remain faithful and Loyal to you; and I declare my love for you, I fasten you hard upon my heart; never to lose grip; my Holy Spirit is my ultimate desire it is my Lord Jesus within, my burning passion, my Messiah, my King, AMEN.

# A God to Worship

**WE HAVE COVERED** a many Topics and a few to go; but this one is very important; we are talking about our Lord God, and he has to be respected and worshiped; if he on Earth we think that we need to out of respect bow and curtsy to our Queen then really how important is it to honour and worship our King; Jesus Christ; we are his children and this he expects out of us, amen.

There are many topics in the Holy Bible regarding worship, and on many levels however the one to never be confused about is to worship anything; in other words any objects other than God himself; there is only one God, and that is our Father in Heaven our Lord Jesus Christ; understand many people do worship other Idols other than our God; let me explain deeper; in theory it is everything that you love hear in our world; the love you have for your house; the love that you have for all the material things in your house; the love you have for all your jewellery, the love that you have for your partner, your children, your family; the love of money; holidays, parties; these are just a few examples; you see God says love your neighbour; but however God is a jealous God which he states in the Bible; but I have had someone say to me but isn't jealousy a sin; and yes it is, but God is our creator; he is the disciplinary.

**EXODUS 20:5**
You shall not have any other Gods before me,

You shall not make yourself any graven image (to worship it) or any other likeness of anything that is in Heaven above, or that is in the Earth beneath, or that is in the waters under the Earth.

You shall not bow down yourself to them or serve them; for I your Lord God am a Jealous God.

Our Lord is greatly to be praised, he is to be reverently feared and worshiped above all (so called Gods); for all the God's of the nations are Idols, but the Lord made the Heavens; honour and majesty are before him; strength and beauty are in the sanctuary; ascribe to your Lord, all you families of people; ascribe to the Lord Glory and strength.

Give to the Lord the Glory due to his name; bring an offering and come before him into his courts; worship the Lord your God in the beauty of holiness; tremble before and reverently fear him, all of you on Earth.

## PSALM 95:6

O come; let us worship and bow down; let us kneel before the Lord our maker; for he is our God and we are the people of his pasture and the sheep of his hand.

## PSALM 97:7

Let all those be put to shame who serve graven images; who boast in Idols; fall prostrate before him, all you Gods.

All you people do not understand or know what you are truly worshiping; you worship what you do not comprehend; we do know what we are worshiping for we worship what we have knowledge and of understanding; for after all salvation comes from among the Jews.
**John 4:22**

A time will come however actually it is already here, when the true genuine worshiper will worship the father in spirit and in all truth; reality is for the father to seek just such people as those who will worship him; God is of spirit a spiritual being; and those who but love trust and faith in the Lord God, should worship him in spirit and in truth which is reality.

## SPEAK THE WORDS OF GRACE

My Lord God Almighty, I worship no other God but you; and I confess this with my mouth, and I ask of you to keep me on the right path of righteousness; in accordance of the will of you my gracious lord and Saviour; I have my many struggles; and it grieves me much; but my Love and my faith, turns to the one that I worship and are in fellowship with; and that is my Lord Jesus Christ; you are the one that I trust and Love and put all my hope in; you are the one who saved my life, you are the one who took me by the hand, and lead me to knowledge and understanding, you saved my life and took away all my sins, I praise and I glorify your Holy Name, as I pray AMEN.

# Inner Spiritual Warfare

**THIS TOPIC IS GOING** to be a long and intense one because it covers a vast area in people's everyday thoughts and struggles of your mind, your body and your soul, and it's an area which every single person goes through on a day to day basis and these are struggles of your life and your mind, this effects people on so many levels whether it's in your relationship, your work, your family, children, your health; and for children at school, it could be bullying, and pier pressures; problems with family ect.

But the first thing that I want all to listen to is that God approved of you long before anyone else got the chance to disapprove of you and what someone else thinks of you for whatever reason, it matters nothing, God approves and loves you.

Our Lord he accepts us for who we are, it's God that we have to please not anyone else; although we are placed in some difficult situations when someone is treating you really bad, the other point is that you could be thinking what have I done wrong to be treated so poorly; not only do you feel helpless, but very upset; and dragged down, to the same level as the person who is tearing your life upside down.

Your mind takes over and then this is where darkness comes in putting all sorts of ungodly thoughts into your head, you try to rationalize it over and over again, bitterness, anger, pain, heartache, revenge; cursing; and all because you are hurting; all of these things are not from God; but Darkness, the Bible says that you should bless those who hurt you; I found that hard, although I wanted to obey God, but sometimes the pain is unbearable; people are spiteful, hateful and unforgiving; especially when the pain comes from not understanding why someone is treating you so bad; and in your eyes you are innocent; in your mind it keeps playing the same words over and over( like your mind is torturing you) what have I done wrong; why won't they at least explain to me; but you know something sometimes people cannot explain what you have done wrong, because you are innocent, it is because they are miserable and want to lash out at someone and that person was you, they don't know any different in their behaviour.

God says that you should not worry; who cares what someone thinks about you; God loves you especially the ones that truly love and follow him with all their heart and soul; "Yes you are thinking" I do love God a lot, yes my father I understand that; but I am truly struggling here with what's happening in my life; I am trying to stay in faith, in truth and righteousness; but I am getting dragged back; 1 step forward and kicked back 3.

I love you my Lord with all my heart and soul, I pray for peace and harmony; but life isn't dealing me a good hand; "right". I pray every day and thankyou everyday for I truly understand that I am not wanting for anything, except peace, joy and happiness; is it too much to ask for; oh Lord.

The ones that say they love me are hurting me continuously, it's ok for a time and then it blows up in my face and I truly feel helpless and the only one that I can turn to now is you; I read in the bible Lord that the world hated you long before it hated me, (yet I still feel totally helpless).

I feel betrayed, defeated, unloved by the world; mistreated by the ones that say I love you; I try hard to do my best by everyone, I work hard to accomplish everything I put my heart into, yet Lord I find that it does not matter what I do; I am always wrong, I cannot please anyone, Is this the way of the world; am I really meant to be here, tell me Lord, what am I to do; I really do only have you to turn to; do you at least understand me.

You have probably said many of these things or even know someone so close to you, or It could be a child or a young adult suffering and is going through things; it doesn't matter what your age many people feel this way; not many if not any go through a blissful life without any upset and struggles; I know I have been through much of this and this is why I am writing it to you, I could easily write another book just on this subject; but I guess no matter how I have felt in my heart there are many me's out in the world feeling the same; but do you know it doesn't really matter, what I mean is that if someone is hurting you and you cannot break free from the pain, it's not really your problem it actually is really all about them; they like making you feel bad; because they are feeling worthless and want you to feel the same.

They actually have a bigger problem than you, and you need to become stronger and feel worthy; and God will make you feel like you are someone special because you are special to him; he loves you and he wants you, do you understand what I am telling you; pray for them instead turn it around, take control, take back your freedom and peace of mind, remember you have someone very powerful on your side, Jesus the son of God.

I started writing this book about 12 months ago and I also had the prayer book on the go and worked 7 days a week, and look after my 14 animals to feed and the house and family; and not one holiday in fourteen years of working in my business; the only day we close is Christmas day; so with all the problems I have had to face including my stress and health issues, I said to God; God I have prayed for them, I have done what you have asked, I pray and I pray, but nothing has changed, I would think today is just another day, I feel exhausted and run down; but yet I am at my computer writing to my readers (complaining) about the topic that I am going through, wow, is this meant to be, praise the Lord and how great does he work, to show you all that we are not alone in this subject; to personally be able to express these feelings to someone else, not just write to someone about a subject and never have had to experience it firsthand.

# INNER SPIRITUAL WARFARE ✝ 199

I just love the way God works, in understand how I can walk away from my book Jesus son of God and work on the prayer book and come back to it 6months later in more knowledge, and give it so much more in what has happened in my life a calling by God to go back now and finish the book, you are ready.

Even to cover of the book I didn't have; it was given to me during the Night on the style and the cross; Jesus is an amazing teacher; spiritual warfare is the most difficult emotional ride that you can go through it can without any doubt tear you away from God, even if you have God always in your mind and heart; God requires 100% of you, to keep you in faith and to have the power to fight darkness; if you become emotionally weak then you are at the mercy of darkness, and he will turn your life upside down, and I am aware of this very much so; he almost destroyed my marriage not long ago and ruined my life with my family; darkness will work on them as well, just to achieve what he has in plan to keep you away from God; the family members will not understand what is going on when they want to cause you upset, because if they love God; but do not want to follow him on a full time basis, then Satan will have his way, regardless of what they think or will acknowledge; you will be a target; and if you are an unbeliever of God completely, then Satan will think you belong to him; he will not cause that person to much grief but he will certainly cause you to cause someone who loves God, grief and heart ache through arguments or another options of grief, and stress; to touch a nerve.

Physically, emotionally, mind, body and soul; sometimes people can just wake up either first thing in the morning or in the middle of the night and feel totally miserable and not understand "why" you are just not happy, you are not enjoying life the way you should be, everyone else around you is happy, smiling, laughing, joking with one another, but you on the other hand, find it hard to crack a smile when someone has said a really funny joke, a rib tickle that cannot even cast a smile on your face; you know you should be in on the joke and you know people are looking at you thinking why are they not smiling, which makes you feel worse.

Many people will also wonder around in a dazed state asking themselves what is wrong with me, and sometimes this is very common in young adolescence children; why am I feeling this why, Satan loves to get in children's heads at an early age because they are innocent and vulnerable, and he can do so much damage; you or someone you may know; and these children will start to question their mental status; you have this dreaded heaviness in your heart; what is wrong with me; but listen rest assured you are not alone.

I just served a customer not long ago, and I had God say to me ask her if she wants a cross; (I haven't given one away all day) and I was thinking no she doesn't want one; (but that was how I was feeling, not to mention I was disagreeing with God) but the Lord God said it again; so I asked the Lady; I said to her I give away free crosses; would you like one; the lady replied; I won't say no; I need a little faith in my life right now, I hope it can bring me some luck.

Wow I though God really knows everything he reads people's hearts so well, he knows what is going on in everyone's lives, doing this has given me so much knowledge and understanding in how our Lord God works in everyone on different levels and he will reach you if you let him in and have faith and trust in him, God will heal you; If that cross brings that lady love, faith and trust, and God he already knows the answer to that, he sent her to me; so whatever this lady got out of the cross of Jesus Christ our Saviour, then I thank God for sending her to me and her receiving the cross of her Messiah.

That day it changed my demeanour I felt amazed at how wonderful God works, he not only helped that lady but he called me to give her the cross, so he worked on the lady and me as well; praise the Lord; amen, however it is all about faith in our Lord and trust; it benefits his children to feel this way for him; he loves us very much; he only wants to work in us through the Holy Spirit he gives us, this is where is resides "in us" he doesn't want us grieved because it grieves him as well, we need to feel the peace and the harmony and the joy to keep us in faith and believing, live in me and I will live in you.

# INNER SPIRITUAL WARFARE ✝ 201

Inner spiritual warfare is being taken away from our loving God, because you can actually on a personal level go through a lot; you may even say that you hate life, that you do not want to be here anymore, you have already exhausted all avenues to fix what you are going through; (trying it all by yourself though "right") but in the end of this experience you still feel unfilled and very bitter; believe in it emotionally because it is real, I gave up on life, I wanted to not be here anymore, I was suffering terribly, I hated life; I wanted to be with the one who I knew in my heart really loved me and that was God; I begged him to take my pain away; I begged him so much in my heart to relieve me from this world that hated me, I thought up things to take my life away from everyone that was hurting me, but God had another plans for my life and that was to teach you his readers about this wicked spiritual darkness that destroys the lives of his children.

Many people of today do experience this same emotional turmoil; and if you are not going through it and you know someone who is close to you that is, it can even be stressful to watch for you, making you feel emotional and just as vulnerable; one way or another inner spiritual darkness can affect many; I love being a minister/pastor for God, I love talking to people who God brings through to talk to me on a spiritual level (godly Level) I know I am doing God's work for him.

I have had many people say that they were going in another direction but felt draw to go in the direction of where my business is; and they said when they saw my shop they knew they had to come in; some said they felt the nice energy as soon as they opened the door, I told them that they were feeling the energy of God; because I do a lot of my church work here and I write my books here and God's church is in the business, it's within you.

People think that me being a minister for God's work; that they are surprised that I have and do go through what they do and the level of turmoil that I have endured; but believe me so was I, until God taught me that I with endue much because I have given myself to him; Satan does not like that, he wants to destroy what God loves, and that is his children; however when you come to this understanding God will give you the power to defeat Satan, he will become the defeated foe.

We are still in our fleshly bodies so Satan will try his best; it's like he holds you for ransom; god will help you ever step of the way, he is patient and he will not give you up to the clutches of Satan; have no fear at all for Satan; he is relying on your fear; give your fear to God and fear only God; it is the fear of God that will keep you closer to him, that right path of righteousness will give you what God is fighting for you for and that is "Life Everlasting" in his kingdom.

What truly is the secret then to having a happy and joyous life while you are still in your fleshly body? Well it is still having the power, which is love; faith and trust in Jesus the son of God; trust in your deliverer to deliver you out of the hell that you keep putting yourself in; "Oh you of little faith" I am saying these wonderful word's because God has said them to me a few times especially in the first few months of becoming a new minister in faith; and they are powerfully strong words; "the truth hurts to" yes changing you and your life to become stronger in your "faith" leading you, and to trim off the bad stuff going on in your life; to give you a fresher life, to fill you and your home environment with the love and light of God almighty; I know I want it, so how could you not want love and light, letting God come and cleanse everything with light.

To trim of the dead branches for new growth to take hold, but listen, you need to hang on to these new branches given to you by our Lord God Jesus Christ; people are what they are, and the people who cause you grief need their own dead branches cut off (pruning is another good way to explain it) cut away all there badness; to give a better flesh life of abundance that God wants you to have.

God is there for you and we need to call upon him much more often, to ask him to help cut away and to help you to make a new clear pathway for you so you do not trip over all these unwanted dead branches; for all you need is a clear visual pathway; unwanted thick dead branches will only cause your life to become hectic, trapping you in thick negative and emotional darkness, clouding you and draining you physically, which with lead you to think unclearly.

What are you waiting for; even though we still have a bit to go on spiritual Darkness; let's get started now; put this book down and call upon God in prayer; ask God to clear away from you all your unwanted negative darkness, tell Jesus that you want it gone out of your life, it is a space waster, you rebuke it out of your life, and you want it replaced "right now" in the name of Jesus Christ; replace it Lord with what is more needed in your life; the love and the light of God almighty; he is all you need in your life; you are now filled with the love of Jesus Christ; Amen. This is a guide, you use what you need and want but put force love and power in Jesus name behind all your prayers to God, he is always with you; your faith is very important to God; your trust that he can do anything for you is going to be the strength behind your prayers, your willingness to believe in the healing of Jesus, remember Jesus words to his disciples "oh you of little faith" BELIEVE and climb the tree of life, remove all your dead branches, have a clear and a clean life with your Saviour.

Never start thinking in your old ways again; (for you are a new child of Jesus Christ, reborn in your faith as a Christian) believe in him for his promise is that he will work in you, you will realize after awhile when he reveals it to you that you are feeling different; he has changed you in every essence, you will realize that you are not the same person, I found this the most phenomenal experience when he showed me what he has done in my life, and more surprising is that he had this planned for me all along; I might have gone through much heartache; but if it wasn't for all that and hitting rock bottom and turning to Jesus; I would not be the person I am today; Jesus brought me to him, to do his work, and do you know that without Jesus we are nothing; we cannot do anything without him; we thing we do but we are so wrong, I needed our Lord to show me the truth, to wake up and realize what Is dark forces and the truth; the word of God and the light of goodness.

God is so full of Love and mercy that he also does not want you hating life, he gave you life he knows too well the forces of Darkness, remember he kicked them out of heaven; he only wants you to receive him; so he can help you through your troubled times, he loves his children; and

God loves his children who love him unconditionally; we as people of flesh are always wanting to please most; and to be accepted by others, and some think that they are being godly by doing so; and then you have other people who do not give it to much thought, but God does want us to be good to people; (love one another as I have loved you) helping others who are in need is being Godly; and our love for God, is to please his "right".

Now understand; God wants us to please people right? But on the other hand God also doesn't want anyone to be more important than him; I have explained in this book, if we do not rely on God for all our problems; asking God for his help, then we would not be relying on our Lord God for anything, God will be less important in our lives; this will lead to chaos in our lives and there is a lot of that already, leading us all into the hands of God's enemy Satan, and people without faith will become rife.

The Bible already shows us that those who believe in God will enter in peace and into rest, and an unhappy life is not peace, joy, and happiness or rest; however experiencing God's rest is the only way you can tell whether you are truly in faith, or whether you are just trying to have faith; ah strong word's right; this will give you something to think about, what is the difference; Plenty' it all comes to trying to live your life in God; not of what the world has to throw at you; keeping your peace; treating people differently no matter what they say or do; you have turned your life around, you want to live a new life in Jesus Christ; then you need to think like the son of God; how and what he would say in the circumstances; to think like God; to live and meditate on his words not the words of the world.

Live in the life of God, live in the word of God, and pray to God everyday not just when you are in the mood; if you do not go to church that is fine, maybe there isn't a fellowship church around you that you like; that's fine, God will not condemn you for that, however there is plenty of fellowship churches on daystar TV and other channels; where you do not have to even leave home; really you have no excuse; church is also in your Holy Spirit where God resides; he loves you, but he also doesn't want you to live a life in sin; (getting drunk, abusive, partying, as an example ect;) then you go and pray to him or go to church in repentance thinking well ok; I have done the right thing in God; I am a Christian, and then continue the following week in sin; understand the difference now; live a true life in Jesus Christ, make a steadfast commitment to the son of God, not a part time faith commitment lifestyle; have God working in your favour; not the world, so that you can truly enter into the heavenly realm of faith and enjoy the rest of God; Peace.

One has to now ask, who do you now think wants your life to be filled with this turmoil God, or Satan; Satan is what causes you unrest of the mind, and frustration, worry and fear; these mixed emotions cause you to struggle in your everyday duties, with all this going on in your mind; you do not even want to get out of bed, never mind going to work or looking after your children; or any other commitments that you may have to deal with; however the rest in your mind which God wants for you gives you the freedom, and it is only God that can and will give you this freedom; you need to give in to this darkness and recognize what it is doing to you and rebuke it; cast it out of your life; and turn to God for peace and rest in your mind and your daily life; he will hear your prayers, trust me and trust God; I know because I have been through it all; the peace of mind and the calmness and the strength that only God can give you is complete transformation to get you through all your problems; God gives it all to you, not just a little bit here and there, he gives his "all" to his children who love and follow him on an everyday basis; not a part time basis, God wants a 100% of his children; God comes to give you life; it is Satan that comes to steal your life.

Do you know when you find the Lord the feelings that you have are so much different than the feelings you had before; sometime I sit back and think of the way I use to live my life; and I cannot believe that I use to act and think that way, the change God brings to you is a miracle in its self; you most certainly are transformed into a new person when you find God; when he says that he cuts away the old you (branches) and replaces it with new branches; this is when you become new born in Christ ,when the transformation starts taking place; and it is a gradual process; and God is not kidding; he does exactly what he says he is going to do for you; when God says he promises you these transformations he does not change his mind; he loves his children and he wants the best for you.

    I use to ask God things especially when I first turned to God for help; I remember thinking things like there is no way God could ever fix that about me; I want it change but this is a big task even for God; "wrong" I didn't even realize that a few weeks later that it was gone; god had answered what I was thinking; no this was not a prayer that I had done, it was a thought; he knows what you are thinking; you read this in the bible but it is harder to comprehend, until you are actually given it on a personal level by God; when he tells you; that he has fixed it; and you didn't even realise; you were not even doing that again, (I am talking about my cursing).

    You cannot know when God will actually help you, if you asked God he will tell you it is not for you to know; he works when he feels you are ready; God knows when you will believe and accept his working in you; but like me if you have accepted the working from God you will feel the change ; and it is a welcoming one; you will notice the calmness in you; and this will come from the depths of your inner self and your body, and rest assured, God will always be working in you; because you have a long, long way to go, pretty much until you enter the kingdom of Heaven; never think you are fully restored to Gods perfection; this comes with the glorification and purity when you lose your fleshly body; and whether we like this or not our sinful body.

    Many people want the feeling of accomplishment when we become strong in our faith, we like to feel the confidence that we are on the right path of righteousness, we do not like the thought of failure in ourselves when we are close to God; because we do not want to fail God; our faith and our security within God is strong in us; many believers do understand that without our faith and our believing and trusting in our Lord Jesus we are nothing; let's face it if you do not have these, then you are not a believer of our Lord; **Hebrews 3:6** says; But Jesus is faithful as a Son over his (fathers) house; and we are his house, If we hold fast and firm to the end; our joy and exultant confidence and sense of worth and triumph in our hope in our Lord Jesus Christ; ( God is saying to us that he will do things for us if we also do what we are suppose to do in our walk with our Lord).

We must also in other words to the end; believe, trust and have continuous faith; we do have the power to live in the house of the Father in the kingdom of Heaven; but how bad do we really want this gift that we can receive from God; how bad do you want it; what does your Holy Spirit tell you, do you want God more or the world and what it has to offer; if you heard God's voice tomorrow; what choice would you make? Would you believe him, would you walk strong in faith as a new child in Christ; would you repent of all your sins, or would you still deny him and question all that you have learnt, this is a strong question because the world of darkness will always interfere in your faith and walk with God, so God is asking you to stand firm in your faith to fight of the unbelieving thoughts of darkness.

Rebuke these manifestations that build up within you about what you read in the bible or anything that has to do with your faith believing in God or what has been given to you by God; learn to understand the difference in what is a positive thought (godly) or a negative thought (evil); these negative thoughts are of doubt and unbelief; sometimes these thoughts do not come straight away after reading the bible or after you have prayed for instance; sometimes these thoughts are mocking what you have read or done in your Christian faith; later on in the day for instance, saying; do you really believe that?

Sometimes a manifestation will build within yourself of doubt and unbelief because what you have asked God for has not come straight away after you have prayed to God; but always remember as I have already explained previously God will in his own appointed time answer your prayers; consider God waiting to see how your faith and believe is going to pan out, your confidence in him; to see how you manifest God's himself in you.

What would God think about the manifestations of your mind; could God also be testing you to see what you will do with your thoughts, will you rebuke the negative thoughts or will you manifest them further; because if you do take them further then you would be receiving and believing the lies of Satan, you would be believing Satan over God; this could be in unbelief but never the less it is happening to you; you would still be believing the messages which are causing you grief and invasion of your faith and not believing in what God can do for you; which is trusting in our Lord and Saviour.

The strength of your faith in God must stay steadfast even when you are receiving these messages from Satan; actually reverse them and still thank our Lord because if Satan is annoying you, then you know for sure that your faith in Jesus is steadfast, and by thanking God then you are recognizing the work of Satan and he will lose his strength each time; so continue to fight the good fight of faith.

Your faith in Jesus Christ is inside of you, for he resides in you, this is his promise to you; reside in me and I will reside in you; live in me and I will live in you; is this not a promise, Is this not of Love; this is the love he gives to you in your Holy Spirit; this is love, faith, joy, happiness, trust, reliance; guidance to a life everlasting; However when Satan is working on your mind you can lose all of this and only receive a hardened heart and lose all that God is trying to manifest into you, and you can become untrusting and you will eventually start to ignore the workings and calling of God.

You will need to stay focused believing that you need God's help, and believe that he will never leave nor forsake you; he will still stay with you and wait patiently for you to recognise you're wrong and to repent; through the powers of your words in prayers; God will read your heart to see how sorrowful you truly are and how deep are your prayers in your Holy Spirit; for this is faith believing at its best form; this is the healing power of prayers reaching our Heavenly father.

So try not to wrap your heart in the unbelief of darkness, do not anger God by hardening your heart; he is trying hard to keep you in your faith; you keep trying hard to stay in faith; some people in their unbelief refuse to even consider learning Gods way; so search your heart for as long as you have to, but open it to the truth of God; I am

# INNER SPIRITUAL WARFARE ☦ 209

trying for all readers the different level of being in God to teach you to stay opened and in faith of the wonderful God that we have and his levels of mercy and patience; and to keep all away from the destructive forces of Satan; and getting all to search your thoughts, making sure that no evil is hiding in your unbelief; because it is these dark forces that wants to keep you away from God.

The inner spiritual warfare of Satan is what he wants to keep you away from our God; it will only want to keep you angry, sad; crying and depressed and so on; ask yourself "Why" there is only one answer "God" If you keep any of these thoughts in your heart you will not think about anything on a good level "right" of cause not because these thoughts are negative; destructive, and not from God; Amen.

This is spiritual warfare at its best, full of doubt, mistrust, deception, and unforgiveness sound familiar; many older people have lived in the world long enough to understand that it isn't becoming a nice place to stay in , but Satan wants to keep you these; he really does not want to lose you to God; and God is waiting for you to let go of what you are hanging onto; God will be patient and wait until (like me) you hit rock bottom, waiting for you to call upon him, when you cannot take the pain and suffering anymore, utterly defeated; you may be really lucky and not end up that way and turn to God; however regardless of the situation, sadly there are many people who do not think about God at all or his deep love and compassion that he has for his children; many believe he doesn't even exist.

Some people chose to blame God for their suffering; guess it's easier than blaming themselves or the situation they may have put themselves in or the situation that someone else put them in; whatever the case lets blame God; if he loves me and is a compassionate God why am I suffering; my answer is blame who controls this world Satan and look at what is going on inside you and your surroundings before you blame God; I have suffered a lot and not once did I blame God.

One of the greatest answers to "why" we suffer; that answer is also; "you" you didn't love God enough to put all your trust and faith; your hopes and belief in him, it was easier to put blame onto God; you also had more faith and belief in the darkness rather than the healing power of God; you alone are allowing darkness to take control of your thoughts in blaming, rather than in the compassion and faith.

This is the reason we should not blame the one who gave life to us and he is the only one who can take it away for eternity or in following him and loving his in trust and faith, can give us life through the blood of his son, our saviour and messiah Jesus Christ; God is not to blame for our suffering, this suffering can also give us life when we turn to him; I never knew any better even though I never blamed God; however I like many others never knew the knowledge that I do today; neither the wisdom regarding the realms of light and darkness and how they can have so much control over an individual.

I knew that God existed and I certainly knew Satan existed, I believed in them both period, I guess I allowed God in to rescue me God knows us so well he knew that I was ready; he knew I believed in him and that my faith was still strong enough to accept him to be helped; and in the knowledge given, the power to fight and rebuke darkness, and allow God to work in me.

I called God and asked him for help, which we his children must do; however I need you to understand these words now; Satan he put up a good fight; to try and destroy me and my families strength and love for each other; he worked hard on myself and my husband and our son, he was destroying the relationship between my husband and our young son, and that was tearing my heart apart this alone was enough to almost completely tear us apart as a family unit; it became very nasty and serious, it didn't matter how much love we still had for each other, Satan he still worked to crush and destroy; it was only my faith, my love, and my believing that become stronger in our Lord Jesus and his words of healing, his love and compassion and in his baptism that won this battle, I was not going to let Satan win and neither was God.

I strongly and spiritually felt this darkness; I feared this darkness (bad mistake), I physically saw this darkness; God gave me the spiritual sight to see what was destroying us, and from that time on I thanked God, I did not fear it anymore as hideous as it was; I woke up and looked right at it and said to it I know who you are, I turned then away from him, I prayed the Lord's prayer to God and I realized then I had no fear at all of him; he was as clear as if you were standing next to me; God gave me the physical strength to fight and protect my family; my spiritual connection to our God, Our Lord and our saviour Jesus grew ever so deeper.

I knew then not only my heart belonged to God; But I knew that I belonged to God, I knew he loved me; I knew when he showed me what was attacking me; my husband/family that he wasn't going to allow darkness to hurt us no more he was going to help us win this battle; and our lives began to change dramatically, darkness had to leave; it lost its power to God and our strong faith and belief; we started to feel the difference, our home felt lighter, my son wanted to hear the word of God, which my husband reads to him, and he is happy and smiling; my marriage is strong, we are a happy family unit; our faith is strong in our Lord God, my husband and son know me and believe what God had shown to me to help fight and win this battle; in our strength, faith and with the power of our Lord Jesus.

My health become well, my stress levels had dropped; and I trusted everything in my practitioner Jesus Christ; I turn to him always for healing, I turned to him for all my entire problems, whether Business related, family or staff related problem; and Jesus always answers my prayers; I do not no longer dwell on anything or allow anything to get to out of control; I have more control, I may still get annoyed at things, but I definitely have been given a more balanced attitude; we all work together united as one, in love; faith and trusting in our love for God.

The best is watching the relationship between my young teenage son and husband blossom; I have never seen that, there was always too much negative energy; and it was making them both depressed, they loved each other always; but the forces of darkness was destroying them; Satan did not want to give us up for his enemy "GOD" my son and husbands relationship is now the best I have ever seen; they talk greatly, they work out together in the gym, they talk about cars (boring) no seriously it's great, (praise the Lord) and we always tell each other how much we love each other more than once a day; God has worked miracles in our life and family; our Church is in our business area; I minister at home; I am an author in my home writing the words of God; my business which is a fuel/takeaway business is full of the word of God on the counter; we are surrounded by God; in prayers; faith, love and worship; our son is a different child and he believes in God and he knows about the forces of darkness; and he is aware; to always fight with the word of God.

God he does answer prayers; repentance and to help rebuke all darkness; trusting in our beloved Lord God is a must; remember you are a beloved child of God, he is your teacher and he loves and wants "You" he wants to change you, save you, and bring you home to where you belong; who will you turn to for this peace and love; because to put it bluntly one wants to love you, and the other only wants to destroy you, to keep you from the one who loves you.

I believe that if you are reading this book, you want God; you need God and the love and faith and compassion that he gives; I cannot live, nor do I want to live my life without my Lord God; he is where he promised he would be; residing in me, in the Holy Spirit he gives to you out of his/yours love faith; trust and believing.

Jesus he says; live in me and I will live in you; Jesus never goes back on his word; he is pure love, he forgives you, if you have repented and sorrowful in your heart, he will remember your sins no more; and believe that, do not question God's words; you have become a new child in Christ; and it does not matter your age group, I am 58 years old and I am his child; he loves me and I love him very much; I am a mother of 4 lovely children, a grandmother of two teenagers, I have seen a lot and been through a lot, and I believe I am living the best years of my life now, in faith, love and believing in Jesus Christ and not only with Jesus but with all my family, becoming a minister for the Lord was the best decision I ever made; the path of becoming an author was another great surprise given by God, to share with you, the words of God and the life path he has taken me on.

# INNER SPIRITUAL WARFARE ✝ 213

One thing I can honestly express deeply to you all and the Lord God almighty is thank you so much for opening my eyes physically and spiritually to share who I am now and what God has achieved in me; thank you for my journey of the Good and bad; to teach me the knowledge and the wisdom, and the transformation; because without going through all that I would not be the person that God intended for me to be or my family, we all belong to a wonderful family in Jesus Christ, our Saviour and our King; we can fight together the forces of darkness because we have our mighty God to help us win this battle; darkness has no power because God is and always will be mightier, he is and always will be Lord over all, he wins the greatest battle which is yet to come, he fights for all his children; this is how much he loves and wants us, this you must have faith in and believe with all of your heart and your soul.

Do you know some people ask the question how do I know that God really loves me; Go to **Romans 8:35:39**

Who shall ever separate us from the love of Christ? Will tribulation, or distress, or persecution, or famine, or nakedness; or danger, or sword? Just as it is written and forever remains written; for your sake we are put to death all day long; we are regarded as sheep for the slaughter; yet in all these things we are more than conquerors and we gain an overwhelming victory through him who loves us so much that he gave his life for us; for I am convinced and I continue to be convinced and beyond any doubt that neither Death, nor life, nor angels nor principalities, nor things present and threatening nor things to come, nor powers; nor height, nor depth, nor any other created thing, will be able to separate us from the unlimited love of God; which is in Jesus Christ our Lord.

How wonderful is that readers to have the clarification in the Holy Bible that our Lord Jesus Christ loves us that much; to have it written in the most famous book in the whole world; our Lord God loves us very much, he gave his life for us; and it is the truth, the words of our Father in Heaven, saying how much he loves us, yet so many people still question his love, they still cannot except the words of

God, people have so much going on in their lives and yet when it does not go in their favour they start to question God his love and his faith, saying why is God not letting their lives flow more smoothly and in their favour if he really loves us; people have fear and worry, we all have this and not many of us get through life and do not experience this; I believe that people have no faith in their lives if they are going to feel such pity in their lives to blame God for all their ups and downs.

If people made changes in their lives and started to think about putting love and faith in their lives and in themselves, then they may also find more love and trust in God; so one must ask themselves can you find trust in yourself to let God work in you; sometimes in general we admit that we are not unable to solve our own problems, but many still just sit around complaining, and worrying because it is in all our human nature to do so, we have become a very complaisant world; we should put more focus on God than in all our problems and figure out other strategies to solve these problems ourselves with the guidance and love of God; some people actually do, but it only lasts for such a short period of time and their problems usually happen again; all God wants to start to work in the areas of your life is for his children to put all their love and focus on him and have faith and trust; God clearly states that without him you are truly nothing and he is correct, we cannot doing nothing without him; many will always be arrogant enough to think it is their body and their thoughts so they are in control; how wrong they are.

Leaning to be patient in everything in your life is a good focus point and a good start to your Christian faith and life because trusting in our Lord will certainly bring forth peace and relaxation; you have to ask yourself, do you want to be happy or are you so use to the stress and the darkness in your life that you do not know any difference, do you really want the change; do you want the miracles that God can give you; you know many do want the miracles when it comes to God doing things for THEM, but many do not want to lift a finger and receive him as their Lord and Saviour.

# INNER SPIRITUAL WARFARE ✝ 215

    It is not for us to even understand God's will, for instance everyone hates the thought of getting a disease, or cancer, or losing a loved one to any kind of circumstances; it is a huge fear in our lives; and God understands that, do you think it was easy for God to see his only son Jesus suffer at the perils of mans torturous behaviour in what they classed as punishment, and all Jesus taught was about LOVE; faith, trusting in his father, giving people the chance to have life forever in the kingdom of God; believe in him, makes you wonder what we really have to complain about doesn't it, makes you feel like a real winger; how do we feel when we see our children become very sick, some have seen their children suffer and die at a very young age, how defenceless they really must feel; however many have faith and love in God, and then because they have suffered such tragedy they turn their heads on God and their faith, because of their heartache; Blaming God for their loss; they don't even consider Satan; or circumstances; however they expect God to accept their loved one to be in Heaven; is life not a mystery; God did not let us have life to cause us misery; he wants us to have love and faith; maybe sometimes we need to consider ourselves; and the way we think instead of pulling Gods love apart and wondering in our times of troubles how much he really does love us; the bible explains everything and all circumstances, his love for us is more real and true to how and what we believe to be truth and love, he never changes, it is us that lives life in sin, not Jesus our Lord and God; it is God that is sinless, what he says is steadfast, so do not ever question God's love for us, look within and make changes; for it is only our doubt and faith that is actually being tested with God; our true love and faith in him.

    The power of prayer is the most important step to changes being made in your life, Jesus never stops praying for all his children; Jesus sits at the right hand of his/ our father and he intercedes for us; this should actually give us peace and comfort to relax us knowing that Jesus is praying for our salvation, how wonderful is that, is this not love at its grandest; and it should not actually surprise us, because Jesus came to minister not to be ministered too; the Church is our Lord Jesus Christ.

To make changes in becoming a Christian, a new child in Christ; this is a trust and faith, and believing lifestyle, whether you understand it or not; all this you must have in our Lord; I know I have said this over and over again so many times but it must sink in; God wants this to be clear for you so he can work in you and your lifestyle; this will be your new walk with Jesus.

Taking action in the word of God, learning the truth and walk of God so he can put you finally on the right path of righteousness; the spiritual warfare that takes place in people's lives is no laughing matter it is a serious problem and one of the biggest problems many have to face on a day to day basis; it's a fight you cannot win without the power the faith and strength of our Lord Jesus Christ in your life; you know I was just talking to someone regarding the spiritual warfare that takes place on a day to day basis, now and then it does really hit home how severe this can be; I could not have got through life without Jesus; unless I had turned to him without any doubt at all I would still be in this dark place; no medication in the world can give you the help that our Lord Jesus can; unless I received him and called on Jesus to help me and have the deep sorrow in my heart that he can read and know that I am ready to receive him fully in my heart; I would still be in a terrible place; and Jesus would still be waiting patiently for me, so reach out to God now.

# Draw your Strength from Jesus Christ

**MANY PONDER ON** in the lifestyle they live especially when they become stressed in their lives or maybe knowing someone who is dealing with high stress levels, however studies show that the stress in people's lives around the world is a massive 70% so in one way or another it affect people of all ages from very young children to the elderly; can you imagine what it would be like to live in a 3rd world country where there is hardly any food, water, living arrangements, money to buy what we class as luxury items, or clothing, medicines, all these things that many of us have at our finger tips, how many people even comprehend what they must go through, to actually have to rely on people who have just maybe even a little more than they do, which in general is a huge amount; can you imagine the stress of these families, watching their loved ones die at an alarming rate, it is unimaginable; but they need us, to help them, support them and give a little that we do not really need.

We all need to care and think why we are depressed, some get depressed because they want more than they have, the next door neighbour has a new car, how can I get the same, it sound outrages but it is truth; we are becoming a more selfish world wanting more and more regardless of how we can afford it, many put their faith in the world than the faith in our Lord; how much do we really need; these third world countries draw a lot on the faith and the love of God, and the hearts of the people in the world to have the strength and the love in their hearts that God gives to all to help feed them; these people believe in God, they draw their strength from God to reach people to have love and compassion for all our brothers and sisters.

## PSALM 39:4

Lord let me know my life's end, so as I can appreciate the extent of my days; let me know how frail I really am; for behold my days are as short as hand's widths, and my lifetime is as nothing in your sight; for surely every man even at his best is merely as a wisp of smoke a vapour that vanishes into thin air.

Surely every man that walks around like a shadow, pretending to be respectable, an absurd pretence; surely they make an uproar for nothing, each one building up their riches for nothing; not even knowing who will eventually receive them; now Lord, for what do I expectantly wait? For my hope is in you, save me from all my transgression.

We do not know what will happen tomorrow; really then what is the nature of our life, if the Lord is willing to help us should we not be also willing to do more in our lives as to not worry and stress ourselves in things we cannot change; or if we are willing then we should at least help others, many people not only put stress on themselves but also their family members; and also worrying about everybody else and what has been said; and all that get accomplished is making everything worse.

We are only here for such a short time and all we do is waste our lives in stress and anxiety; how often do we think about Jesus and call on him for strength and help; we try to rely on ourselves and most of the time fail and miserably; so how much differently are we than the person who can cause us the stress and worry? Why should we even worry and waste our breath on such insignificant issues, and turn to our Lord to have a decent life that he promises to give us; we are nothing without him; we cannot accomplish much without his strength, love and above all forgiveness in ourselves and of others.

# DRAW YOUR STRENGTH FROM JESUS CHRIST ✝ 219

Let's not also forget about our last subject of Satan he will always have his way and try to keep you in stress and anxiety, if he keep you in this state he has you just where he wants you; away from faith in God; if we want total freedom in Jesus to keep us on the path of righteousness, we must stay clear of the turmoil; and be lead by the Holy Spirit; remember also that Satan and God understand that without us never having trouble in our lives, we would never need faith.

The battle of Good and Evil; how many run away from their problem, not many could honestly say they have never push it under the carpet so to speak, we are all guilty of that, hoping it will just go away, tomorrow is another day; However Jesus also says that we are to go through them; our Lord also tells us that in love and faith if we call upon him and draw our strength from the Holy Spirit given; we do not have to go through our problems alone; to trust and rely on him, to love him with all of your heart and soul; to pray and he will hear our prayers; he knows your heart and your thoughts, our Lord will always be there to help us in every way; he says to us "fear not" for I am your Lord God and I am with you.

Our Lord God he created us all and he loves you and you must not forget that; he knows all your faults and all your weaknesses, he reads your heart and he knows if you want to change and he is willing to wait for you as long as it takes; if you are ready to give your life of turmoil away, then when you ask God to work in you and you accept Jesus as your Lord and saviour then you must have trust and faith and believe that he can work miracles in your life, he will change your life around; he worked in me every day bit by bit cutting away the dead branches and replacing it with the new growth, remember that Jesus is the vine dresser and he wants to change you and love you; and he wants you to enjoy your new life in him.

When Jesus comes into your life you will come to realise that you had many faults and some not to pleasing, you have lived a life as a sinner and you will die a sinner, but God forgives you of these sins through the shed blood of his precious son; he died to forgive and take your sins through repentance; now you must forgive yourself; and now live a new life in Jesus Christ, overcoming all your weaknesses; never to be discouraged again and to not dwell of your failures; If your Father in Heaven forgives you, then you forgive yourself; God knows if you are truly sorrowful in your heart for all your sins; and if you are then you are on the right path of righteousness and a new child of God, Amen.

Your new life will transform your life and your thinking; you will not worry too much about what other people think or say, it might annoy you but I promise you this the more you live your life in the Lord the less it will bother you, Jesus says to live more in your life thinking and acting like him and I believe he says this for a reason, can you imagine God acting and behaving like we do; No, he was sinless, and we are far from that, however we can draw our strength on Jesus for his promise is that he will never leave us or forsake us.

If you pray to God you can tell him your deepest thought even though he already knows them; he needs you to express your love to him, ask him to be your teacher; tell him that you will try harder; tell Jesus that you did not like the person that you where becoming, and that you are glad that you turned to him and received him as your Lord and saviour; tell father that you believe that he sent his son to die and take all of our sin; and that he rose again to give us life; thank God for all that he has planned for your life, and that you will fulfil it to the best of your ability; and that you will be all that you can for all his mighty glory; because God will give you talents to fulfil what he has planned for your new life, these will also be to help others, and it's our Lord God's will for you to fulfil them.

Don't ever be too hard on yourself because even with all your faults your Lord God in his eye's he loves you very much, you are everything to him; you are a child of God and do not forget that; it will be one the most important things to remember in keeping with your faith; the trusting in your Lord to hear him and to do what you have been called to do for him.

I know that there are many areas of my life that I still need to fix and change and through the grace of my father, I will strive to do even better and maintain balance of work and rest, trying to even eat more

# DRAW YOUR STRENGTH FROM JESUS CHRIST ✝ 221

well balanced meals, not to even spend more than I earn for this is a problem with many people, they get to complaisant and borrow from banks way above what they can afford to even pay back; this is the new way in which people live in today's world; and this is what also causes pressure at home and stress, while people should be living a stress free life and start to enjoy people more and smile even if someone isn't being as nice back to you, Jesus says to turn the other cheek, and to have solitude.

I will always put father God and Jesus above everyone first at all time, for they are wonderful loving, caring, and faithful, merciful; I know that if it wasn't for the grace and the glory of God I wouldn't have what I have today, for without them I am nothing.

I owe everything to the Heavenly kingdom; I thank Jesus for my life, for saving me from all my sins, so that I have a second chance to live a life of abundance in the kingdom of my father; glory to God, however understand also that regardless of what happens in a person's life, that you can bear up under the pressures of this world and the dark forces that cause you grief and heartache, you must draw strength to have a strong spirit within yourself to help sustain you in troubled time.

When you become a devout, Christian in Jesus Christ; people are so different between you or me, this answers the big question why are so many people having so many problems today; it is as simple as believing in Jesus Christ and how deep is their faith and Love in our Lord and what he promises that he will do for you and will you believe in him? When you lose faith you lose so much power and you will become weak;

To understand how you end up feeling when you haven't put Jesus first in your life everyday is an experience you will have when you receive him as Lord and saviour; you need Jesus everyday to keep you in righteousness; to keep you in faith, and trust; you can become moody and angry if you fade away from him on days, could be as simple as going out to party or visit someone who isn't in faith or your mind is elsewhere because you become too wrapped up in what else is going on around you, whatever the reason it does happen; if this happens to you, then you need to focus back on our Lord; I have even received messages from the higher realm telling me that you need to receive Jesus now; to change my thoughts back to our Lord and saviour.

That is what faith believing is all about, not just relying on what people would class it as all in your mind; that these are just your thoughts, no they are not; it is discerning the good from the bad, Jesus also says love worketh by faith alone; you need your peace, joy, and your happiness, and this is where Jesus wants you, you need him to keep you balanced and away from Evil.

We need to recognize our thoughts and our weaknesses and this is where Jesus works in us; he brings it back to us stronger each time we recognise the difference and call upon him; he will lift our spirits, giving us back our faith, and trust; Jesus will not give up on us, you can be guaranteed that it is us that lets him down and go; our faith and trust in our Lord has to be a continuous learning program and he is the best teacher we can ever have; he was a teacher to the disciples and he still has disciples today "us" he knows exactly what we want and need, he resides in us and there is nothing he doesn't know about us; it is like having your own church inside you lifting you up when your spirit is low to strengthen you, putting you back where you belong on the right path heading back to Jesus, which will not only make you happier but certainly everyone else around you will be happier to, they will see the radiance that Jesus gives you, his light shining through.

How great is it to know and think on the level of having your own church of Jesus Christ inside of you, it however is his promise to his children; your Holy Spirit, the Christ in you; this is where Jesus resides, "in you" not enough people understand the power of this; even many people who go to church on a very regular basis, it isn't taught enough about the power of the Holy Spirit and the power of the blood of Jesus Christ.

How you perceive the messages is from your level of thinking in your Holy Spirit; it is how you are willing to use this power given by our Lord Jesus; he resides in you releasing this power all the time and the strength; faith and trust; he also gives to you the power of healing,

# DRAW YOUR STRENGTH FROM JESUS CHRIST

peace and joy; and its given for all the days of your life, so if you use your mind properly and use this to your advantage and do not waste it, then you will achieve a lot of this power, and wisdom given and in the name of Jesus Christ.

Drawing your strength from our Almighty Lord by calling upon him with faith and believing in your heart, and by doing so it will bring to you an increase in your hearing and your learning, because it's the person of understanding that will receive skill; and will attain to sound counsel so that you will be able to move yourself in the right direction, the direction of life and wisdom, in your Lord Jesus Christ.

Experience and unlock blessings of God in your life, many people have lowered their expectations because they have been disappointed so many times before being surrounded by everyday life battles however God can restore your hopes and he can give you a new life to enjoy which will fill your hopes and dreams, and this is because Jesus loves you; you cannot expect to live a perfect life; however God he does promise that he will walk through those hard times with you, a parent will protect his child and God is your father; and he will love and protect you.

God will always be there to give you strength on the inside to face all problems, he will give you a new prospective on all your sufferings in your heart, he sends in the comforter and he turns all that pain into a life with him as blessings; he reads your heart, he knows your inner most secrets; he is willing to give you a second chance to accept and belong to him.

So now what you need to remember is that it is impossible to change your life unless you listen to your inner knowing from the Lord, God says he will help those who help themselves; and changing your thoughts and rebuke the bad thoughts, and all your good thoughts strengthen; by bringing them into the grace and the love of our Saviour and king Jesus Christ, he is our game changer, bring you a sense of worthiness and calm, helping you to renew your mind; keeping you focused on the positive words of God the father, your clear thinking is the works of God; remember that nothing is impossible with Jesus Christ.

If you chose not to live in Christ the alternative is only misery; **proverbs 23:7** says for as a man thinks in his heart so is he; so what and how you chose to live your life and think in your circumstances will determine whether you are going to live a life of peace and harmony or whether you are going to have dysfunction and negativity surrounding you day by day; for me I have lived a life surrounded by negativity, and this is no way to live a life, Jesus truly is a game changer for your life, he is the only way, what are you waiting for.

The bible shows you the way to live a good life in peace and harmony; many become conformed to living in this world, adapting to its superficial customs, the change we need to be accepted and perfect in the will of God, which is transformation of our minds, new attitudes, and proving ourselves to God that we want this change and that it is for the better, we can prove for ourselves and accept that we can feel this goodness transforming us into better people living a life in Christ Jesus; feeling acceptable and perfect in Gods sight.

This transformation it has clarity, it brings to us peace, joy and confidence to continue the walk in Jesus Christ, he leads you on this path; he knows he is working good in you and that you are accepting him; this transformation leads to a healthier mind and making better decisions' to become a better person in general to how you once lived your life, you will feel the relationship that you have become stronger in the Father and our saviour Jesus Christ; there presence is nurturing, and remember that our father is merciful, he gives his blessings to all who call on him with a sorrowful and genuine heart.

Staying strong is what God wants from you; he doesn't want you to have anxiety and worry in your life he doesn't want you to even have worries about your body, or to even worry about what you wear; for God says is not life better than food or even clothes, wise words from God "right" he says also to look at all the birds in the air; that they neither sow nor reap; yet he still loves and feeds them, he says that you are more worthy than they are, so why then do you worry, for your father already knows what you need.

We therefore should seek and strive for the kingdom in heaven first and his righteousness, because this is the right path to take and it is God's doing for you, it is the path he has chosen for you to walk to him to be accepted into his holy Kingdom, for life everlasting; this peace and calmness god wants you to walk on now, and not to have worries and burdens, or to even have concerns about what tomorrow will bring, because they will have worries all on their own; so take each day as it comes; live a life of peace, joy and happiness in God; cast all your worries on to him, he will ease your burdens, Jesus he care and he knows what worry does to the children of God and how destructive it can be, look at Gods faith and provisions as your medication.

Jesus says in Matthew that those who are strong and healthy have no need for a physician, but only those who are sick; go and learn what this means, I desire compassion for all in distress; I can not to call and invite the righteous, those who are upright and in right standing with God, but for sinners, those who are not free from their sins.

God's mercy is full of kindness and sometimes it takes people a very long time to understand the deep meaning of God's mercy until you start to experience the change in you; you may even think that someone you have known or met is a merciful person until for example you get to know them; for another example I was a caring person I always cared if someone was suffering and I gave a helping hand, but with all that was going on in my life I was becoming a different person, I still cared about others suffering and always has a soft spot for the little ones; but I was still changing to someone I didn't like, I knew in my heart I needed someone who truly knew me; knew me inside my heart and spirit, somewhere where no one else could possibly know the true me; and there is only one who can know me deep down and that is my and your creator; Jesus Christ our king and our God.

You know when you are going through a lot of pain and suffering; you can become so involved in yourself and your troubles, that you forget about all the loved ones around you; and other people who you come in contact with especially if you are in a job like me when you are dealing with people on a every day basis, which can add to your troubles because there is many out there who are dealing with the same issues as yourself; but you become so focused on how people are treating you that you do not even consider anyone else's problems; sometimes this makes you more bitter, I treated people with great kindness, I gave away presents; I helped people financially even if I really could not afford it, I gave away things for free, especially to children, and gave food to people who were hungry; but people do abuse your goodness and take you for granted, they refuse to see the goodness in you; until God showed me that you should not look for acknowledgement from what good you have done in this world because your rewards are noted in Heaven; and that has changed my feelings regarding people, you simply pray for them instead.

Having a hardened heart, and becoming bitter did me no good at all I was only getting more deeply hurt thinking why are people treating me so badly; do they not know that I would help them before probably their best friend would; these people know how I have helped others; they really do not know my heart'; and this is the problem when you have a good heart; like Jesus did" people refuse to see the good side of you, they really do not want to know you, in Jesus day they acted the same way, Jesus spoke of love, compassion for others; kindness, Jesus was lowly in heart; he loved and cared for the homeless, the poor and the suffering, he healed, and he loved children, he forgave sins; and they sentenced him to death, he suffered unimaginable cruelty and he did this for us; our Lord Jesus; he is simply the best; he is our king and Messiah.

Pain and suffering how deeply this can affect you, Jesus shed many tears not only with what he knew he was going to experience, but he shed many tears for the dying and the suffering, tears we all have when you have a compassionate heart; but many do not think that even the cruellest of people/ murderers have compassion and love for their own children ect; they may hurt or kill someone, yet if someone did the same to someone they love this is different to them, they're feelings become focused in a different direction.

# DRAW YOUR STRENGTH FROM JESUS CHRIST

Within my feelings I would cry and cry because I knew I was feeling differently and I didn't like it; I didn't like being the person I was becoming, it was an inner calling from God to turn to him, and I did need God in my life, I knew that God didn't want me to be this way, I felt that; I needed mercy, I needed to draw my strength from Jesus Christ; The mercy I needed from God is to learn to be able to have more mercy towards others, regardless of how they are; you may be thinking that this is very unfair though; but in Gods eyes it isn't; it is to make you become a better person in all areas of your life, and I can see that now; we have to learn how to receive God's mercy before we can give God's mercy; all people are our brothers and sisters, the bible does state that you have to love your neighbour as you love yourself, if you cannot do this or accept this then you will become very hard in your heart, and this isn't a good place to be, you must show mercy if you want to receive mercy from God; and this is what God wants from us; and really think about it; God loves us we have a calling from him, he wants this change in us; so it is very important to look at how you do treat others in your life, we will be judged by God for our actions, so changing and repentance should be a must as a new child reborn in Christ; learning to bless all who want to curse you doing so with love and forgiveness in your heart; the power of believing and faith in the love that God has transformed into your spirit with most certainly be transferred to others, this will change them to think about their actions as well when they see that you are not reacting like you use to because of your love and faith in our Lord and Saviour Jesus Christ.

Rejoice in the Lord with all the teachings of your heart, embracing his mercy and compassion when you turn to someone who has caused you grief and heartache before; the new you will want that person to find God to have the transformation that he has embraced you with; you will want them to ask god for forgiveness of their sins, because you already know that God will forgive them as he forgave you; because our God is a merciful God and he "listen" LOVES US ALL" yes the good and the bad; he wants all to change and receive him as Lord and Saviour, so even the people who have hurt us have a very good chance to be saved and loved by God; amen.

All God's children have to refuse to live under condemnation and must ask for forgiveness of their sins and after they have done so must not continue to make the same mistakes as before; God wants you to learn by your mistakes; and when you do recognise that you have made a mistake (your Holy Spirit will let you recognise you have done wrong) then you admit your mistake and immediately repent and feel sorrowful in your heart; and you will without any doubt receive God's mercy and forgiveness and then you can move forward; always remember he loves you for your honesty and he is patient.

Do not fret or have any anxieties about anything that is written in the bible in Philippians; for it also says; but in every circumstance and in everything, by prayer and petition, definite requests, with thanks giving, continue to make your requests known to God, God's peace shall be yours through the salvation of Jesus Christ, so fearing nothing from God and being content with its Earthly doings of whatever sort that is, that peace which transcends all understanding shall protect over and guard over your hearts and minds in Jesus Christ.

So for the rest; Children of God, whatever is truth, whatever is worthy of reverence and is honourable and seemly, whatever is just, and whatever is pure whatever is lovely and loveable, whatever is kind, attractive, appealing and gracious, if there is anything worthy of praise, think on and weigh and take account of these things, fix your mind on them and practice what you have learned; meditate on what you have received and heard and seen in me, and model your ways on living on it; and you will have the God of peace of untroubled, and undisturbed well- being, will be with you always.

What a great way to really live your life in God; how peaceful we would all be living, but the thing is we can; if we chose to live in the way of God, that God really has chosen for us to live from the beginning of creation; it is only as hard as we want to make our life; do we live in the way of God or do we continue to live our life in the world? Learn how to be content and satisfied, satisfied to the point where you do

# DRAW YOUR STRENGTH FROM JESUS CHRIST

not become upset or discouraged no matter what is happening around you, let God bring you to a state of enjoying your life in abundance, learn through the grace of God in all your circumstances to face every situation in peace and harmony, let God be seen on your face his radiance shining through.

God can and will inspire you that much, it is what he wants for all his children; say to yourself as much as you have to in prayer and in your thoughts talk to God, and say; I have the strength to get through all my challenges, I can fight darkness; I have the power to rebuke what God and myself are not pleased with; I have the power and the strength through our Lord Jesus Christ, and by his mighty power, given to me in his Holy and Righteous Name; Jesus empowers me; and I am ready for anything, I am infused with inner strength given to me through the Holy Spirit; we are united as one; and I love him with all of my heart and soul; I am nothing without Jesus by my side, he loves me and he wants all this goodness for me, he covers me with the white light protection, he answers all my prayers with love, I draw my strength from Jesus Christ.

> I have hope in God, which they themselves also accept, that there will be a resurrection of the dead, both of the just and the unjust.
>
> ACTS 24:15

Choosing God, being adopted; is the spirit of adoption given; this is assurance that we are children of God; for all who are led by the spirit of God are the sons of God; if we are his children, then we are God's heirs; Heirs of God and also heirs of Jesus Christ we share our Lords inheritance, and we must also share in his suffering if we are to share his amazing glory; God he chooses us; how amazing is that; nothing could ever compare with his glory that can be revealed to us; in us or for us, consider our flesh; and why it doesn't like it, our flesh controls us, but the Holy Spirit is given by God, and the holy Spirit is willing, but the flesh is not, we are willing in Jesus suffering but the flesh will deny it; however when we walk with our Lord Jesus Christ and pick up our cross and follow him, our Holy Spirit is more than willing to walk with God; our inner voice leads us on the right path of righteousness, and our flesh let's say loses its power to control us, because the Holy Spirit our God within leads us in the right direction, it leads us

# DRAW YOUR STRENGTH FROM JESUS CHRIST ✝ 231

to obey God, we are made in his image and it's his image leading us to become more like Jesus instead of our weak fleshly form, we want to think and act how Jesus would have behaved, with more love and peace and forgiveness; sin will become less frequent in our behaviour, so the more we think and obey God, the less our flesh will control us, sometime our flesh puts up a good fight so trying to stay obedient to God is a struggle, darkness will always try to keep you away from God, he doesn't want to lose to God; but God is more powerful and you must always remember this; **there is no battle "God" wins;** you will always here Gods calling to you, that inner voice leading you, teaching you what is Godly and what is not Jesus will lead you right back on the right path; Amen.

This is all what is being a new child in Jesus Christ is all about, being reborn again, a Christian you; your faith and strength, you're trusting, and your wisdom, which is leading you to faith believing; you will find yourself loving the new person you have become; you will feel God's empowerment in you, trust me you will love the walk with God; it is the Jesus Christ in you, the Church of Jesus Christ; your Holy Spirit that is given to you.

Let's talk about the flesh, the flesh (our bodies) gives us carnal thoughts, and it is these thoughts that are hostile to God, he cares not for our fleshly bodies, only our spiritual bodies; let's call our flesh for a minute our sinful body; thoughts that gratify the flesh these are unholy desires set by our minds, these thoughts are not set by the Holy Spirit; only flesh and it is death; this death comprises us with misery; and if you continue in this behaviour and live accordingly to the dictates of these thoughts; you will surely die it is only through the power of the Holy Spirit that you can put that death sentence away forever through repentance and a sorrowful heart; this will give you a sense of peace that you can genuinely live forever in Jesus.

This is the power in the word of God; his promises; many who study the Holy Bible understand and will learn something different each time they read a passage, however the bible is the word of God and the word of God will speak to you differently each time you read it; it teaches you something different each time you open and read it even years and years later; "why" because of your wisdom; you may have read many passages and not understood hardly anything; then gone back and read it again a year or two later and found that you have got it; I comprehend it now.

The word of God grows with your understanding, your faith and believing; it teaches you; if you do not understand the Bible you are simply not at the level of understanding; this however does not mean that you will never reach the level of understanding; because God wants you to have faith; love and strength; this is your training; so to fully understand the word of God, we must walk in faith believing; and when we finally meet God face to face then all will be revealed, we will fully understand.

The true meaning of Love is when you are in his presence; you feel him ever so deep inside; we will not understand while we are in our flesh everything, but we can walk with him so closely on a day to day basis and meditate on the word at night, the fear of God is that our father wants us to walk with him, not against him, love him with all your heart and soul; and do not have be unbelieving walking in no faith and trust, because one day we will all face him and it could be much sooner than we can even imagine; I understand that many fear the unknown, but understand we all make mistakes, but our father he loves us so much. He is the power of true love; he will stand by you and forgive you; Jesus died to give us life everlasting, he is willing to give you a chance; our father he gave up his only son; to give us life; THAT IS LOVE.

As devout, Christians of Jesus Christ we experience deep love and we do not want to fail God in any way; we are in training and we want to walk in Jesus Christs footsteps every step of the way; however our school room is the church of Jesus Christ and he is our beloved teacher; our fear of God is disappointing him and being reprimanded; so we call on him in repentance and forgiveness; but there will be times when we do walk in the flesh instead of in the Holy Spirit given to us by God; and Jesus died for us to give us life and to ask for forgiveness through his precious blood and to repent of our sins.

# DRAW YOUR STRENGTH FROM JESUS CHRIST ✟ 233

Everyone has sinned; yes we are all sinners need not think that you are off the hook like some may; God states this; we all are guilty, and have all made bad choices; but we have to recognise our faults and walk away from our sin, it only leads to death; repenting gives us a chance with God and God is forgiving and the best news is that his promise to us is that he will remember them no more; he will cast them into the depths of the oceans; never to return nor be remembered; so if God can forgive you then you must as well and to also never to continue to carry the burden of condemnation around with you; Jesus has delivered us from all inequity and guilt, he died as a sacrifice for us; he said it is finished.

I suffered guilt for awhile I use to think how could I have done this to God; why did I do this to myself; I could have been living and walking with God for most of my life; I truly felt robbed of A God I so now deeply love; I understand now that this is a wrong way to think, I believe that me going through all this made me stronger and more mature to walk with God, I would never have been in the place where I am today If it was not because of God's will.

I am writing this book because of my love for God and the words of God to be revealed to you by what I have been through, my walk with Jacob on the train is one of the most inspiring truths of God's angels coming to you to listen and walk in the love of the word of God and by trust and faith and definitely believing, I knew all those years ago that he was a messenger from God I actually never doubted that in my heart I knew that one day all would be revealed by the bible I just didn't know when.

I would never have though in all my years that I would be here typing to my readers; God's children to tell them about my walk with God and my journey with Jacob; and all the amazing prayers that God has given me to share with you all; his beloved ones; God bless you all; God has truly blessed us all to be where we are today, the amazing journey which will lead to the best journey in the end; life everlasting with God; the fear of judgement seems so surreal; you know you will see him because of all your sins; you do not know how it will pander out; that's the fear; but on the other side of the coin so to speak you cannot wait to see our father and his son Jesus because they have transformed your life so much and replaced it with love, you cannot wait to feel the love in heaven which is even deeper than the love we feel now; somehow I feel that this love is like an explosion of all kinds of emotions much more than we can even comprehend, I cannot wait for that.

## SPEAK THE WORD OF GRACE

Our Holy and Righteous Heavenly Father I ask of you to please continue to supply me with love and grace in my Life; continue to empower me, my Gracious Lord Jesus; as I bow before you, honouring you with all of my heart and my soul.

I ask Lord to fill me with the truth from the Holy scriptures; placing them upon my heart, be my teacher so that I can continue to grow in such a way to become more worthy in your eyes; oh I pray thee Lord to look lovingly upon me with a merciful heart; keep me on the right path of righteousness, do not let me stray before your eyes; I bow before you with tears of Joy rolling down my cheeks; I look lovingly upon thee oh Lord, as I give myself to you, I have only you who I can rely and trust in, it is only you who has saved me from a life of destruction and death, oh how I thank you for lifting me up and finding me worthy to be loved and saved, how I feel blessed to become a new born child of God, thank you my Lord my God, my king of Kings, Lord of Lords our saviour our Messiah, Jesus Christ the son of God, as we bow and pray AMEN.

Do not fall into temptation; watch and pray to God, to lift you up out of what you are going through; because the Holy Spirit is always willing to keep you safe, but the flesh is always weak and tempted by darkness leading into sin nature; therefore remember that your flesh it is always weak.

I say unto you say's the Lord God, to always think carefully about what is right and to stop sinning for your shame is also because some of you do not know God at all, and I your Lord do not say these things to you to shame you; but to reach out and to teach you as my beloved children and to change your direction.

# DRAW YOUR STRENGTH FROM JESUS CHRIST ✟ 235

If you are in trouble call on my name and I will answer you and I will say, they are my people, and you will say; the Lord is my God.

Oh Lord Jesus you come and save those whose hearts are right; you protect all your children who call on your Holy name as a shield; and you do good to those whose who are good, and those whose hearts are upright; Oh Lord all your saints love you with all of their heart and soul, please keep us all on the right path of righteousness and help us to stay in righteous faith so we do not fall into the sin nature of condemnation.

We pray deeply our God so that the grace of you Lord will be poured out onto me abundantly along with the faith and love that are from our Lord Jesus Christ our Messiah; all these things being spoken (written) to you are for you; delivered by the word of God so that the grace of God is being given to more and more people; because it will bring increasing thanks to God for all of his glory.

Remember our Holy Spirit is being renewed every day strengthened by our Love and the Love of our Lord God; we should never give up, even though we know that our bodies are dying, there is no escape from that, however in faith and believing in our Lord we have life everlasting; all who believe in me says the Lord God will have rivers of living waters flowing out from their heart, and I will lead you there, I will wipe away your tears for the rivers of tears are your tears of love flowing from your Holy Spirit, this is the ultimate gift from God.

## SPEAK THE WORD OF GRACE

Your heart rejoicing and exalting in your love for our amazing God, the precious thoughts he gives you to express his love and compassion to others; he searches your heart and thoughts if you listen and wait patiently he will answer and reveal much more to you, he will take your breath away when you understand and feel deep within the depth of his love for you, we will all understand in time that all things do work together for the good to those who are called accordingly to his promise and purpose, and we are to give thanks to our God almighty for it is his love that endues to all his children forever; this means that anyone who belongs to our Lord Jesus Christ has become a new person, the old life we once lived is gone forever, and the best news is that your new life has just begun.

My Lord God how my soul waits for you in silence for all my hope and faith is in you, you have filled me with support and strength, my heart is stronger because of your love for me; there is no one like you, you are majestic in holiness; you are awesome in all your Glory, praise be to our Lord Jesus Christ our Messiah and to our Holy and righteous Heavenly Father how we glorify you for the wonderful gift of your precious son, we give you thanks for all that you have done to give us a chance to have a life forever in the heavenly realm.

# Jesus Message of Love

**JESUS IS OUR ANOINTED** Messiah and his message of love has always been about love, receiving love, turning darkness away for love, and what we can do for love. We need to trust in his love, and to be fulfilled in his radiant love it is this love he gives to us deeply when we receive love from him and receive him as our Lord and our saviour; our Holy Spirit is transformed, being filled with Jesus who is our teacher.

Many people want proof about the Holy Spirit, this new transformation and how does God change you into a new born child, and so on? I probably though on this same level many years ago myself; how can one be born again when I have already been born; and many say, that's ridiculous; nonsense or its just words; however it is ignorance regarding the unknown, we have no knowledge because we are living a life in unbelief; one answer to all that is "Faith" you cannot experience any of this without the faith or receiving Jesus as your Lord and saviour; without any belief that God exists.

How does one expect to be given something so precious without believing in the most precious one that is willing to give; you cannot expect even in our world to be given something just because you want it; it takes work; trust and faith to receive it.

The love that the Holy Spirit gives is work and it is work to keep it; think of yourself working to keep your Job, your house, marriage together, and even your children, if you fail at one or even all of these you can lose everything you love; you fight for what you love and want to keep.

God works in the same way with you; and your Holy Spirit; if you leave God after you have turned to him and already received your Holy Spirit, then you lose confidence; do not turn to him for help and turn away from him you are leaving yourself open to darkness to cause you grief; and in heading in this direction God will take away the gift of love and loyalty he gave you; and lose confidence in you, and in return turn away from you also.

Let's look at it another way; you deeply love and care about someone; you have faith and confidence and you are very loyal to them but they on the other hand have lost favour in you; and they slowly turn away from you, deceiving you; you become hurt and unsure without answers; would you trust them again; this has probably already happened to you; most people can at some stage in their life associate with this; whether it be a sibling, at your work place; your best friend or even your partner.

Now you may say but God is love and of forgiveness; "yes" this is correct; however what are you expecting from God because it is also what he expects from you which is to love and forgive all (your brothers and sisters) love thy neighbour as you would love thy self; Jesus also says, love and forgive all as I loved you first; however we wouldn't think twice about saying to someone; what comes around goes around "right".

We want and expect so much from everyone; we have become an unforgiving society, selfish and self absorbed; and God does understand this all too well; we however only think on these line's when we are affected and angry; God he sees the big picture 100% because he knows us all individually; he is our creator, our God, he is all seeing and all knowing.

God gave us life and he takes life, 1 in 1 dies there is no way out "or is there? Think on that for awhile.

Once we have our love of the Holy Spirit given to us fulfilled with God's devotion shouldn't we be appreciative and loyal; after all we would expect it in our life, if we were in a situation where we depended on someone to save our life wouldn't you expect help; and if you received that help and they saved your life, gave your life back to you would you not be very appreciative and loyal forever to them, of cause you would it would be a life changing experience, not one that you would forget that easy.

Your Holy Spirit is also life changing as well, God's promise to you is he will give you back your life if you love and receive him; he died for you to give you this life changing experience to have life; everlasting; why would you turn away from this love, why would you not embrace Jesus and the Holy Spirit of life, where our Saviour resides; this is Jesus' message of Love to you.

Is this not the feeling, the same feeling that we feel when we have received this love; the same feeling of Jesus' love that he has for us, is this Jesus' message of love to us he sends "the Holy Spirit".

How do these words feel to you? This same love that I am writing to you is expressed from my Holy Spirit where Jesus resides; it is the overwhelming feeling of love that he is expressing to his beloved children; to never let him go; you fight for whom you love.

Jesus' love for us was worth dying for; he died to give us everything; everlasting love and life; Jesus suffered such cruel punishment, unbearable pain and humiliation; he suffered so we would not suffer eternal death, but to have life eternal. This eternal life is where we will shed no more tears or heartache; no more sicknesses or disease; where children can walk and feel safe; we will never die, we will live, and this is the gift from the son of God.

I know this is real, I know what Jesus will give from his love to his children, and I can express what I feel deeply because he has given me this transformation of love to express; and what also this transformation does to you spiritually when you feel his love and you believe with all of your heart and soul; faith believing is Jesus Christ, faith believing is the Holy Spirit, faith believing is his deep love for you; if you cannot receive Jesus and all that he can give to you; then you have nothing because we are nothing without him, we have no life period; I personally cannot live without him in my life I cannot even imagine my life without him now in it; I now know that I was on a life of death forever; and I am forever grateful to have my Lord in my life; I am grateful to have him love me enough to find me worthy enough to pick up all my broken pieces and to put me back together again in which he found worthy and righteous; enough to work in me casting away what he didn't like and to put in what he wanted (transformation); to unite us again as one; so I can be reborn again "anew" and to have a heart worthy to belong to him.

I am a changed person; I found love in God a love that is so different than the love we think we know now. If you are reading this message from God and you know God already, you will understand; you can already express God's love from your Holy Spirit; your tears will overflow, you can feel you belong to Jesus; it's connection, it is this connection he says, do not let go; don't walk away from me; if you truly love me, you will stay and be saved; by grace.

There is a cost, a price to follow Jesus, he must come first above all; even your own life; we pick up his cross as your own cross, nailed with Jesus, Jesus' parable is great when he says; salt is good for seasoning, but once the salt loses its flavour it is nothing, it cannot be restored; it has no more use, Jesus also says all who have ears let then hear, and if your ears are opened by your Holy Spirit then to be a follower of mine, apply this to yourself.

Passionately with all of your heart seek Jesus and the kingdom of God above everything in your life; and never be afraid, because he will love you and take care of you, it is his promise; you must be willing to open your spiritual eyes to the world in which we live in and look around you, for it is not what it seems to be.

Is the son of Gods deep passion within you; to seek him, again longing deeply in your Spirit his love, and your love for him; this deep burning you feel is the God within; your heavenly realm; do you cry out to him day and night, to forever pray for an answered call, are you faithfully in love with the son of God.

Do you have the child within to be lifted up; will you receive the revelation of the kingdom as a young child would receive? For this is "faith" that the innocence of a child would have; faith believing "put faith in God, receiving Jesus as the son of God, the gift he gives you is the greatest gift of love and this is to be baptized in the Holy Spirit; the spiritual fruit and the spiritual power; the spiritual kingdom, the gift of life given by Jesus Christ; this is the inheritance that he gives to you and all his children.

The power of faith is available for all to embrace if you want to truly desire to be a follower of our beloved Lord Jesus Christ; the revelation of all truth will be revealed to you, your eyes will be opened to light: God's glorious light will shine before you; no darkness will penetrate what belongs to God; for it fears God it has no place or belonging, it cannot harm what belongs to God, you are protected; more aware to be able to rebuke and give to God who loves and cares for you; Jesus says believe in me, not always in yourself; let my light shine through, open your heart, letting me teach you.

The days of a fully transformation are still yet to come; this will be the day when Jesus comes; how we will jump for joy; pure love has arrived; this day we have prayed for with our hearts; this is how Jesus makes you feel; the love of your Holy Spirit transforming within; the most compassionate and love filled joy that is shared between yourself and Jesus Christ; believers who share deep prayers encountering God's heart, to work together and encourage all to listen to God and his heart felt words, a witness for Jesus the son of God.

God's mercy and love is why he chose you; you are worthy to be saved when you believe in him, repentance for all sins and a sorrowful heart, to tell God that you love him deeply; to be reborn again is Jesus' birth of the church; his teachings of prayer with devotion and love, the outpouring of faith believing and a pure heart which is filled with the Holy Spirit given by God, an outpouring of love spreads the word of the Holy Bible, and spreading the word of God saves more children of God.

How important is this to have Jesus' message on love, these are such powerful words to all lovers of God; because faith works with deep love in your heart, believe in him and he will change your life, and he will continue with this love in your next life to come.

## 242 ✝ JESUS SON OF GOD

www.ingramcontent.com/pod-product-compliance
Lightning Source LLC
Chambersburg PA
CBHW071230080526
44587CB00013BA/1552